Mainstream or special?
Educating students with disabilities

This book aims to stimulate debate about educational options for students with disabilities. Taking a critical approach to assumptions underlying special education in both integrated and segregated settings, Jo Jenkinson draws on recent research, current practices and real life examples from Australia, the United Kingdom and Canada.

Part I clarifies important issues including normalisation, least restrictive environment and the right to integrated education. Part II presents four models of educational provision for students with disabilities: the special school, link schools, the special unit or class and the regular classroom. Part III focuses on the debate about curriculum for students with disabilities, and Part IV offers an international perspective on special education and considers possible future developments in provision.

Josephine C. Jenkinson is a Senior Lecturer at Deakin University, teaching graduate courses in disability studies and special education.

Mainstream or special? Educating students with disabilities

Josephine C. Jenkinson

London and New York

First published 1997
by Routledge
11 New Fetter Lane, London EC4P 4EE

Simultaneously published in the USA and Canada
by Routledge
29 West 35th Street, New York, NY 10001

© 1997 Josephine C. Jenkinson

Typeset in Garamond by Routledge
Printed and bound in Great Britain by
T J Press (Padstow) Ltd, Padstow, Cornwall

British Library Cataloguing in Publication Data
A catalogue record for this book is available from the British Library

Library of Congress Cataloguing in Publication Data
Jenkinson, Josephine C.
Mainstream or special? Educating students with disabilities/
Josephine C. Jenkinson.
p. cm.
Includes bibliographical references and index.
1. Handicapped children—Education—Australia. 2. Mainstreaming
in education—Australia. I.Title.
LC4039.J44 1996
371.91/0994—dc20
96–21562
CIP

ISBN 0–415–12835–8 (hbk)
ISBN 0–415–12836–6 (pbk)

Contents

Acknowledgements

This book was begun during an Outside Studies Programme granted by the Faculty of Health and Behavioural Sciences, Deakin University, in 1994. I am indebted to Dr Seamus Hegarty, Director, National Foundation for Educational Research, who provided a base for me to work in England during the summer of 1994, and to Dr Margaret Winzer, who hosted my stay at the University of Lethbridge, Alberta, Canada. I also thank the principals, staff, parents and students of the many schools I have visited who willingly gave of their time and provided many of the practical examples of special education provision that are included in the book.

Part I

Issues and outcomes in special education

Chapter 1

Introduction

The scene is a classroom of eight- and nine-year-olds in a school in a large provincial city. The lunch break is not far off, and the children are playing a miming game. One child mimes an activity, and the others try to guess what the activity is. 'Who would like to be next?' asks the teacher, Ms O'Brien (not her real name). Hands shoot up, Monica's among them. 'Would you like a go, Monica?' asks Ms O'Brien. 'Yes, Monica, give Monica a go!' chorus the children. Ms O'Brien beckons to Monica and whispers in her ear. Without a word, Monica lies down on the floor and closes her eyes. 'I know, I know!' volunteers another child, 'she's pretending to be asleep.' 'Yes, that's right; good girl, Monica! Back to your place now,' says Ms O'Brien, and Monica returns to her seat, obviously pleased with her part in the game.

What is special about this scene? Monica has Down syndrome and has been assessed as having a severe intellectual disability. Her language skills are very weak: she has only two or three words of speech. At twelve, she is older than the other children in her grade, although not much bigger. Twenty years ago, most students with Down syndrome would have attended a day training centre for people with intellectual disability, segregated from the mainstream of education. But Monica is part of an integration programme in her district and attends a mainstream primary school full-time. She is unable to cope with the academic skills that other members of the class are learning, but she participates in most of the other activities in the classroom. Much of her behaviour has been learned from observing and imitating the children around her, and superficially at least there is little to distinguish it from that of the other children with whom she mixes. Monica's classmates realise her limitations and make allowance for her disability. They are usually kind and helpful, ready to show her what to do and often extravagant in their praise for her efforts. Despite her disability, integration appears to be working well for Monica.

But is it? Later in the playground, other children are clambering noisily after each other over a monkey bar, jumping a skipping rope or throwing and catching a ball. Lacking adequate motor skills for these activities, Monica drifts aimlessly around the playground on her own, not consciously rejected, but for the moment forgotten by the other children in the exhilaration of their play. Ms O'Brien worries about whether she is doing the right thing for Monica. She admits to being unsure about Monica's educational needs and her capacity for learning. There are thirty other children in the class who need her attention; two or three are significant underachievers and another two are from homes where a language other than English is spoken. Monica spends much of her time in the classroom working on 'readiness' activities and worksheets that the prep grade teacher has provided. Many of the activities seem too juvenile for a twelve-year-old. Ms O'Brien is frustrated by Monica's lack of progress in even the most elementary of pre-reading and number skills.

The principal believes that Monica should be with her age peers in a higher grade, but fears she may not cope with the more formal atmosphere and tougher demands of the Grade Six classroom. Monica's mother is anxious about the future, especially as Monica reaches puberty. She cannot see how Monica will survive in a secondary school. She is concerned that Monica may be missing out on learning some of the essential skills for adult functioning that she would have acquired in a special educational setting, but that are taken for granted in the mainstream school. But for the present, Monica seems happy at school, and her mother is pleased with her behaviour and the way she seems to be accepted by the other children.

Monica is not necessarily typical of all students with disabilities, nor does her classroom placement represent the norm for children with disabilities who have been integrated into the mainstream. In fact, the scene I have described took place some years ago, when our under-standing of integration and the resources necessary for its support were far less than they are today. In a way, Monica was among the pioneers at the start of two decades of rapid and radical change in our perceptions of special education. But her situation illustrates the many dilemmas faced by both parents and educators in seeking to provide for the education of students with special educational needs. Children with disabilities need the companionship of their typical age peers; they need the same experiences of achievement and opportunities to grow into adolescents and adults who have interesting and satisfying lives. Above all, they need to develop self-respect and a sense of belonging. But to achieve these goals, they need a great deal of support, often far beyond that provided in most classrooms.

In the past twenty-five years extensive practical experience has accumulated in the integration of students with disabilities into mainstream education. An expanding body of research has identified and described factors that help to make integration effective. There has been wide theoretical discussion, although often driven from an ideological perspective rather than from a realistic understanding either of the needs of students with disabilities, or of the social and psychological forces which have prompted the debate in the first place. Ideologists on both sides have left little room for individual choice. There have also been changes in mainstream education which have an impact on provision for special education. Yet, despite the push towards integration, in many western countries such as Australia, the United States and the United Kingdom, substantial numbers of students with disabilities remain in segregated educational settings. In some cases, schools have not taken up the challenge to adapt to meet the needs of these students; in others parents have shown a reluctance to move away from the settings that have provided so much support for their children. There are also many outstandingly successful integration programmes. At the same time, reports of large increases in numbers of students receiving special education in both segregated and integrated settings, of students being pressured into mainstream enrolment without adequate resources, of inequities in allocation of funding, and of budget 'blow-outs' in integration programmes, pose dilemmas for both educators and families.

Adding to this complexity, the debate about integration, originally concerned only with students who had mild disabilities or sensory and physical impairments, now includes students with severe and multiple disabilities – students who have hitherto been quite outside the experience of mainstream education and regular class teaching.

The concept of disability is one that arouses emotions in all of us. By the time a child has reached school age, many parents have become involved with an often confusing range of services designed to address the needs of their son or daughter who has a disability. To their emotional strain may be added conflicting advice about educational options from a number of different sources, some of whom have vested interests in perpetuating their own form of educational provision.

Others may view the child's needs from the limited perspective of their professional orientation, or lacking knowledge of either the child's potential for development or the ways in which that potential may be achieved. Parents are subject to many pressures and may find it difficult to resist well-meant but ill-informed advice from people they perceive to have greater knowledge or expertise than themselves. Options are often presented in value-laden terms that leave little room for consideration of alternatives. My purpose therefore is to provide material for informed discussion and decision making about educational options, in recognition that no single option is ideal for all individuals, rather than to promote one particular view. I do, however, have one view to push, and that is that education, including special education, cannot remain static. We live in a society that is constantly changing, and rather than feel threatened by that change, we should seek ways of making the changes that are currently taking place in education work to the advantage of all students, including those who have disabilities.

In this book, I will not attempt to resolve the dilemmas faced by either educators or parents – indeed, each child has individual needs, and each family has its own set of values and circumstances. The choices parents make about the education of their son or daughter who has a disability must be made in the light of those values and circumstances and in relation to available provisions and resources. Nor do I attempt a comprehensive review of special education. This is primarily a book about options in special education and their advantages and disadvantages, in part based on real-life situations drawn from my own observations and discussions in Australia, the United Kingdom and Canada, and in part on the special education literature. Along the way, I provide some historical background to the changes taking place in special education, I try to explain some of the catch phrases and 'movements' that have influenced or characterised these changes, I discuss curriculum issues and some of the supports needed by students with disabilities to gain access to curriculum, and examine the needs of students with severe and multiple disabilities in education. I have included a chapter on research issues because I believe that decisions in special education should be informed, although not necessarily determined, by the results of systematic, scientifically based investigation. At the same time, I believe it is important to realise that research in special education has unique problems, and does not necessarily provide answers to the many questions that parents and educators face. Finally, I examine current trends and practices in Australia and overseas, and attempt to identify a future role for special education.

SOME TERMS USED IN THIS BOOK

Throughout the book, I refer to 'students with disabilities' as those students who have an identified disability – whether intellectual, sensory, physical or emotional, or some combination of these – that in some way creates a special educational need. That is, the student needs resources or support in addition to those provided to typical students of his or her age group to gain access to education. The need for support is usually recognised in the provision of additional funding for the education of these students, reflected in a variety of ways such as a reduced student–teacher ratio, or provision of special equipment. From time to time, I also refer to students with a specific disability, such as a hearing impairment, or an intellectual disability. This is not to either endorse or reject a categorical approach to disability, or to support a view that students who have a disability-related educational need should in any way form a separate category from those who do not have such needs, or whose special needs are in some way less significant. It is rather to avoid the confusion that results from what the Organisation for Economic Co-operation and Development (OECD, 1994) referred to as the 'new language' of special education. Terms such as 'learning difficulty', 'learning disability' or 'student with special needs' have different meanings in different countries – indeed, even within Australia there is variation between states in their interpretation of the terms 'learning difficulty' and 'learning disability'. Although these terms are intended to remove the focus away from the disability and its implications for individual functioning, and on to the educational provision needed by the student, their use also creates a risk that important needs may be overlooked in the interests of emphasising the similarities between students with disabilities and their more typical peers.

Interpretations of concepts such as 'integration', 'mainstreaming', 'least restrictive environment' or 'inclusive schooling' also differ widely both within and between countries. For example, views of integration range from location of a special class on a regular school campus to the individual student as a full-time member of a regular class. In between, integration has also been used to describe as little as half a day a week in the regular class. Others talk about 'maximum participation' in the mainstream setting. My own view of integration tends to be enrolment in a regular class, with perhaps minimum withdrawal for therapy or special instructional needs that cannot be met without difficulty or considerable disruption to the regular class. Where I use the term differently it should be obvious from the context, or I will explain its use. I also tend to use the term 'mainstream' as synonymous with the regular class setting. In this I differ from some other authors: for example Lipsky and Gartner (1989: 17) who refer to mainstreaming as 'the provision of opportunities for students labelled as handicapped who are in special education settings to spend a portion of their time in general education', or Cole and Chan (1990: 27) who use mainstreaming to refer to 'an educational policy that favours the placement of students with disabilities into regular schools'. Interpretations of some other terms, because they have an important impact on special education provision, will be discussed in more detail in this or subsequent chapters.

We also need to ask what is meant by special education. Much of the debate that has occurred in special education over the past two decades has centred on its location. Although it is now widely recognised that what is important in special education is not so much where it takes place, but what takes place, it is also important not to forget that what takes place cannot be divorced from the environment in which it occurs. For example, opportunities for interactions with typical peers are likely to be fewer in the special school compared to the regular school, although simply being in the regular school does not guarantee that such interactions will take place, or that, if they do, they will be frequent and positive.

Fish (1989) wrote of special education in terms of the nature of provision in special schools and classes, but found it difficult to be precise because of the variety of provisions that could occur in these settings. Biklen (1989) described special education somewhat negatively as providing a 'safety valve' for students who were unable to succeed in the mainstream, or were likely to be disruptive in the regular class. Biklen argued that the function of special education is to identify and remediate individual deficiencies by offering specialist techniques such as language instruction or mobility training or individualised programmes. To this end, additional funding is required to support specialist teaching staff, resources, equipment, transport and so on. School systems must be accountable for how public money is spent, and so in order to receive this funding, a student needs to be identified and labelled as in need of special educational services.

Although many school systems would like to eliminate procedures for identification of students in need of special education, this has proved very difficult without at the same time eliminating provision for these students. The best that can be achieved is to ensure that procedures for identification of students and allocation of funding are as fair and equitable as possible. Biklen (1989), however, believed that assessment for identification implied a decision about placement in the most appropriate setting, and claimed that special education therefore perpetuates segregation of students with disabilities from the mainstream of education, and by implication of society. This assumption can no longer be supported – considerable evidence has emerged that special education can be provided in a wide range of both integrated and segregated settings for all but a few students – those with profound intellectual or multiple disabilities, extreme health needs or severe behaviour problems, for example. Special education might therefore best be regarded in terms of the Warnock Committee's (1978: Section 3) definition of special education provision as 'educational provision which is additional to, or different from, the educational provision made generally' for children of the same age group, regardless of setting.

Chapter 2

Educating students with disabilities
Background and influences

HISTORICAL BACKGROUND

Traditionally, education for students with disabilities has been provided in segregated schools, classes or institutions, often designed to cater for a specific category of disability. Many of these centres were started by voluntary organisations setting up their own schools for students with a specific disability, and were maintained as governments increasingly assumed responsibility for the education of all students. Thus most special schools and classes were category-based.

• Although opinions differ on the reasons for establishing segregated schools and classes for students with disabilities, several advantages were seen in this form of provision. These advantages related not only to practical and economic factors, but also to the perceived effects on both students with disabilities and non-disabled students of an integrated education.

Firstly, it was assumed that economies in the provision of special instructional methods, aids and equipment could be more easily achieved if students with a specific disability such as hearing impairment or physical disability were congregated in a limited number of settings rather than dispersed over many schools. Similarly, specialist teachers could be concentrated in a single school, enhancing the development of professional expertise in a specialised area. There is little doubt that this did occur: some special schools have achieved considerable renown as centres of knowledge and expertise in a particular disability. A further economy was achieved by the fact that ancillary services such as speech therapy and physiotherapy could be provided in one centre rather than being dispersed over schools in a wide area or requiring the student's withdrawal from classes to attend a specialist centre. In addition, paramedical staff could work in close collaboration with an educational team in a special school.

A second major advantage claimed for segregated education was that students with disabilities could benefit from the smaller classes provided in special schools or units, where they would receive more one-to-one attention and instruction could be pitched at a level appropriate to their needs rather than at the traditional age-grade level that catered for the majority of students. The segregated school was perceived as more supportive and less threatening to students with disabilities than the regular school, encouraging a feeling of security and enhancing the self-esteem of students with disabilities by avoiding continual comparison of their achievements with those of other, more competent, students.

Finally, placing students with disabilities in regular classes was seen as disadvantaging non-disabled students by creating undue demands on teaching and other resources. The post-war population explosion, with large class enrolments, made it even more difficult for class teachers to devote time and energy to exceptional students.

Under these circumstances, a marked increase occurred in the numbers of students receiving special education in some form in most western countries in the 1960s and beyond. To some extent this occurred as education systems assumed responsibility for students with disabilities who had previously been in the care of health services. It also reflected the increased life span of people with disabilities. Although specific forms of provision varied, with some systems favouring special schools, and others favouring special classes, for most students this meant being segregated from their non-disabled peers.

INFLUENCES ON SPECIAL EDUCATION

The movement towards integration of students with disabilities came about as a result of a number of inter-related influences. The first was the principle of normalisation of services for people with disabilities.

Integration as normalisation

The concept of normalisation originated in Scandinavia and was at first applied to services within institutions for people with intellectual disability. The concept implied that the patterns and conditions of everyday life that were available to these people should be as close as possible to those available to the mainstream of society. Wolfensberger (1972) redefined the concept to make it more applicable to people with all kinds of handicap. Normalisation was defined by Wolfensberger (1972: 28) as: 'Utilisation of means which are as culturally normative as possible, in order to establish and/or maintain personal behaviours and characteristics which are as culturally normative as possible'.

Categorising people with disabilities into groups that were separate from the mainstream of society immediately removed them from the cultural norms that they should have been following. Segregated settings were seen as artificial and non-normative, as well as counter-productive because transfer from such settings into a normative community setting would require considerable adjustment that would not be necessary if the individual were integrated from the start.

Thus an inevitable corollary of normalisation is integration, and the process of integration, according to Wolfensberger, consisted of those practices and measures that would maximise a person's potential participation in the mainstream of the culture. This would include living and moving about in the community in ways that were typical for the person's age group, and using community resources, including generic agencies – those that serve the general public – rather than specialist agencies for necessary support services. Thus in education normalisation would mean making maximum use of the regular school system – the system that is used by the mainstream community – with minimum dependence on segregated facilities.

Although the validity of normalisation as a basis for integration was questioned from the start, the concept played a significant role in pressures towards integration, and continues to do so. Critics claimed that normalisation did not recognise the fact that society includes a wide range of individual differences; moreover, it did not adequately recognise the diversity of educational, vocational and other opportunities that are available to people in the adult world. The concept itself founders as soon as we begin to ask who, or what, is 'normal'. There is a growing concern with protecting the rights of people with disabilities to express their own individuality. There is also a questioning of the value of programmes that are designed to ensure conformity to some predetermined norm of behaviour that is based on a restricted set of priorities. More emphasis is being given to the enjoyment of learning for its own sake for people with disabilities as they take their place in the mainstream community.

Criticism of special education

A second influence in special education was the much-cited article by Dunn (1968) which pointed to shortcomings in special education, and questioned the justification of separate education for students with a mild intellectual disability. Dunn argued that segregated education could be justified only by the benefits that accrued to teachers and students in regular schools. Segregation relieved class teachers of the need to devise and implement curricula for students who appeared unable to learn from normal instruction in the regular class. Teachers could then devote their efforts to the majority of students who did not have learning problems. According to Dunn, this benefit was at the expense of those slow learners who were removed from the regular class.

Dunn supported his criticism with four main arguments. These arguments concerned academic achievement, the detrimental effects of labelling associated with placement outside the mainstream, the racial imbalance in special education, and recent advances in individually paced curricula which would make it possible to accommodate students with disabilities in the regular class.

Firstly, Dunn cited research which showed that students with intellectual disabilities placed in special classes achieved no better academically than students of comparable ability placed in regular classes. Differences that did occur tended to favour regular class placement. Further, Dunn maintained that homogeneous grouping in a special class was to the disadvantage of students who were slow learners. Encouragement of academic competition, greater emphasis on the acquisition of basic academic skills rather than on the development of personal and social skills, and wider variation in curriculum content were seen as elements in the regular class that would be more likely to favour academic growth.

The problems in much of the research on which Dunn drew to support his argument are now widely recognised. For a number of reasons, which I will expand on in Chapter 5, it is very difficult to make valid comparisons of academic achievement between students in regular and special classes. Moreover, Dunn appeared to forget that students were placed in special classes because they had failed to learn in the regular class. Nevertheless, as Dunn pointed out, unless it can be shown that the achievement of students with disabilities in segregated settings is actually superior to that in regular classes, then segregated placement cannot be justified for academic reasons.

Dunn's second argument was that placement in segregated settings was itself responsible for people with disabilities being labelled and excluded from the mainstream of society. Diagnostic procedures based on administration of standardised tests tended to categorise the student under a particular label, with damaging effects both on teacher expectations and on the student's own self-concept.

Despite Dunn's argument and supporting studies of the effects of labelling students as having an intellectual disability, there is no evidence that integration will in itself remove the stigma attached to disability. Moreover, evidence of a relationship between labelling and negative attitudes towards students with disabilities is by no means clearcut. In a sensitive discussion of the effects of labelling, Hallahan and Kauffman (1994) suggested that labels can also help to explain behaviour or characteristics that appear different, leading to greater understanding of the individual who has a disability. The challenge, according to Hallahan and Kauffman, is for society to learn to use labels constructively rather than as the basis for stereotyped expectations about an individual. The convoluted language that is sometimes produced in exaggerated efforts to avoid labelling can be as misleading as the labels themselves and even damaging in that they may result in a denial of very real needs created by a disability. Disabilities do not disappear simply by removing a label, any more than they do by encouraging a lifestyle that is as close to normal as possible. This fact has sometimes been overlooked.

Dunn's (1968) third argument against segregated special education centred on the disproportionate number of ethnic minority students who were labelled by the education system as having an intellectual disability. This disproportion was attributed to unfair methods of identification, in particular to culturally biased measures of intelligence which favoured white, middle-class children and disadvantaged those from an impoverished or culturally different background. The integration movement in the United States was essentially confounded with the Civil Rights movement of the 1960s (Semmel, Gerber and MacMillan, 1995) – indeed in the United States it would be difficult to separate these movements because of the disproportionate numbers of minority group students included in the special education population. Students who had disabilities, along with people who belonged to ethnic minority groups, were perceived as excluded from many of the rights and benefits of citizenship, including attendance at mainstream schools (Lipsky and Gartner, 1989). Special education was accused of being a legalised form of racial segregation long after racial segregation itself was no longer legal.

The extent of racial imbalance in special education in countries outside the United States is not well documented. A survey by Watts, Elkins, Henry, Apelt, Atkinson and Cochrane (1978) of students with mild intellectual disabilities in the eastern states of Australia found that the proportion of minority group or economically disadvantaged children in special education was no greater than that in regular education, and was well below the proportion in the United States. This does not exclude the possibility that disproportionate numbers of minority children may be included in special education in areas of Australia or other countries – one of the problems in drawing conclusions about this issue is that statistics on minority group participation in special education are not available in some countries. In many areas of impoverishment, minority groups are often over-represented. Mittler (1992) has drawn our attention to the connection between poverty and special educational needs, and the links between inadequate health care, disease and malnutrition on the one hand, and the whole range of learning difficulties on the other.

One benefit arising from Dunn's (1968) argument about over-representation of minority group students, and from legal challenges in the United States to the procedures by which students were identified for special education, was that much greater attention was given to development of tests that, at least superficially, were less clearly biased towards white middle-class children. In addition, educators responsible for placement of students in special education became much more sensitive towards the misuse of test results in isolation from other information about the student's background and educational history. Even so, assessment and referral practices have continued to draw criticisms. Greater sensitivity to assessment issues and changes in the cut-off score for defining intellectual disability have not removed the disproportionate numbers of minority group children in special education in the United States (Artiles and Trent, 1994). The problem is more likely to be solved by addressing the reasons why disproportionate numbers of minority group children are prone to school failure which leads to referral for assessment in the first place, and the changes that are needed both in schools and in the wider community to prevent failure occurring.

Dunn's (1968) final argument against segregated special education and in favour of integration was that advances in the development of individualised, self-paced curricula in regular education would allow students with disabilities to be accommodated in the regular class, if they were provided with a programme designed by a specialist teacher to meet their needs and in which they could progress at their own pace. Integration could be made possible by radical departures in school organisation, involving a greater emphasis on team teaching, ungraded classes and flexible groupings.

Despite legislative provision in the United States for the development of individual educational programmes for all students with special needs (Public Law 94–142 – Education for All Handicapped Children Act, 1975 and its successor, the Individuals with Disabilities Education Act, or IDEA, 1990), implementation of this concept in the regular class was limited by lack of training of regular class teachers, and lack of time to give each student the necessary individual attention. Nevertheless, radical school restructuring involving concepts such as collaborative teaching has continued to play a major role in the argument for integration of all students with disabilities.

With hindsight it is easy to be critical of Dunn's arguments, or to regard them as over-simplistic or unworkable. It is also easy to dismiss them as irrelevant outside the United States, where segregated education was far less widespread and less confounded with the issue of minority group over-representation, or as applying only to students with mild intellectual disabilities, who were the focus of his arguments. The crucial issue is that, regardless of their validity, Dunn's arguments were taken up by educators and advocacy groups both within and beyond the United States and had a far-reaching influence on integration as a general principle for all students with disabilities.

As the move to integration gained impetus, a sociological perspective of special education as a means of social control emerged as a further influential force. This perspective also gained its support from the prevalence of minority group and impoverished students in special education. Barton and Tomlinson (1984) espoused the view that special education had been structured to cater for social and political interests by excluding from the mainstream students who for various reasons did not fit readily into the norms and practices most valued by society, particularly in terms of economic productivity. The social control theory was reflected in the eugenics movement of the 1930s which sought to limit reproduction of supposedly hereditary disabilities by segregation of people with disabilities in residential institutions.

The view of special education as a form of social control is not well founded in empirical evidence and indeed would be difficult to prove. In a historical review of special education, Cole (1989) claimed that legislation in Britain in the late nineteenth and early twentieth centuries to establish segregated schools for students with disabilities was prompted largely by humanitarian motives, however misguided. Segregated education was not seen as a means of placing children with disabilities 'out of sight', but as the best way of providing for needs which were beyond the expertise of the regular classroom teacher. Legislation enacted in 1893 which made education compulsory for children with visual and hearing impairments provided residential schools in the belief, according to Cole, that these children were best educated with others of similar age and abilities, and that they would receive good physical care and protection in such centres. Most important, it was argued by educators that these centres were the best way of preparing students with disabilities for ultimate integration into the community as self-supporting adults. In his review, Cole found that only limited practical support was given to the eugenics movement and the associated concept of permanent segregated care, and concluded that the aim of social control was overridden by a genuine concern to help students with special needs. Further, in a number of instances integration was advocated by nineteenth-century educators, an example being the education of individual blind children in Scotland in regular classes (Cole, 1989).

To give unqualified support to the social control view of segregation is therefore to do an injustice to early special educators. A theory that is not easily tested is not a good theory, and should certainly not be accepted as fact. But in fairness to those who advocated this view, it has to be acknowledged that one effect of segregated education for students with disabilities was to create an attitude of ignorance or indifference to disability, simply through lack of contact, even though this may not have been the primary motive underlying segregation.

THE LEAST RESTRICTIVE ENVIRONMENT

In the United States, reactions to Dunn's (1968) paper, as well as a number of legal cases in which it was claimed that students had been wrongfully placed in special education classes, were reflected in the enactment of Public Law 94–142. This Act asserted that, as far as possible, children with handicaps should be educated with their non-handicapped peers. Central to the Act was the principle that students with disabilities should receive their education in the 'least restrictive environment'. In 1970, Deno had proposed a model of special education provision in the form of a cascade or continuum of services, which ranged from full-time residential care through various forms of special placement to full-time education in the regular class for students with disabilities. Within this continuum of educational services, Deno proposed that there should be a continual upward movement of students with disabilities, the aim always being to move a student out of a more restrictive setting and into a less restrictive setting.

The principle of least restrictive environment was interpreted in a number of ways. Although the Act appeared to favour regular education, it also recognised a need for a range of alternative placement options (Hasazi, Johnston, Liggett and Schattman, 1994). On the one hand the least restrictive environment was seen as the environment which least restricts the interaction of students with their non-disabled peers – that is, the regular school (Sailor, 1989). On the other hand, the concept was seen as implying a continuum of settings, with a more segregated environment being appropriate for students with the most severe disabilities. Biklen (1989) strongly criticised the least restrictive environment principle for focusing on physical settings and handicaps, and for failing to focus on the supports needed by students with disabilities to function in integrated settings. A common criticism of any continuum of provision in special education has focused on the implication that, in order to move to a less restrictive environment, the student must display appropriate competencies and behaviour expected of that environment. Since students will always be in a more restrictive environment than the one to which they aspire, the opportunity for developing appropriate competencies and behaviour will never occur, and the student will remain locked into the more restrictive placement.

Biklen's view is a simplistic one. But there is no doubt that there is confusion in interpreting the principle of least restrictive environment. In the United States, Hasazi et al. (1994) conducted a semi-structured interview of over three hundred administrators, educators, school principals and parents in six states representing different approaches to special education. They found a wide range of interpretations of the concept. One approach viewed the least restrictive environment as a series of placement options arranged along a continuum that included separate facilities, schools and classrooms as well as a range of supports for students in integrated settings. Another, more pragmatic, approach took the view that, since many facilities in regular education did not have the ability to serve all students, decisions regarding the least restrictive environment for any student should take into account the capacity of the system as well as the needs of the student. Yet another approach saw the least restrictive environment as representing a continuum of supports within the neighbourhood school rather than in isolated programmes. Those who took this approach also disagreed as to whether it meant placement in regular classrooms with varying degrees of support, or placement in resource rooms or special classes for part of the day and in regular classrooms for specific activities.

An examination of court decisions on placement of students with disabilities by Brady, McDougall and Dennis (1989) also found that legal interpretations of the principle of least restrictive environment varied according to whether the court focused on the benefits of integration or on the severity of the individual student's handicap. Diamond (1995) pointed to the difficulty of defining what is meant by the word 'least', while Zigler and Hall (1995) suggested that in a climate of economic stringency 'least restrictive' might be interpreted to mean 'least expensive'.

Furthermore, the cascade model does not necessarily represent a progression in amount of contact with typical peers, or in degree of participation in mainstream activities. In the United Kingdom, the interpretation of least restrictive environment as representing a continuum of educational provision was paralleled by the proposal of the Warnock Committee (Warnock, 1978) for a continuum of services ranging from full-time education in an ordinary class with necessary help and support to home tuition. However, Warnock also distinguished three separate dimensions of integration. Locational integration referred to special units or classes set up in regular schools, or a special school and a mainstream school sharing the same site. Social integration referred to students with disabilities sharing extra-curricular activities which were designed to encourage social interaction with their typical peers. Full integration could be achieved only through functional integration, in which students with disabilities would participate with their age peers on an equal basis in educational programmes, using the same facilities and resources.

Warnock thus drew attention to a perspective of special education that now seems so obvious, yet was neglected in the early debates about integrated versus segregated education. The locational setting – special school, special class or regular class – does not in itself determine the quality of education that is received. What occurs in that setting is of far greater importance. This belief is now so widely accepted that we have to conclude that the concept of least restrictive environment has outlived its usefulness.

CATEGORIES OF DISABILITY

In the United Kingdom, a comprehensive review of special educational needs carried out by the Warnock Committee (Warnock, 1978) played a major role in changes to special education. Although the review and the 1981 Education Act which followed it embodied a number of new provisions, including provision for drawing up a 'statement' for individual students with special needs, one of the most far-reaching recommendations made by Warnock was the abolition of disability categories. In this, as well as in other respects, the Warnock report had a strong influence on the review of special education subsequently carried out in Victoria (Collins, 1984), although the latter became far more radical in its proposals for integration.

Warnock (1978) argued that the traditional categories of handicap did not adequately describe a student's educational needs. Instead, special educational needs were viewed as resulting not from a medical condition, but from a broad concept of learning difficulty which might in turn result from a range of emotional, behavioural or social problems as well as cognitive difficulties (Fish, 1989). Thus an individual's special needs would be determined by the nature of the learning difficulty rather than by a category of disability. Although Warnock (1978) recognised some advantages in the use of categories, including helping to focus attention on the needs of different groups of children and safeguarding their rights to an appropriate education, the Committee also identified four major disadvantages in their use (Norwich, 1990). Firstly, many children have more than one disability, making it difficult to place them in any one category. Secondly, the use of categories as a basis for education suggests that children in the same category have similar educational needs and fails to take account of differences among children within a given category. Thirdly, categories draw resources for special educational provision away from children who do not readily fit one of the specified categories. Fourthly, and most important from Warnock's point of view, categories assign labels to children which have lasting negative connotations.

The alternative proposed by Warnock (1978) and embodied in the 1981 Education Act was to consider all students with special educational needs as having a learning difficulty, although for administrative purposes it became necessary to subdivide this concept further into mild, moderate and severe learning difficulties. The result, in the view of a number of educators, has been to replace one set of categories with another, much less precise set (e.g. Norwich, 1990). In a detailed analysis of Warnock's arguments for the elimination of categories, Norwich pointed out that relevant information about the student's educational needs is lost if traditional categories are abandoned. The assumption that children in the same category have similar educational needs is not removed by assigning the label 'learning difficulty', which fails to distinguish, for example, the educational needs of a student with a severe hearing impairment from those of a student with a severe intellectual disability. The existence of multiple disabilities only creates a problem in relation to category-specific schools or units. Problems in the allocation of resources, according to Norwich, arise not from the existence of categories, but from the way in which they are allocated to organisations.

Norwich (1990) acknowledged the difficulty of avoiding value judgments in assigning a student to a category. But it is also not clear that the more educationally relevant categories of specific, mild, moderate and severe learning difficulties will be any less stigmatising than those that have been discarded. A number of educators have disputed the claim that categorisation leads to labelling and all its negative connotations (e.g. Stobart, 1986). Stigmatising and negative attitudes are claimed to arise not from labelling, but from the deviant behaviour and inadequate social skills that often accompany disability. The way to deal with this problem is not necessarily to eliminate categories but to address the behavioural and social problems that produce negative attitudes through appropriate integrated pro-grammes. If categorisation does lead to labelling, the question arises as to whether or not the negative aspects of labelling outweigh the problems raised for teachers and administrators by the loss of information about a student's special needs.

In Victoria, the review of special education services by Collins (1984), which in effect determined policy for the years that followed, adopted non-categorisation as one of its five guiding principles. The review proposed that legislation, service delivery structures and procedures should not refer to students by a specific category of disability. Support services should be determined by a student's additional requirements rather than by categorical assignment. Special education teachers should be able to teach across categories, dealing with a range of students with different educational requirements.

The full impact of this principle should have been anticipated. Indeed, in the absence of supporting legislation, the principle was resisted, particularly in areas of low-incidence disability such as hearing and vision impairments, in which a high level of category-specific expertise had been built up through the establishment of special schools and visiting teacher services. In practice, it was impossible not to consider specific categories of disability in making decisions about allocation of resources. But because students were no longer formally categorised, allocation of funding in terms of specific needs became impossible to monitor. In addition, there were inequities in funding that were not related either to category of disability or to extent of individual needs. A subsequent government review of the integration programme in Victoria concluded that the policy of non-categorisation made it extremely difficult to evaluate the programme in terms of both educational and social outcomes, and cost-effectiveness:

> The [Education] Department needs to reassess the appropriateness of its position on non-categorisation of students with disabilities which has led to a lack of comprehensive data for performance evaluation. Such data is essential in view of the Department's obligation to ensure that public resources are being applied in the most cost effective and efficient manner for the ultimate benefit of students on the integration program.
>
> (Auditor-General, Victoria, 1992: para. 4.6.24)

What this review brought home was that special education is not just about providing for special educational needs in ways that encourage learning and maximise community participation. It is also about expenditure of government funding, and administration must be accountable for how that funding is spent to ensure just and effective allocation of limited resources.

CONCLUSION

In this chapter I have outlined some of the changes that have occurred in educational thinking over the past quarter century and have had profound implications for students with disabilities. As the following chapters will show, many of these changes have been positive in terms of both attitudes to integration of students with disabilities, and the implementation of successful models to meet their educational needs in the regular school. From Dunn's (1968) influential arguments against segregated education, to the inclusion of students with the most severe disabilities in regular classes, it must be acknowledged that the integration movement has grown far beyond its earliest expectations. However, the changes have not been without problems.

Criticism and concern about the feasibility of integrated education for all students continue, and segregated special education settings remain the preferred option for a substantial number of students. Critics of integration have questioned the capacity of the regular education system to take on additional responsibilities associated with the education of students with disabilities, to cater for an increasingly diverse range of abilities and accomplishments, and to ensure that financial support for students with special needs is not reduced (O'Shea, O'Shea and Algozzine, 1989). Although many social benefits have resulted from integration, as O'Shea et al. point out, stigma results from failure to meet normative standards of performance, rather than from the setting in which performance takes place, and it may be unrealistic to expect that it will be diminished to any major extent in the regular school setting.

In times of economic setback, the provision of support for students with disabilities, whether in segregated or mainstream settings, is as likely as any other aspect of education to suffer from funding cuts. In Western Australia, for example, a task force set up by the Ministry of Education (1993) to examine educational provision for students with disabilities and specific learning difficulties acknowledged the difficulties of making sweeping changes in the current economic climate, and proposed that maximum use should be made of existing resources, consistent with the aims of maximising educational achievement of all students and ensuring social justice for those with special needs.

At the same time, a concern with academic standards, differing interpretations of school effectiveness and a drive for greater economic efficiency all raise questions about priorities for the allocation of resources. The issues for the future provision of education for students with disabilities, in Australia and elsewhere, are by no means clear. One issue that will need to be faced as education moves through the 1990s into the next century will be how the special needs and entitlements of students with disabilities can best be met within a common curriculum framework.

Principles of social justice demand that all students with disabilities should be enabled to take their place in integrated educational settings. But ideology always needs to be supported by evidence that it will work. The last decade of the twentieth century has seen political ideologies swept away in many countries as evidence accumulated that they did not work. We know from many individual studies that integration does work under the right conditions. But opinions are divided about whether there are some students for whom integrated education will have little benefit, either educationally or socially, and for whom the intensity of support needs is such that the cost of their provision over widely dispersed local schools cannot be economically justified. Some educational systems have retreated from an integration-only stance to one that allows choices in special education. This is less of an about-face than a recognition of the very real concerns that some parents have about mainstream education. One of the purposes of this book is to identify practices that are effective or not effective in both special and mainstream settings, so that the choices that are made are informed by a considered integration of ideology and what is feasible in practice.

Chapter 3

Integration
From the right to education to inclusive schooling

In this chapter I present an overview of two of the influential movements in the United States that have had wide repercussions for integration, the regular education initiative and the inclusive schools movement. But before I discuss these movements, I examine two other issues that continue to be of crucial importance in integration and its implementation: these are the issue of rights to education in the regular school, and attitudes to integration.

THE RIGHT TO INTEGRATION

The International Year of Disabled People in 1981 influenced the community to think more deeply about the way in which services should be provided to people with disabilities. The United Nations Declaration made during that year included the right to receive an education that would enable students with disabilities to develop their skills and capacities to the full. This right was also embodied in the United Nations Convention on the Rights of the Child in 1990 (Herr, 1993). Like the principle of least restrictive environment, however, the rights issue has been interpreted in different ways. The right of students with disabilities to receive an education had already been implemented in the establishment of special schools and services. But for many children with disabilities, education had consisted of training programmes that had little to do with future participation in the mainstream community. The assumption of responsibility by education authorities for the education of all children in part reflected a realisation that, with appropriate instructional techniques, many students with disabilities had a far greater capacity for learning than had previously been thought possible. It also reflected the right of all students to an education for a future that offered more than a lifetime of custodial care or unsatisfying repetitive work.

For the advocates of integration, however, the right to education meant the right of students with disabilities to receive an education that was comparable in every way possible to that received by the majority of students. Again, this right was interpreted in various ways. For some, it meant the right of parents to choose between regular and special settings. The extent to which parents were able to exercise this right in an informed fashion, free of any form of coercion, is debatable. The rights of students to choose an integrated setting as a separate issue from the rights of parents was not always considered (Goacher, Evans, Welton and Wedell, 1988). But Goacher et al. also noted that even parents' rights to choice of school were curtailed by the 1981 Education Act in Britain in the interests of the rights of the child to receive an education that was 'appropriate' to his or her special needs. The rights of students included the right to appropriate assessment of educational needs, but not to choice of school. Parent and student participation was to be encouraged in the decision-making process, but was only part of the overall input into that process.

A similar view is taken by the New South Wales Department of School Education (1993). The Department's policy acknowledges that all children have the right to attend a regular neighbourhood school, but also maintains that for some children their interests will be served best in a segregated educational setting. To this end, a commitment has been retained to the provision of services in a continuum of special educational settings which included regular classes, support classes in regular schools, and special schools.

Similarly, a report on integration in Tasmania (1983) recognised the rights of all students to be educated in their local school, but at the same time advocated the retention of special schools for students for whom the regular school was not considered appropriate.

Those most vocal in demanding integration of students with disabilities into regular schools often referred to the rights of children to attend their neighbourhood schools. In Victoria, the Collins (1984) review of special education rejected the concept of appropriate educational setting, finding it incompatible with its guiding principle that 'Every child has a right to be educated in an ordinary classroom in a regular school' (Collins, 1984: 13). The principle placed an obligation on schools to make the necessary provision to integrate students with disabilities, and on governments to ensure the necessary resources were available to schools. The principle also acknowledged parents' right to choose the setting in which their child was to be educated: 'The principle does not require children with impairments and disabilities to be educated in the regular school if this is not their parents' wish' (Collins, 1984: 13).

Other states in Australia have also acknowledged the right of all children to be educated in a neighbourhood school, but have generally been less radical in their implementation of this principle.

It is clear that the issue of rights is one which continues to pose dilemmas for many individuals concerned with special education. While documents concerned with both policy and practice speak glibly about rights, Australia, unlike the United States, has no Bill of Rights. In Victoria, for example, the right to an education is not embodied in legislation for any student (Sykes, 1989). Rather, parents have a legal obligation to ensure that their children receive an education. To confer legislative rights on students with disabilities would make them different from the majority of students, a situation which the advocates of integration are clearly trying to avoid. Furthermore, there is a danger that statements about the right to an education in the regular class can be interpreted to mean that all students must be educated in the regular class. Such confusion is evident in Collins's (1984) original proposal that special schools should eventually be phased out, while also implying that parents should continue to have a choice of educational setting. Moreover, rights that are part of policy but are not the subject of legislation may be qualified by special conditions – for example the right to an education in the regular class might be accepted as subject to resources being available, rather than be given unqualified acceptance.

Statements about rights can therefore be enforced only if they are embodied in legislation. Unless legislation is enacted, and there is a corresponding obligation on the part of the regular school to provide an appropriate education for a student, the right of a student with a disability to be educated in the regular school carries no more than moral weight. Under these conditions, the right to an education in the regular school may be considered an ideal to strive for, rather than a reality.

Even if rights legislation exists, its influence on practice may be limited unless it is directly concerned with education. Black-Branch (1993) examined school principals' views of the impact the Canadian Charter of Rights and Freedoms, enacted in 1982, had on special education. Most principals believed the Charter to be important in expanding the rights of students with disabilities, and in influencing policy changes at both provincial and school levels. Its influence on special education practice was less apparent. There had been a greater focus on meeting the needs of students with disabilities, but principals disagreed on the extent to which this focus was a direct result of the Charter itself, and the extent to which it reflected a larger role played by parents in improving educational practices and opportunities. Canada has no federal legislation relating directly to education (Winzer, 1994) and, except for two provinces, there are no guarantees in provincial legislation for students with disabilities to receive an 'appropriate' education, although appropriate education is strongly encouraged in individual policies.

In the United States, where the rights of students with disabilities to an education have been established in legislation, there is still a lack of clarity about the meaning of these rights in practice. This lack of clarity is reflected in the variety of interpretations of the principle of least restrictive environment, discussed in Chapter 2. It has also been reflected in a concern that rights might be reduced if category labels are eliminated for students with disabilities (Reynolds, Wang and Walberg, 1987).

The extent to which integrated education is recognised as a right will in turn depend on people's attitudes, and, as the following section will show, this is an equally complex issue.

ATTITUDES

Ben, a ten-year-old boy who has an intellectual disability, recently moved from his local school to another mainstream school in a neighbouring suburb. Ben's father described the situation at his previous school as 'dismal':

> The attitude of the teachers, and especially of the principal, to all students was extremely poor. To children with disabilities it was even worse. The staff were only concerned with their own problems and with the problems of their school. They had no time to consider Ben's needs or to develop a programme for him. When we pushed for the resources he was entitled to, they employed a teacher's aide to support him in the classroom, but the aide had no idea of what to do with him or how to encourage his learning. It wasn't her fault – she was just seen by the rest of the staff as a babysitter. They really had no interest in Ben's

progress. He wasn't challenged enough either in the curriculum, or in developing physical skills. Other children in the school were friendly and supporting, but because Ben got no encouragement from staff to take part in their activities, he became very unhappy, so we decided to move him. Now Ben is in a school where attitudes are quite different – there is a definite commitment to integration, and lots of effort is put into working out how to adapt programmes so that Ben can be a part of the school. He's so much happier, he's learning all the time and can hardly wait to get to school in the mornings.

Ben's story shows that the right to an education in the regular school, and even the provision of support staff, are simply not enough. While the formal acknowledgment of rights is likely to be important in encouraging integration, it does not ensure that integration will be successful. Positive attitudes, reflected in a commitment to encouraging the progress of students with disabilities in the mainstream, are essential. Full integration, because it inevitably requires radical changes in thinking about special education, has not always been accompanied by positive attitudes among those most closely involved. Principals may see a need for major modifications to school organisation and environment to provide for children with disabilities at a time when they are faced with competing priorities and limited resources. Teachers may feel threatened by having to cope with a child who has special needs that they feel ill-equipped to deal with, while at the same time providing instruction for as many as thirty other students who also have a wide range of individual needs and abilities. Parents fear the loss of facilities and expertise, and the security of knowing that their child is being educated in an environment that is specifically geared to dealing with the problems associated with having a disability. Students may look on the child as less competent than themselves, or reject a student whose behaviour is regarded as inappropriate or even embarrassing.

Not surprisingly, then, the early stages of the integration movement were accompanied by numerous investigations of attitudes towards disability, and in particular towards the practice of mainstreaming. These studies have been concerned with the attitudes of professionals, including principals, teachers and support staff, as well as of students, especially in relation to contact with disability. Results have been mixed.

Attitudes of professionals

Comparing professional groups in the United States and England, Norwich (1994a) concluded that contact was only one of a number of interrelated factors which influence attitudes towards integration. Complex interactions were found between social views, contact with disability and professional role in determining attitudes in both countries. Overall, attitudes to integration were positive, slightly more so in England compared to the United States. There was a small tendency for professionals with more liberal social views to have more positive attitudes, but those with predominantly conservative views who had contact with disability or were employed as special education teachers also displayed more positive attitudes. Professionals who favoured social control (more use of discipline and punishment) had more negative attitudes to integration in both countries, but a relationship between favouring personal liberty and positive attitude was evident only in the English sample. Professional position was important, with regular class teachers having least positive attitudes, and advisory and administrative staff most positive. Different patterns of relationships between the two countries also suggested that cultural factors might play a part in influencing attitudes.

A study by Leyser, Kapperman and Keller (1994) confirmed that cultural influences are likely to affect teachers' attitudes to integration. The study explored attitudes of teachers in six countries, and found differences which suggested that cultural factors, such as religion and overcrowding in schools, might be related to attitudes. However, these factors have not been systematically explored as determinants of attitude. Other cultural differences may have equal claim as influences on educational practices. In the same study, a number of common influences were found across cultures – more positive attitudes towards integration were held by teachers who had more training in special education, taught at higher secondary rather than junior secondary or primary levels, had more experience in teaching disabled students, were younger, and had less teaching experience.

The role of the professional is also likely to influence attitudes towards integration, as Norwich (1994a) found. For example, the school psychologist is often involved in the processes of assessment and decision making, as well as playing an advisory role in recommendations regarding curriculum adaptations, but less likely to be involved in direct teaching of students with disabilities. This role difference could explain the more optimistic attitudes towards integration found by Center and Ward (1989) among school psychologists compared to teachers in New South Wales.

However, one study found similar attitudes between regular and special teachers (Semmel, Abernathy, Butera and Lesar, 1991). Although both groups of teachers supported education of students with disabilities in the regular classroom in principle, both also questioned assumptions underlying regular class placement, claiming that it would be unlikely to produce improvements in achievement of either special or regular class students, that it would not necessarily produce social benefits for students with mild disabilities and that full-time placement of special education students in regular classrooms could slow the rate at which curriculum objectives were met for regular class students. Fewer than one-third agreed that the regular classroom with support from a special education consultant would provide the most effective educational environment for students with mild disabilities.

The similar attitudes of regular and special class teachers could be explained in part by the results of a complex study by Thomas (1985) of factors which determine teachers' attitudes towards integration of students with intellectual disability. Thomas found the best single predictor of class teachers' attitudes was the perceived attitude to integration of the special educator who taught or acted as adviser in the school and with whom the class teacher had contact. If the special educator was perceived to have a positive attitude, then the class teacher also showed a positive attitude. Negative attitudes were related to a perception that the special educator held either a negative or a neutral attitude to integration. That is, to encourage a positive attitude in teachers, the special educator must be perceived to be positive as well, not simply neutral. The relationship between class teachers' positive attitude and the perceived positive attitude of the special educator was further strengthened when teachers saw themselves as competent in teaching students with intellectual disability, or if they rated the quality of special education support as high. High-quality support appeared to compensate for class teachers' lack of confidence in encouraging positive attitudes.

Although Thomas's (1985) study was limited to two samples in widely differing geographical locations, it did suggest that the perceived contribution and enthusiasm of support staff can be crucial in influencing the attitudes of other professionals. Anecdotal and case study evidence supports this conclusion, although more systematic evidence is only indirectly available. Center, Ward, Parmenter and Nash (1985) found a high level of support for integration into the regular class among school principals in New South Wales, with over 88 per cent favouring integration as a desirable goal. Principals of Catholic schools and country schools showed slightly more positive attitudes, and slightly less positive attitudes were found among those who had been a principal for more than seven years, who had a special class on the site or who had previous experience with a special class.

Although endorsement of integration was very high, the majority of principals believed that integration should be conditional on the provision of appropriate support services. Consideration of the effects of integration on other students was also emphasised. Students with mild or moderate physical disability were rated as most acceptable for integration. Mild hearing impairment and mild intellectual disability were also regarded as acceptable. In general a disability appeared to be acceptable provided that no extra competencies or extra-curricular demands were required of the regular class teacher, and no building modifications were needed. This condition was consistent with the principals' relatively pessimistic expectation that extra support services would be unlikely to be provided. Thus students with moderate or severe disabilities whose needs might exceed the capacity of the regular school staff were regarded as less acceptable.

Center et al.'s (1985) findings contrast with those of Desai (in press) in Victoria. The discrepancies may reflect differences between the two states in special education provision and integration policies. Desai found that positive attitudes of principals towards integration were best predicted by the length of experience the principals had in integrating students with disabilities, with formal training in special education, experience with students with disabilities in formal study programmes, and completion of in-service training in integration also predicting positive attitudes. Gender, age, years of experience as a teacher or principal, and location and size of school, had no effect on attitudes.

Further, a study of Israeli teachers disputed the conclusion that positive attitudes towards integration are necessarily dependent on availability of adequate support. Schechtman, Reiter and Schanin (1993) found concerns about the difficulties of class teachers in providing for students with disabilities were unrelated to attitudes towards integration. Positive attitudes were more likely to be determined by school policy and a personal conviction of the importance of integration. Teachers who saw the success of integration

as being dependent on external support were more likely to hold
negative attitudes, but those who perceived themselves as having
more control through their conviction that integration could be made
to work were more likely to hold positive attitudes.

A sense of personal control and ownership of an integration
programme may therefore be at least equally as important as the
amount of available support. Harvey (1989) compared changes in
attitudes of teachers, student teachers and non-teachers over six years
following introduction of the integration policy in Victoria. Practis-
ing teachers and student teachers were generally more positive after
the six years, particularly evident in greater acceptance of students
with a mild intellectual disability in the regular class. Non-teachers,
however, showed no change. Harvey attributed the change in teachers'
attitudes to three possible factors. Firstly, with the passage of time
integration policy was perceived to be more flexible than was
originally thought. Special schools had remained open, allowing
parents to continue to choose this option. As a consequence, teachers
may have felt less pressure to accept all students regardless of the
severity of their disability. Secondly, widespread employment of
teacher aides to support students with disabilities in integrated
settings could be seen to lessen the impact of integration on regular
class teachers and schools. Thirdly, teachers had had greater exposure
to students with disabilities, and this may have reduced their
apprehension about integration. Non-teachers would not have had
this experience to moderate the attitudes they held at the outset.

In fact a common finding in studies of attitudes is that teachers
report a change in their attitudes after some experience of integration.
In a qualitative study by Giangreco, Dennis, Cloninger, Edelman and
Schattman (1993), teachers of students with severe and multiple
disabilities in regular classes described their initial experiences of
integration as primarily negative. Their first reaction to having a
student with a disability in their class was to have minimal
involvement with the student in the expectation that someone else
would take responsibility. During the first year, a gradual change
occurred as teachers began to notice benefits, not only in acceptance of
the student by non-disabled members of the class, but also in the
greater responsiveness of the students with disabilities to social
interactions. Teachers made an effort to include the student in more
class activities. At the same time, they began to value the opportunity
for teamwork, rather than expecting someone else to take prime
responsibility for the student.

The importance of teachers' attitudes cannot be over-estimated. Moreover, it is difficult to find a successful 'inclusive' school in which positive attitudes are not present from the top down. The principal's attitude is crucial in ensuring that students with disabilities encounter a climate of acceptance and warmth within a school. If the principal is responsible for allocation of resources, it is also crucial in ensuring that both staff and students receive the support they need to make integration work.

Attitudes of students

The attitudes of school principals and teachers are likely to be reflected in the attitudes of students. Teachers may unwittingly create negative attitudes in non-disabled students by the way in which they interact with a student who has a disability. For example, Lynas (1986) found that although regular class peers of students with hearing impairment were generally favourable towards integration, their attitude was qualified by class teachers who showed positive discrimination towards the student (for example overlooking a student's failure to respond to instructions on the assumption that the student had not heard). The students with hearing impairment were aware of problems in being singled out for attention by the teacher, and even developed strategies to avoid attention such as pretending to understand or copying other students. Teachers themselves did not seem to be aware of the effects of their actions.

The assumption that increased contact will improve the attitudes of non-disabled students towards students who have disabilities by increasing familiarity and understanding of disability has been only partially supported. Early studies in the United States of attitudes towards mild intellectual disability suggested that increased contact may result in negative attitudes as classmates become more familiar with the less acceptable aspects of behaviour of students with disabilities (Gottlieb, 1981). Weisel (1988) examined attitudes towards students with hearing impairment of three groups of non-disabled students with varying amounts of contact. One group consisted of students in regular classes in which a child with hearing impairment was integrated full-time (high contact); another group consisted of students in the same school but not the same class as a student with hearing impairment (moderate contact); and the third were students who had no contact with hearing impairment. The study examined attitudes from a multi-dimensional perspective, and found differences between the three groups according to the attitudinal dimension being measured. Although all groups were relatively positive in their attitudes, the group with moderate contact showed more 'generalised rejection' than the other two groups – consistent with previous findings that superficial contact is likely to have negative effects on attitudes to disability. The high-contact group was higher on a measure of 'distressed identification' – a dimension that reflected sensitivity to the disability and an awareness of one's own vulnerability. Subsequent investigations have confirmed that it is the nature of the contact that is important, rather than the amount of contact. For example, Fenrick and Petersen (1984) found peer tutoring was associated with more positive attitudes towards students with disabilities compared to free play situations, and concluded that a structured situation in which students were given a definite role would be more effective in changing attitudes than simply providing opportunities for social interaction.

A limitation on studies of students' attitudes towards disability and integration is that students may have limited understanding or misconceptions about disability. Kyle and Davies (1991) carried out a study of secondary students' attitudes towards intellectual disability (mental retardation). Students had limited knowledge of the causes of intellectual disability and confused it with both mental illness and physical handicap. Although they expressed 'kindly' attitudes towards people with intellectual disability, they also revealed feelings of discomfort, embarrassment and uncertainty.

Research on attitude change has had some promising results in improving attitudes of peers towards students with disabilities. Kyle and Davies (1991) found discussion sessions to be valuable in alerting students to important issues and facts about disability and in assisting them to question the appropriateness of their own attitudes and feelings. Gash (1993) implemented a programme which included dramatisations and videotapes of situations involving specific disabilities, such as impairments in hearing, vision and speech, with the aim of increasing understanding and awareness of disability. Students were encouraged to explore the feelings and emotions of the person with a handicap. The students were then asked what they would do if a child with a mental handicap was placed in their class. Those who had participated in the programme showed more concern for the welfare of the disabled student and generally a more positive attitude towards the disability than those who had not participated. However, students not in the programme were more positive about friendships, sharing of secrets and reading the same books. Age, gender and prior experience with disability also influenced attitudes. Concerns with intellectual disability, being more sociable, and school arrangements for the student with disability increased with age, but more so for girls than for boys. Students who had no previous experience of disability and did not participate in the programme preferred special class placement for students with disabilities, whereas students with no previous experience who did participate had no clear preference.

These studies indicate that efforts to create more positive attitudes will have to take complex factors into account. Experience with disability has both positive and negative influences. The factors that create negative attitudes will not necessarily go away with increased contact, and need to be addressed if contacts are to be productive. For example, social skills training or programmes to reduce the challenging behaviour of some students with disabilities have been suggested as helping to remove barriers to successful integration. Short-term contact is more inclined to produce negative attitudes, whereas long-term contact improves attitudes.

The contribution of attitude research to the success of integration is nevertheless problematic. Much of the research has been carried out without a theoretical orientation. An important question is the extent to which attitudes expressed in response to questionnaires and surveys are actually reflected in a person's behaviour. Negative attitudes may be expressed in rejection of people with disabilities, or in indifference or insensitivity. Teacher attitudes as expressed by ratings or questionnaire responses may represent a global attitude towards integration rather than an attitude towards an individual student with a disability, but it is the individual attitude that is more closely related to acceptance or rejection of disabled students by their peers (Roberts and Zubrick, 1992). Teachers interviewed in an early integration programme in which few services were available to support students with moderate and severe disabilities often expressed hostility towards the programme (Jenkinson, 1982). Yet their concern for individual children in their care and their commitment to achieving the aims of integration were equally evident.

Trickey and Stobart (1987) pointed to evidence that attitudes follow rather than precede behaviour change, and that attitude change in itself does not automatically produce changes in behaviour. This conclusion would support research that has shown positive effects of contact with disability, but not those studies that have found negative attitudes to be associated with more contact. Where educators and students are forced into behaviour changes by their daily contact with disability, attitude change is more likely to follow. However, positive changes are more likely to occur if both teachers and students feel themselves to have some control over the situation in which interaction occurs. Educational awareness programmes which are not accompanied by opportunities for behaviour change may well founder. What is needed first, according to Trickey and Stobart, is organisational change, with new patterns of responsibility and new working relationships. Attitudinal and awareness issues can be attended to once this has occurred.

TWO MODELS FOR INTEGRATION: THE REGULAR EDUCATION INITIATIVE AND INCLUSIVE SCHOOLING

The belief that negative attitudes to disability have been created and perpetuated by segregating special education from the mainstream underlies the more radical reforms to special education proposed in the latter part of the 1980s and the 1990s. Inconsistencies arising from different interpretations of terms and procedures in special education, frustration at lack of progress in integration, and an inability to resolve many of the dilemmas created by ambiguities in legislation, have also contributed to two movements in particular. These movements are respectively the regular education initiative and the concept of inclusive schooling. Although these terms have often been used interchangeably, and often confusingly in relation to their meaning and intent, they can also be distinguished by some unique features which represent a progression towards the elimination of special education, as it has traditionally been known, altogether. Fuchs and Fuchs (1994) have clearly distinguished these two movements according to their major advocacy groups, goals and tactics.

The regular education initiative

The regular education initiative had as its chief goal the merging of special and general education into a single organisational structure, with all students with disabilities being educated in the regular school. This was not to deny the continuing need of many students with disabilities for additional services and resources: rather, the merger would be achieved by integrating into the regular school special education personnel and resources as well as students (Stainback and Stainback, 1989). This was not as simple as it may at first appear. The complexity of the regular education initiative is illustrated by the fact that even within this model several different perspectives can be identified. Kubicek (1994) identified at least three approaches. The first, the most conservative, called for minimum change in the status quo, acknowledging that regular education, even with radical changes, could not on its own solve the problems of learning failure, classroom diversity or over-representation of minority groups that have beset special education. At the other extreme it was argued that, if students with special needs are not a separate category of student, then special education should not form a separate or segregated system. In between these two approaches, the more moderate advocates of regular education called for a significant reduction in special education, particularly for students with mild disabilities.

Thus at least two distinct advocacy groups for the regular education initiative could be identified (Fuchs and Fuchs, 1994). The first consisted of educators and others concerned with high-incidence disability – learning disabilities, behaviour disorders and mild intellectual disability – students who were considered to be part of a mainstream population which also included at-risk students with no identifiable disabilities. The goal of this group was a large-scale increase in the number of students with disabilities being educated in mainstream classes, rather than individual, case-by-case integration. Students in the mainstream would be supported by special educators in a restructured, unified system. This would help to strengthen the academic performance of underachievers without disabilities as well as those with mild to moderate disabilities.

Strategies proposed by this group for implementing the regular education initiative included the introduction of co-operative learning structures, in which students would work in groups of mixed ability helping each other in their academic tasks. The overall intention was to strengthen regular classroom teaching by making it more responsive to individual differences. This could be done by transferring specialist resources previously only available in segregated settings to the regular class.

The second group identified by Fuchs and Fuchs (1994) were those concerned with low-incidence disabilities, especially severe intellectual disability. This group advocated the integration of students with severe disabilities into local neighbourhood schools, based in self-contained resource settings, and the collaboration of special and general educators to achieve this aim. In effect, they advocated modifications to the continuum of service provision, with elimination of the lower levels of the continuum so that students in residential or day special schools would move to resource rooms in mainstream schools. The more extreme advocates saw this as part of a progression towards complete abolition of segregated resources, with all students sharing the same resources for learning on a full-time basis.

The regular education initiative was confronted by several obstacles. The diversity of interests concerned with its promotion was reflected in confusion and inconsistency in both goals and strategies (Fuchs and Fuchs, 1994). Academic excellence was beginning to replace equity as a significant issue in regular education. The regular education initiative was not a concern of regular education; furthermore it risked being perceived as motivated by economic rationalism and a somewhat superficial view of equity (Kauffman, 1995).

The inclusive schooling movement

The objectives of inclusive schooling were similar to those of the regular education initiative, but its advocates went further in promoting the elimination of special education and special educators altogether. Its primary aim was to abolish the continuum of services, which it saw as no longer useful, with the placement of all students with disabilities in the regular classroom (Fuchs and Fuchs, 1994).

The proponents of inclusive schooling claimed that the existence of a separate system of special education was responsible for many of the problems in general education, with schools placing 'troublesome' students in segregated settings rather than attempting to modify their curriculum and instructional strategies. Specialist support services would be retained in inclusive schooling, but would operate alongside the regular class teacher in the mainstream, where services would be available to any student in need. This practice was expected both to change the attitudes of students and teachers without disabilities, and to enhance the social competence of students with disabilities and increase their community participation. Inclusive schooling was thus concerned, but not exclusively so, with the integration of students with disabilities:

> It [inclusive schooling] also means providing all students within the mainstream appropriate educational programs that are challenging yet geared to their capabilities and needs as well as any support

and assistance they and/or their teachers may need to be successful in the mainstream.

(Stainback and Stainback, 1990: 3)

It goes beyond integration to focus on:

new conceptions of ordinary schooling, not with developing individual programmes for particular pupils; it is a matter of school reform, not pupil placement; it is about fitting schools to pupils, not socialising pupils to pre-set norms of learning and behaviour.

(Hegarty, 1991: 90)

In this context, special educators would continue to provide support to students with disabilities, but would be integrated into the regular education system as educators with specific expertise in areas of curriculum and instruction.

Unlike the regular education initiative, the inclusive schooling movement in the United States was advocated primarily by a clearly identified body: The Association for Persons with Severe Handicaps (known as TASH). This organisation was concerned with promoting the rights and well-being of people with severe intellectual disability, and its adherence to the principle of normalisation was reflected in the belief that all children had a right to attend their neighbourhood school and participate in class activities together with their chronological age peers.

In addition to structural changes in education, the inclusive schooling movement advocated radical changes to curriculum to accommodate all students in the regular classroom. The standard curriculum was seen as emphasising the division between those who were able to attain its objectives and those with severe disabilities who clearly could not. It was further rejected on three grounds: firstly, that no single body of knowledge could be identified that children should be required to learn; secondly, that it did not allow for individual differences in students' needs, prior experiences and learning styles; and thirdly, that it lacked meaning and interest for many students (Fuchs and Fuchs, 1994). The inclusive schooling movement proposed that the standard curriculum should be replaced by an emphasis on the processes involved in students learning what they can, rather than on the acquisition of specific skills, so that students would come to enjoy learning for its own sake.

In the inclusive school a disability would be perceived as part of a continuum of difference rather than implying a separate group or category (Stainback and Stainback, 1989). While some homogeneous groups might be desirable for specific instruction, these should be minimised and heterogeneous groupings encouraged, with students contributing according to their capacities. Teaching methods, materials and programmes should be adapted according to individual needs rather than for specific categories of disability, and assessment should be criterion-based rather than norm-based to reflect a focus on individual progress rather than on placement decisions.

Inclusive schooling differed from the regular education initiative in two important ways: firstly, in proposing the abolition of special education altogether; and secondly in emphasising a broader curriculum that included functional and social skills rather than exclusively academic skills. The change in focus on learning reflected a concern with students with severe intellectual disability, rather than those with mild or moderate disabilities. Although its organisational strength, its political connections and the consistency of its aims and strategies allowed it to have a profound impact on policy in several areas (Fuchs and Fuchs, 1994), many of its proposals were unrealistic, failing to recognise the needs not only of students in the mainstream of education but also of those with severe disabilities whom it claimed to represent. Its proposals for curriculum change did not reflect a growing community concern with improving academic standards. Nor did they recognise the need of students with severe intellectual disabilities for often intensive instruction in specific skills that are taken for granted in students without disabilities, or the need for more tangible sources of motivation than an intrinsic interest in learning. The inclusive schooling movement has therefore not been universally accepted by either professionals or parent groups concerned with the education of students with severe disabilities.

Inclusive schooling also raised organisational issues which, according to Jenkins, Pious and Jewell (1990), had not been adequately dealt with. These included willingness of the regular class teacher to take responsibility for all students, and of the special teacher to collaborate and communicate while at the same time relinquishing final decision making about instruction. In addition, Jenkins et al. maintained that multi-disciplinary teams should acknowledge that some students could not develop competency in basic skills, and should be segregated from their regular class peers in order to protect regular class teachers from unrealistic demands.

Other writers have suggested that to regard disability, particularly severe disability, as part of a continuum of individual differences is to deny the extent of needs of some students with disabilities (Mostert, 1991), and is more likely to work to their disadvantage rather than to remove any stigma associated with the disability.

Paralleling the concept of inclusive schooling has been a change in views about the nature and purpose of education, and a greater concern with school effectiveness. The concept of school effectiveness gained prominence in the late 1970s and 1980s, partly as a counter to claims that outcomes of schooling were largely determined by individual student characteristics including home background (McGaw, Piper, Banks and Evans, 1992). Initial research focused on a relatively narrow conception of school effectiveness as measurable academic achievement, especially in basic skills. A renewed concern with academic standards, though much needed, poses a potential threat to the participation of students with disabilities in the regular school system unless adequate provision is made for their educational needs. Research by McGaw et al. indicated that parents perceive academic standards as only one element of school effectiveness: students' social and emotional well-being is equally valued. Although it is doubtful if special needs provision is seen as a priority by mainstream schools striving for greater effectiveness, improving school effectiveness has been viewed as the key to accommodating a wider range of students with disabilities in the regular class (Ainscow, 1991). Ainscow's view suggests that an even broader conceptualisation of school effectiveness may be required if schools are to cater for the full spectrum of students with special needs.

Chapter 4

Outcomes

Kate is the youngest of four children, and has lived all her life in a small country town with her parents and older brothers and sister. Now twenty, Kate was diagnosed at birth with Down syndrome. The town where she lived had no special school and no early intervention programme, and when Kate was four it seemed to her parents the natural thing to do to enrol her in the pre-school centre that her brothers and sister had attended. The pre-school had a warm and welcoming climate. Kate was an easy-going child, and although her speech and motor skills were delayed, she enjoyed being with the other children at the centre. At the end of the year, when the other children would be moving on to school, the pre-school director suggested to Kate's parents that she too should be enrolled in the local primary school that the rest of the family had attended.

The school principal knew Kate's family, and was happy to have Kate in the school. For her class teacher it was 'no big deal' – in the small town where Kate lived there were no other options, so the teachers were used to coping with any child who came to the school. They knew that their expectations of Kate could not be the same as for most of the children in the class, and that she would need to be given extra encouragement and help to participate. As she moved through the primary school, Kate lagged increasingly behind her classmates in academic skills, but she also learned a great deal from them, especially by copying their behaviour. The other children took their cue from their teachers, and accepted her as one of the class. She was a part of their community, she had friends among them, and if she ever behaved in ways they found unacceptable they soon let her know. They shared in her achievements and always encouraged her to try new skills and join in their games. They made allowances, because they knew that somehow Kate could not always keep up with them, but they accepted her disability as part of life.

By the time Kate finished primary school, she could read simple sentences, and had learned some basic number skills. Her vocabulary had increased enormously, and although she still had some problems with speech, her family, teachers and friends were patient and usually understood what she was trying to express. Kate also had many practical skills which meant she could care for herself at school with very little prompting from her teacher, and with the help of the local shopkeepers who knew her she was quite competent at making small purchases. Kate's brothers and sister had gone on to the high school in a nearby city, travelling there by bus each day. Kate's parents were uneasy about sending Kate there because they feared that both academically and socially she would fall further and further behind the other students, with little to gain from the curriculum offered at the high school. Then they heard about a smaller secondary school that emphasised vocational training and independent living skills. The school had a programme for disadvantaged girls, and Kate was accepted into this programme. A sociable girl, she made new friends, and learned many useful skills that would prepare her for her life as an adult in the community.

Since leaving school, Kate has been employed in the kitchen of a fast food outlet where she helps prepare orders. Her fellow workers accept the fact that she is slow at some tasks, but they are willing to help her when necessary and prompt her when she forgets what to do. Kate still lives at home, but her parents are looking ahead to the possibility of her sharing a flat in supported accommodation closer to her work.

Both Kate and her parents are pleased with the outcome of her schooling. She was given every opportunity to learn useful skills that now stand her in good stead, she was given help in obtaining a job in open employment, and friends from both her primary and secondary schools keep in touch. She still needs some support, especially in making important decisions, but Kate's parents are satisfied that she has never been held back in any way. In a climate that places heavy demands on resources to support integration, the comment by Kate's mother may seem a little unusual:

> I'm glad Kate went through the school system without getting involved with all that bureaucracy. We didn't worry about funding, and neither did her teachers. There were no teacher aides, and not even any special programme until she went to the secondary school. We didn't have any of the hassles. She just went to school like anyone else, and now she's come out of it like anyone else – with a job that is suited to her ability, and as much independence as she is capable of at the moment. We have no regrets about missing out on all the resources students like her are getting now.

Ray, like Kate, is twenty, and has a moderate intellectual disability and problems with motor co-ordination. Ray also started his schooling in a mainstream primary school, but, in the words of his father, was 'totally out of his depth' there. He made no friends and was unable to cope with the academic work. He felt isolated and unhappy. After two years of plummeting self-esteem, Ray was moved to a special school. It was a move that Ray's parents have never regretted. He is now in a vocational preparation programme, and near the end of his schooling. Ray's father describes him as 'an independent, socially able person with confidence and well-developed living skills. Because he was educated in a special school, he has a group of close peers who have an active, exciting social life. They are able to draw on one another's skills and support to foster their own independence, and live fulfilling lives. We would never have thought in his first two years of school life that Ray could achieve what he has.'

These two very positive outcomes result from two different school backgrounds and settings. They also illustrate two quite different sets of expectations about the outcomes of education for students with disabilities – for one it is as a member of the mainstream community; for the other a satisfying and fulfilling life is also important but is not dependent on being part of the mainstream.

Concerns about rights and resources tend to overshadow concerns about outcomes in special education. Outcomes are often described in vague terms of satisfaction with a particular school setting or programme. Yet evaluations of outcomes are important, not just to support or reject a particular view about special education, but also to identify ways in which special education provisions need to be improved.

Dunn's (1968) criticisms of special education, described in Chapter 2, were based on what he interpreted as the absence of any positive outcomes in segregated special education, and indeed some perceived negative outcomes. Lipsky and Gartner (1992) also argued that special education, compared to regular education, had poorer outcomes for students with disabilities. For example, students with disabilities in special schools or classes were less likely to complete secondary education, and when they did leave school were likely to be unemployed, to live at home rather than independently, and to have few friends. Few were likely to be enrolled in post-secondary education, or were engaged in any productive activity after they left school.

The problem with many conclusions about outcomes is that they fail to show how outcomes are determined by educational setting. Linking unemployment with segregated education is not simply a matter of showing that students who were educated in a special class or school are more likely to be unemployed than students educated in the regular class. Instead, we need to consider all of the factors that produce particular outcomes, including those that are an essential part of the educational setting and those that are quite independent of it. These factors include the goals and objectives of a programme, the expectations of students enrolled in a programme and the criteria used for evaluating outcomes. For example, the poor outcomes of special schools and classes were seen by Lipsky and Gartner (1989) as reflecting a common set of attitudes and expectations – that students with disabilities were unlikely to achieve the goals of education aspired to by the majority of students. We also need to examine the extent to which outcomes can be attributed directly to characteristics of a setting, such as instructional methods used, or opportunities provided to students, and how far they are related to characteristics that are independent of setting. Outcomes of special education are most likely to be determined by complex interactions between what goes on in the educational setting and individual student background and characteristics.

This chapter considers outcomes of special education in relation to each of these issues – goals and objectives, expectations, criteria for evaluating outcomes, and characteristics of both educational environ- ments and students, concluding with an examination of the long-term outcomes of special education. No definitive conclusions are offered –

rather the aim is to highlight some of the factors that need to be taken into account before any conclusions about outcomes can be made. Finally, I will briefly consider outcomes of integration for students in regular classes who do not have disabilities.

GOALS AND OBJECTIVES OF EDUCATIONAL PROGRAMMES

Outcomes of programmes and settings in special education have traditionally been measured in terms of goal attainment (Smith and Noble, 1993). Goals and objectives of a programme are defined and strategies for their achievement devised and implemented. At the conclusion of a programme, or at some predetermined point such as the end of a year, achievement of goals and objectives will be measured. In special education, programme objectives are often formalised in individual educational programmes or plans.

For a number of reasons we need to be cautious in making claims about the outcomes of integrated or segregated special education based on this model of outcome attainment. The goals of individual programme plans are likely to be influenced not only by the student's abilities and needs, but also by the extent and range of resources available. In turn, achievement of goals will differ according to the perceptions of administrators, educators, families and the students themselves of what those goals are. In a survey of integration in its member countries, the Organisation for Economic Co-operation and Development (OECD, 1994) identified three kinds of outcomes which reflected variation between countries in the aims of integration. Attitudinal outcomes emphasised increased community participation of people with disabilities. Educational outcomes could include improved learning and academic performance, as well as advances in the methods and techniques used to teach children with special educational needs. Recent reforms in education suggest that a further educational outcome might be increased participation in, or access to, a common curriculum. Social outcomes formed a third category of outcome identified by the OECD, and included socialisation skills, improved self-image and autonomy.

Of these, academic outcomes have received most attention. The absence of any demonstrated superiority in academic performance of students with disabilities placed in special schools or classes compared to those remaining in regular classes has been well documented. Reviews in the late 1970s and early 1980s (e.g. Semmel, Gottlieb and

Robinson, 1979; Strain and Kerr, 1981) of a wide range of studies of mainstreaming concluded that students with disabilities placed in special classes achieved no better educationally than those placed in regular classes, and in fact the dominant trend was in favour of regular classes. This trend was attributed to several factors, including fostering by the regular class of a social climate that encouraged competition, greater emphasis in the regular class on the acquisition of competence in basic academic skills, compared to an emphasis on personal development and growth in special schools and classes, wider variation in curriculum content in the regular class, and selective placement, with more able students remaining in the regular class. The major exceptions to this trend were students with emotional–behavioural problems, who generally showed greater long-term academic benefits from special class placement, and students with learning disabilities, who showed improved academic performance at least in the short term from special class placement, although there was no evidence that this improvement was maintained on reintegration into the regular class (Semmel et al., 1979).

The trend towards more positive academic outcomes for students with disabilities in regular classes was confirmed in further analyses of research studies (Carlberg and Kavale, 1980; Wang and Baker, 1985–86). Wang and Baker's study examined academic and social outcomes, environmental and student characteristics associated with positive outcomes, and the method used in each of the research studies included in their analysis. They found overall gains in integrated, compared to segregated, settings, but could not identify any single factor other than the setting itself that would account for this difference.

Following Dunn's (1968) influential paper, these studies offered further persuasive arguments to the supporters of inclusive schooling, despite flaws in methodology which will be discussed in more depth in Chapter 5. While these early studies have now been discredited as being based on invalid comparisons, the fact that special classes could not demonstrate superior outcomes was used as justification for large-scale integration and the elimination of segregated settings except for students with the most severe disabilities. Equally important were the assumptions made about the regular class environment that lacked the support of investigations of environmental or other factors conducive to school achievement. Thus Wang and Baker (1985–86) were unable to identify any factor other than setting which could account for differences in educational outcomes between integrated and segregated settings. If important characteristics are not considered in an original study, then no amount of re-analysis will make up for that deficiency.

While studies of academic outcomes for students with disabilities have generally favoured the mainstream setting, the same cannot be said for social outcomes. The concern with social adjustment of students with disabilities arises in part from the stigma apparently associated with the disability, which marks the person with a disability as different in the eyes of those not so disabled. One of the goals of integration has been to remove that stigma by making the person with a disability part of the mainstream community, so that the focus is on similarities between individuals rather than on differences. Further, it was assumed that integration would result in students with disabilities exhibiting more acceptable behaviour acquired through modelling the more typical behaviour of their peers.

Acceptance of students with disabilities by their non-disabled peers in mainstream settings has been a major focus of outcome studies. Studies of social outcomes during the 1970s tended to focus on the social acceptance of students with mild intellectual disabilities integrated into regular classrooms. The conclusions were not promising. Following a review of forty studies, Gresham (1982) summarised three main outcomes. Firstly, students with disabilities interacted less frequently and more negatively with non-disabled students than with their peers in a segregated setting; secondly, they were more poorly accepted by their non-disabled peers; and thirdly, there was no evidence that students with disabilities modelled the behaviours of their non-disabled peers as a result of increased contact.

More recent studies have also raised doubts about integration achieving its aim of promoting social interactions for students with severe disabilities. Bless and Amrein (1992) examined the social and academic outcomes of students with learning difficulties in three settings which varied in the degree of integration: self-contained special classes which co-operated with regular classes for some activities; regular classes with resource room programmes in which children were withdrawn for therapy or remedial programmes; and regular classes without special support. In all settings, students with learning difficulties received fewer choices on a sociometric test than non-disabled children, and their own assessments of their relations with peers were less favourable than those of non-disabled students. The danger of assuming that increased social acceptance or improved academic performance will follow simply by integrating students with disabilities, regardless of what occurs in the setting, is evident. Further studies have led to the widely accepted conclusion that social acceptance of students with disabilities as an outcome of integration will not be achieved of its own accord.

Danby and Cullen (1988) examined the extent to which five assumptions underlying integration could be supported by evidence of outcomes. In relation to the first assumption – that integration avoids the negative effects of labelling – they could find no studies which specifically described the effects of using different labels in an integrated setting. The second assumption – that integration results in social benefits – also lacked clear supportive evidence, partly owing to weaknesses in studies of sociometric choice which included students with disabilities, and to the fact that many qualitative studies of this issue tend to be difficult to interpret. A third assumption – that integration would give parents more involvement in their children's education – was also found to be not supported, except in legislation. In fact, according to Danby and Cullen, some reports described efforts actually to reduce parents' participation in the type of education chosen for their children. The fourth assumption – that educational outcomes would improve – and the fifth – that non-handicapped students in regular schools would also benefit from integration – were also found to lack supporting evidence.

The absence of support for either the aims or assumptions underlying integration does not mean that integration has only neutral or negative outcomes. It is virtually impossible to demonstrate that one type of setting is more or less effective than another. While it is important not to make unjustified claims about integration, it is also important to explore ways in which placement can determine outcomes – that is, the practices and procedures that have been successful in producing positive outcomes, and factors associated with negative outcomes that need to be addressed if integrated education is to be more successful.

OUTCOMES IN RELATION TO EXPECTATIONS

Our judgment of the value of any experience is inevitably influenced by what we expected to get out of that experience. This is particularly true in special education. Anticipated outcomes are likely to vary between educational systems and indeed, as schools acquire greater autonomy, between schools. Differences between settings in curriculum and instructional approaches are likely to produce different expectations about what is possible in the setting. There are also likely to be differences in the expectations held for individual students, and for any one student there may be differences in the expectations of parents, teachers, other professionals and the students themselves regarding the outcomes of education. Like the goals of education, expectations may also be vague or unrealistic, and offer little that is useful in deciding whether an educational programme has positive outcomes. This is particularly likely when a programme has been implemented on the basis of a philosophical principle, without thinking through the expectations for all of those involved in the programme. For example, the normalisation principle, if taken too literally, may create unrealistic expectations and in doing so foster a sense of disillusionment and discouragement with education.

A common criticism of segregated special education is that curriculum and instruction in these settings are based on relatively low expectations of students. Low expectations can lead to satisfaction with an outcome that is less than optimal for the student (Evans and Weld, 1989). But unrealistic expectations can occur by either over-estimating or under-estimating a student's potential. Even students themselves may under-estimate their potential achievement. For example, in one study, students with learning difficulties in integrated classes rated their own academic skills more negatively than they were rated by their peers (Bless and Amrein, 1992). Further, the students' ratings of their own abilities were lower than self-ratings of comparable students in special classes, with the lowest self-ratings occurring among students in the regular class who received remedial support. In reality, the academic achievement of the students with learning difficulties placed in regular classes, either with or without support, was better than that of the students placed in special classes. Thus settings can have both positive and negative effects on outcomes because of the different expectations they produce.

For many students, particularly those with an intellectual disability, an expectation that performance will be comparable to that of non-disabled peers will almost certainly produce an unfavourable result. As Evans and Weld (1989) pointed out, expectations in regular education are relatively straightforward: students are expected to achieve at a level that is appropriate for their grade. For many students with disabilities achievement at grade level is an unrealistic expectation. Hayes and Gunn (1988) compared the progress of five students with intellectual disability integrated into the first year of a primary school with the progress of five non-disabled students with whom they were matched for gender and position in family. At the end of the year, the students with disabilities had made minimal gains in academic learning, and significantly less than gains made by non-disabled children. Despite this somewhat negative outcome, teachers were generally positive in their ratings of the students' progress, and parents expressed a high level of satisfaction with the programme.

Expectations of the social benefits of integration have been high, and have consequently met with some disappointment as well as satisfaction. Reviewing studies of integration outcomes, Danby and Cullen (1988) found no support for the hypothesis that increased contact would enhance acceptance of students with intellectual disability by mainstream students. Nor was there any clear evidence that these students had benefited socially from interaction with their non-disabled peers. Frederickson and Woolfson (1987) found no differences between primary aged students with physical disability and non-disabled students in integrated settings in the amount of time they spent either alone, with one non-disabled classmate, with an adult or in a negative interaction. However, the students with physical disability spent less time interacting in groups, and more time interacting with other students who had a disability than with non-disabled students – not a surprising result since the students with disability had previously attended the same special school. On measures of sociometric status there were no differences in the number of rejections received, but the students with disability scored lower on friendship nominations and peer ratings of acceptance.

Although negative findings of social acceptance are probably well balanced by studies which have found high acceptance, there is little evidence, and most of what exists is anecdotal, of firm friendships forming as a result of integration. Expectations have often failed to take into account the reciprocal factors that are involved in friendship formation, and in particular the limited understanding that young children have about disability and its implications (Lewis, 1995). Studies by Lewis and others suggest that children do not fully understand disability and its impact, and may interact with students who have disabilities in the same way as they would with children younger than themselves.

We need to take into account these very human aspects of social interaction in our expectations of integration, especially for students with severe cognitive or communicative disabilities. It is unrealistic to expect that integration, even when accompanied by structured programmes to encourage social interaction, will necessarily result in students with disabilities having the same social experiences as students without disabilities, or that these students will be able to interact on an equal basis with non-disabled students. Although genuine friendships do occur, for example between hearing impaired and normal hearing students (Lynas, 1986), friendships are not easily forced. The circle of friends concept developed in some integration programmes provides immediate support for the student with a disability in the regular school, but there is no evidence that this concept creates reciprocal or lasting friendships beyond the school environment. The story of Ray earlier on in this chapter provides a useful lesson about friendships, and warns us not to neglect the mutual support that people may gain from others who share similar concerns.

CRITERIA FOR EVALUATING OUTCOMES

Differences in expected outcomes, as well as variations in the aims, administration, interpretation and implementation of integration policy will be reflected in differences in the criteria used for evaluating outcomes. Criteria may include the quality of participation in class activities, the student's relationships and interactions with peers, greater independence and improved educational performance. They may also include long-term outcomes, such as economic independence, a satisfying occupation or a lasting relationship. Criteria are often defined without much precision, for example in terms of the student's happiness in the current placement, or the satisfaction of parent and school personnel with the placement, adding to the difficulty of evaluating outcomes in any meaningful way.

In particular, claims about academic outcomes are difficult to interpret because of the different criteria by which success or improvement have been judged. Standardised tests are rarely appropriate in this context. Students in segregated settings are unlikely to have been exposed to the same range of academic instruction that is assumed by the tests; further, interpretation of most standardised achievement tests is based on the performance of students in regular classes. Other studies have used self- or teacher-ratings of academic skills. More relevant criteria might be the mastery of clearly defined functional skills or the elimination of unacceptable behaviour. Evans and Weld (1989) suggested that individual outcomes might best be evaluated by comparing competencies mastered, not with those demonstrated on a previous occasion, but with the range of competencies needed in the future.

Improved self-concept has often been used as a criterion of social adjustment of students with disabilities in regular classes. A positive self-concept is believed to be related to learning, although the direction of the cause–effect relationship is not established. That is, a negative self-concept may result from learning deficits, and it may in turn exacerbate deficits by leading to poor motivation and lack of confidence in one's learning ability.

Lalkhen and Norwich (1990) studied the self-concept and self-esteem of secondary students with physical handicap in three settings: full integration into a regular class for at least a year with the support of a resource department; a segregated special school which had no links with a mainstream school; and partial integration in regular school activities of students based in a special unit. Students in each setting were similar in physical health, upper limb functioning and socio-economic status, although there was a slightly higher tendency for the special school students to be in wheelchairs and to have secondary difficulties, for example in speech. An interesting finding of this study was that adolescents in fully integrated settings had the poorest physical self-concept, but the highest overall self-esteem. Self-esteem among fully integrated students was based more on satisfaction with characteristics and activities that were valued personally, rather than on physical self-concept. Physical self-concept was more related to general self-esteem in partial integration and segregated settings. The access to two comparison groups appeared to complicate relationships for the partially integrated group, with self-esteem similar to that of the segregated students.

The complex findings of this study suggest that a low self-concept in a specific area is in itself not necessarily indicative of a negative outcome. Students may have a low self-concept in a particular area, but attach relatively little importance to that area in assessing their general level of self-esteem. This study is important because it illustrates the complexity of interactions between different outcome criteria. In particular, no matter how hard we try to steer clear of comparisons with non-disabled peers in determining outcomes, we are unable to avoid these comparisons being made by students themselves.

Many sociometric studies have fallen into the trap of making comparisons of peer acceptance of students with disabilities between settings without considering the peer group in each setting. A sociometric questionnaire asks children to nominate other students in the class with whom they would like to interact – for example, to sit next to in class, or to play with. The focus is usually the number of choices received by a student with a disability. Most studies have suggested that students with disabilities in regular classes, including those with physical and sensory as well as intellectual disabilities, do not receive as many choices as their non-disabled classmates. Furthermore, they are not as well accepted as their peers in special classes. Other studies have found sociometric ratings to be negatively related to competence in areas such as communication and responsibility (Jenkinson, 1983). That is, the more severe the disability, the more likely the student is to be chosen by classmates, especially in early primary school. Choices may reflect the student's perceived need for support, or a wish by non-disabled students to impress the class teacher, rather than acceptance on an equal basis. In making these comparisons, it is important to note that the choices are being made by students without disabilities in the regular class, and by students with disabilities in special classes. Thus the outcome measure itself can be influenced by the setting.

Interpretation of outcomes also depends on the amount of detail that is included in criterion measures. Ware, Sharman, O'Connor and Anderson (1992) examined the social interactions of partially integrated students with severe disabilities in integrated and special class settings. In the total number of interactions taking place there was no difference between the two settings. There were, however, differences in the type of interaction. When students with disabilities were in the integrated setting they received more interactions (usually verbal) from other students, but initiated fewer, than when they were in the special class setting. In free-time situations, they received more interactions, but also initiated fewer, than their non-disabled classmates, although during class activities they participated in fewer interactions of both types. Ware et al. concluded that students with disabilities are able to participate on a more equal basis in special class settings with other students who have a similar disability than they are with non-disabled students in a regular class setting. In the regular class, they are likely to be passive recipients of interactions rather than equal participants.

Perceptions of the social benefits of integration do not always reflect the results of quantitative studies. York, Vandercook, Macdonald, Heise-Neff and Caughey (1992) obtained feedback from special and regular class teachers as well as classmates about the outcomes of integration for students with severe intellectual disability. Both regular class teachers and special education teachers who provided classroom support reported more interactions between integrated and regular class students than the students themselves, especially outside the classroom. Non-disabled students reported positive changes in the disabled students which were mainly social and behavioural, as well as positive changes in the behaviour and perceptions of other classmates reflected in a greater number of social interactions. The results of this study need to be considered in the light of the more pessimistic results of studies based on observations of interaction, and the possibility that teachers and students asked about their perceptions of integration may respond in terms of what they think should be the outcomes, rather than on the basis of objective observations. There is unfortunately no evidence about the accuracy of perceptions compared to more objective evidence. This is not to say that the perceptions of all those concerned with special education programmes are not important — clearly positive perceptions are important if such programmes are to be successful.

SETTING CHARACTERISTICS

The composition of classes is one obvious characteristic in which mainstream and segregated settings differ. Special classes are usually smaller than regular classes and enrol only students with an identified disability. There is greater opportunity for one-to-one teacher–student interaction. These differences will in turn affect other aspects of the setting, such as classroom structure and instructional methods.

Studies of classroom variables have attempted to clarify the role of setting, although the results have not always been consistent. In a large-scale investigation of the relationships between classroom environments, children's background characteristics and the progress of over three hundred students with a mild intellectual disability in regular and special classes, Kaufman, Agard and Semmel (1978) identified a number of environmental factors that were related to performance. Students with disabilities who were integrated into regular classes had more academic difficulties in classes in which teachers emphasised structure and orderliness. Their attention to academic tasks was greater in resource rooms and special classes in which class sizes were smaller, more support services were available, student–teacher interactions were more frequent and instruction was less demanding on cognitive skills. Social status of students with disabilities was higher in classes in which there was more liking and cohesiveness among non-disabled students, and they were rejected less frequently in classes in which more time was spent in being taught in one large group than in small, self-directed groups. More anti-social behaviour was exhibited in classes in which children showed less harmony.

The curriculum and instruction to which children are exposed, rather than the setting in which instruction takes place, are more likely to explain differences between mainstream and special settings in achievement of students with disabilities. Studies of children with Down syndrome which have taken the developmental level of the students into account support this argument. Historically, children with Down syndrome were thought to have little potential for academic learning, but this assumption has been challenged by reports of unexpected academic achievements since the more wide-spread implementation of integration. Casey, Jones, Kugler and Watkins (1988) monitored the cognitive development and academic achievements of children with Down syndrome over two years. Half of the students were integrated into mainstream schools, and the other half remained in special schools. A baseline measure at the beginning of the study established that the two groups were equivalent in mental age. Each student was retested at five six-monthly intervals on standardised tests of intelligence, language, numerical ability and reading. While both groups showed steady increases over the two years on all of these measures, the increase in mental age was significantly greater for the mainstreamed group. Larger increases for this group were also observed in basic numeracy skills, and in language comprehension. Differences were less clear in reading, and tended to be confounded by sex differences, with girls showing greater gains in reading than boys.

Casey et al. (1988) did not explore differences in the nature of the curriculum offered in the mainstream and special schools, and attributed the greater gains in language comprehension by students in the mainstream to increased opportunities for verbal interaction with a more linguistically competent peer group. Sloper, Cunning-ham, Turner and Knussen (1990) investigated factors related to an Academic Attainments Index among children with Down syndrome in a variety of settings, including mainstream classes and special units in regular schools. The strongest predictor of academic success was the student's mental age, but this was followed by their school setting. Students in mainstream schools were more likely to have higher academic achievements than those in special schools, even when developmental level was similar. At the same time, there were no differences between school settings in behaviour problems, self-sufficiency, health or family functioning.

Although poor outcomes in integration are often attributed to inadequate resources, the experiences of Kate described at the beginning of this chapter suggest that resources are not always the most crucial factor. According to Ward and Center (1990), the way in which resources are deployed is more important than the extent of available resources. Ward and Center developed an index of integration based on several converging academic, social and physical access measures. The index was applied to a small sample of students with mild to moderate intellectual disability, and results examined in relation to amount of support received and teachers' instructional styles. Although students who were most successfully integrated were rated highly as receiving the most appropriate support, other factors also contributed to success. Effective instructional strategies appeared to compensate for reduced resources. Where adequate resource staff were available, successful integration could be jeopardised by poor co-ordination between resource room and classroom teaching, or by over-dependence on an untrained teacher aide.

Other studies have found that classroom structure is effective in enhancing both learning and social outcomes of integration. In a series of studies, Johnson and Johnson (1986) demonstrated that co-operative learning in small groups, compared to competitive, individual learning, promoted more verbal interaction and greater interpersonal attraction between students with disabilities and non-disabled students. Structuring activities so that all students were given tasks in which they could succeed also promoted mutual liking and self-esteem.

There is clearly a need for more studies of how students with disabilities can be encouraged to participate in a greater number and variety of interactions with their non-disabled peers. Staub and Hunt (1993) provided four non-disabled, volunteer students with training in social interaction. Each student was then paired with a student with a severe disability whose social behaviour was observed. The same students with disabilities were also observed with a control group of non-disabled students who had not received the social interaction training. Interactions with the trained students, compared to the untrained students, showed an increased frequency of initiations and proportions of interactions that were social in nature, and an increase in targeted social behaviours. The authors concluded that planning for reciprocal social interactions must be structured. However, the study showed some limitations in this type of training – for example the improved social behaviour was not transferred to interactions with students who had not received the social interaction training.

STUDENT CHARACTERISTICS

Integration has become so widely accepted as a principle that very little attention has been given in recent research to the individual factors which make for success. Although it could be argued that individual characteristics should not determine whether or not a student is integrated, intellectual and personal factors are important for the educational outcomes of all students including those with disabilities. A difficulty in determining which specific characteristics are most important is in identifying those that determine successful outcomes, and those that are in turn the result of positive educational experiences. This problem is made more complex by the interaction of personal factors with goals and expectations.

An earlier review of individual factors related to academic outcomes in integrated settings (Jenkinson, 1987) concluded that the nature and severity of a disability was important only when the disability involved neurological impairment, other cognitive dysfunction or reduced communication. In other respects intellectual ability was the main determinant of academic success, especially if it was supported by motivating factors such as a favourable home background and a high degree of parental involvement in the student's education. Generally, these factors were important regardless of the educational setting.

Much attention has focused on the academic performance of students with sensory or physical disabilities in regular school settings. For students with hearing impairment, communication skills are a crucial factor. Semmel et al. (1979) concluded that academic success of students with hearing impairment was related to the development of good communication skills prior to integration, especially when this was accompanied by parental support. It has also been suggested that students with hearing impairment will benefit more from individual integration, where they are forced to interact with their peers, rather than being integrated in pairs or larger groups. Communication difficulties play a large part in limiting social interaction and acceptance. Deaf adults interviewed by Foster (1989) about their experiences in mainstream and residential school programmes frequently mentioned feelings of social isolation in the regular classroom. Their communications with teachers and other students were described as largely superficial. Being unable to join in the day-to-day conversation and laughter of their classmates, embarrassment at their own efforts at speech, and having to work through an interpreter, were perceived as barriers to social integration.

Behavioural characteristics have been one of the most frequently mentioned barriers to successful integration because of their potential to disrupt a class. In addition, it is often forgotten that students with disabilities may be particularly vulnerable to problems of adjustment. School carries some degree of stress for all students, but for students with disabilities normal levels of stress are likely to be exacerbated by the disability itself. Inability to perform some essential activities, or to perform them as well as other students, and greater dependence on others, can lead to reduced self-esteem and the development of inappropriate behaviour to cope with the additional stress thus created. There is clearly a need for a greater understanding of the role of individual factors, and their interaction with other factors in the school environment, in determining the outcomes of education for students with disabilities.

TRANSITION: LONG-TERM OUTCOMES FOR STUDENTS WITH DISABILITIES

The benefits of various forms of special education provision have usually been considered in terms of the immediate benefits within the school context. Of equal importance are long-term benefits to students.

The majority of studies have focused on long-term outcomes for students who have received their education in segregated settings. However, one study examined the effects of transition from a segregated primary setting to a mainstream secondary school (Sheldon, 1991). Aspects of the regular school which contributed to difficulties in adjusting included large class sizes, negative attitudes of peers, organisational aspects and difficulties in coping academically. Although most students reported that they had eventually adjusted, many with academic successes, they also believed that the segregated unit had provided poor preparation for the regular secondary school.

Retrospective perceptions of schooling by students with disabilities indicate mixed feelings about special school and mainstream experiences. Deaf students interviewed by Foster (1989) who had been integrated in the mainstream were generally satisfied with their academic education, but regretted that they had not been able to

develop social contacts with other deaf students. These students saw a
need for more support services to facilitate integration, as well as
greater sensitivity on the part of teachers and other students in the
mainstream. Students educated in a residential school, on the other
hand, were dissatisfied with the academic quality of their education,
believing that too much time had been spent on communication skills
and not enough on academic content. These students were positive
about their experiences of social interaction and the sense of identity
they had developed with other deaf students.

These mixed perceptions of school placement are also typical of
former students of special classes (Mithaug, Horiuchi and Fanning,
1985; Liebert, Lutsky and Gottlieb, 1990). Most students in these
studies perceived special educational and vocational classes as more
valuable than time spent in the regular class, and the help received
from special educators useful in obtaining employment. However,
many also felt that they had not been adequately prepared for their
post-secondary experiences through exposure to peers without
disabilities, and believed that they would have benefited from a less
sheltered environment.

Despite a relatively high level of satisfaction with schooling, long-
term outcomes for students with disabilities in terms of employment
status, independence and community participation appear to be less
than satisfactory. Sitlington, Frank and Carson (1992) examined the
adjustment of students who had received resource room support one
year after completion of secondary school. Although most had found
employment, jobs were primarily unskilled or semi-skilled. Unemployment was higher for students with a mild intellectual disability or
behavioural disorder, compared to those with a learning disability.
Few students participated in post-secondary training. Most lived with
their families and did not contribute financially to their upkeep. These
findings are typical of the results of recent outcome studies involving
students with a mild intellectual disability (Edgar and Polloway,
1994), and studies by Mithaug et al. (1985) and Liebert et al. (1990) of
former special education students with a range of intellectual,
behavioural, communication and physical disabilities. Many of those
who were employed had part-time jobs with marginal salaries. Most
did not have financial independence and relied on their families for
support.

Long-term studies of outcomes are likely to be confounded by other
circumstances associated with the disability, so that poor outcomes
cannot necessarily be attributed to the fact of having participated in

special education. Nevertheless, successful programmes need to address long-term issues to ensure more satisfactory outcomes. Whether more widespread participation in mainstream education will make a significant difference remains to be addressed. There are a number of problems in attempting to attribute long-term outcomes specifically to any form of educational provision rather than to individual circumstances or to situational factors that have occurred after the completion of compulsory schooling. However, it is clear that students with disabilities should be supported during transition periods and that support should continue well beyond compulsory schooling if positive outcomes are to be maintained. A study by Knox and Parmenter (1990) using structured interviews with former students has confirmed the need for links between schools and community agencies to support transition, and the involvement of transition services in all aspects of the individual's life, not just vocational aspects.

OUTCOMES FOR REGULAR EDUCATION SYSTEMS

One of the major benefits of integration predicted by both the regular education initiative and the inclusive schools movement was that all students in the mainstream, including those who were not necessarily regarded as having a disability, would have access to specialist support. It was assumed that adaptation of instruction to meet a greater diversity of needs would benefit all students in the classroom. These claims have received little attention in outcome studies, and have not been identified as priorities in the implementation of special education reforms. For example, OECD member countries did not include benefits for the regular school system among important outcomes either in terms of greater individualisation of instruction, or in improved access of students without identified disabilities to specialist support when needed (OECD, 1994). Indeed, there is no evidence that improvements in academic achievement have actually occurred as a direct result of inclusive education practices. Recent trends towards standardised curriculum suggest a move away from individualisation of instruction rather than a greater focus on provision for individual differences. Although many studies of students' attitudes and interactions suggest that contact with students who have disabilities broadens and enriches students' experiences, longer-term outcomes such as increased community acceptance of disability have yet to be established.

Other benefits of proposed changes include increased collaboration between regular and special education systems. Although questions have been raised about the willingness of special educators to relinquish responsibility for special education students to the regular class (Jenkins et al., 1990), collaboration between regular class teachers and special educators has been seen by both groups as a positive outcome of placement of severely disabled students in mainstream classes (York et al., 1992). With close collaboration, special teachers learn more about the regular education system and become more a part of the school community, while regular class teachers gain a better understanding of the needs of students with disabilities and ways in which they may become more involved in class activities. Class teachers may also acquire new strategies for dealing with a range of learning problems by observing special teachers.

Much work remains to be done in establishing causal links between educational settings, instructional processes, individual characteristics and outcomes in special education. At the same time, we need to ensure that the objectives and expectations of education for students with disabilities are realistic, regardless of the setting. Many of the studies that have produced negative outcomes in both integrated and segregated settings have failed to look beyond the setting to ask if more could have been achieved in another setting. The answer may well be that it could not.

Chapter 5

Research in special education provision

Some years ago, I was asked to evaluate an integration programme that had begun five or six years earlier in Ballarat, a city of around seventy thousand people situated in the central highlands of Victoria. The goals of the evaluation were to document adjustment and progress made by twenty-one children with moderate to severe intellectual disability who had been placed individually in sixteen primary schools, and to make recommendations about the future of the programme (Jenkinson, 1982).

As I approached this project, my background in traditional methods of scientific research was well to the fore. How could I evaluate the progress of these children, and how could I link their achievements to their school experiences? Would their progress and experiences have been similar if they had remained segregated in the day training centre? That few children of primary school age remained at the centre was testimony to the persistence of the teachers, parents and principals who had formed themselves into a group to oversee the integration programme. There was no possibility of finding an appropriate comparison group. There were wide differences among the children in age, in previous educational experiences, in family backgrounds, in amount of time they had been integrated and in the severity of their disability. It would be impossible to find another group that had the same variety of background and experience. It also became clear that even if there were not logistical problems in obtaining such a group within the relatively short time span of the evaluation, any group from another location would not reflect the unique social context of Ballarat and the surrounding towns and villages in which this programme had been nurtured.

One alternative to comparing the integrated children with a segregated sample was to consider the evaluation as a series of twenty-one separate case studies, so that each individual story could be captured in all its richness. This approach, too, had its problems. As the evaluation began, a number of sensitive areas emerged. Teachers felt hostile because they had been obliged to take on a task for which most felt ill-equipped, and for which they had little extra support. Support services felt threatened because they had not had the staff or resources to provide individual programmes for the students. Parents felt guilty because of the burden they felt they were imposing on the schools. But it was also obvious that suspicion and resentment of the programme were outweighed by the dedication of individual teachers to fostering the acceptance and well-being of each student, and the overall satisfaction felt by both teachers and parents with the progress made by each child. More acceptable social behaviour, friendships with non-disabled students and unexpected successes by some students in learning basic academic skills were often mentioned.

The material certainly existed for detailed case studies. But here there was another problem. Teachers would agree to being interviewed only if they were not identified as the source of comments about students or schools. Parents wanted to have their say about the programme, but preferred their contributions to be anonymous rather than risk reactions by schools that might adversely affect their child. Even if individual students were not identified by name, the uniqueness of each child's story made it impossible to report a detailed case study without enabling the child concerned, and his or her school and teachers, to be identified by others involved in the programme, if not by the wider community. Further, I needed to go beyond individual case studies to draw out general trends on which I could base recommendations for the future of the programme, not just for individual children.

Previous research offered little guidance to the methods I should use for collecting data, although it did confirm the futility of much of the so-called 'efficacy' research – no study had been able to demonstrate conclusively the superiority of either integrated or segregated settings for educating students with disabilities. Indeed, at the time, most of the published research focused on students with mild disabilities. Standardised measures of educational achievement would not be appropriate for this group, and in any case would not reflect the many facets of behaviour that are important in classroom adjustment.

I settled on a descriptive study, with the aim of presenting a picture of the integration programme, drawing on as many sources of information as possible to ensure that the views of those most closely involved, and most knowledgeable about each child in the programme, would be taken into account. I observed each of the children in the classroom and in the playground. I interviewed parents and class teachers, using structured interview schedules which sought information about a whole range of issues. Parents and teachers completed behaviour checklists, and class teachers rated the children on a checklist of school competencies especially designed for use with students with moderate intellectual disabilities. Students in each class in which a child with a disability was placed completed a sociometric questionnaire. From all of this information, I was then able to draw out general trends which seemed to apply to most of the children involved, and to identify individual items which were related to specific circumstances.

The dilemmas I faced in planning this research seemed to reflect two very different sets of values and beliefs in special education (Reid, Robinson and Bunsen, 1995). On the one hand, traditional research methods have been employed to evaluate specific programmes or to demonstrate the superiority of various settings or practices in special education, often with no clear conclusions. On the other hand, policy and practice have been justified by value-laden concepts such as social justice, normalisation and inclusiveness. It is not difficult to enlist popular support for these concepts, even in the absence of evidence that they work. Policy and practice depend on the prevailing social and economic climate, rather than on the findings of research. For example, in the United States, the Civil Rights movement and subsequent litigation had a far greater impact than research data on the integration movement.

In the face of such political strength, the contribution of research to special education has often been undervalued. Indeed, sound research findings have tended to be swamped in the proliferation of publications in the whole disability field over the past two or three decades. As MacMillan and Hendrick (1993: 41) suggested: 'Another characteristic of the period [involving criticism of segregated special education] was that "data were out" and "stories were in" as research evidence was discounted while anecdotes, often relaying atypical experiences, were persuasive.'

In fairness, it must be acknowledged that the lack of interest in research findings by policy makers may to some degree reflect the poor quality of much research, the fruitlessness of investing large amounts of funding in attempting to resolve debates about educational settings without investigating what goes on in those settings, and the bias of many so-called 'research' studies of special education programmes. Part of the reason why research has not been given priority might also lie in an inadequate understanding of research itself, and the fact that useful data can only emerge from research if the right questions are asked in the first place.

In the remainder of this chapter, I will look at some of the important issues facing research in special education, in particular the problems in using traditional research methods, the move towards qualitative approaches to research, and ways in which research can usefully contribute to knowledge and practice in special education.

WHAT IS WRONG WITH EFFICACY RESEARCH?

Efficacy studies attempt to demonstrate the effectiveness of specific programmes, settings or models of implementation, often in comparison with alternative programmes, settings or models. The earliest advocates of integration sought justification for their beliefs in research which showed that special schools and classes produced no more positive outcomes for students with mild learning difficulties than regular classes. Much of this research originated in the United States, and consisted of comparisons of students with disabilities in integrated and segregated settings on various academic and social variables.

The rationale for much of the efficacy research dictated the use of traditional scientific methods. Scientific method, either implicitly or explicitly, involves the formation of hypotheses about causes of behaviour or events, and the testing of those hypotheses through empirical research – that is, through the collection of data. In order to establish that one variable causes another, it is necessary to rule out other possible causes, and to do this the researcher usually sets up a controlled experiment. The most basic experiment consists of two groups; one, the experimental group, is exposed to the hypothesised cause of whatever the researcher is interested in, and the other, the control group, is not. To rule out other possible causes, the two groups must be equivalent in all relevant aspects except the causal situation.

When this design is translated into studies of the efficacy of integrated compared to segregated education for students with disabilities, problems soon become apparent. The rigorous requirements of comparative designs in educational research can rarely be met in special education. Questions of educational placement do not easily lend themselves to experimental methods. Valid comparison between groups requires random assignment of subjects to groups or classes to ensure true equivalence on all variables other than the variable under investigation, which is educational setting. In practice, integration is usually selective – certainly students with disabilities are rarely allocated randomly to special or regular classes. Students who remain in segregated settings tend to be those with the most severe disabilities or with the most serious behavioural and adjustment problems. Matching integrated and segregated groups by age, gender and intellectual ability, or the use of statistical techniques to control these factors, is rarely adequate to ensure comparability on all relevant variables. The study of complete classes rather than random samples of students raises additional problems. Regular and special classes differ not only in student composition, but in many other important variables: for example curricular goals and content, student–teacher ratio, teacher expertise and training, and incentives for learning. Thus even in the most carefully designed comparative research, one group may still have an advantage over the other that influences the final results, but that cannot be accounted for strictly in terms of integration versus segregation.

Interpretation of research is made more difficult by inadequate descriptions of the samples studied. Groups of students with disabilities, even though categorised in terms of a single variable such as intellectual disability or hearing impairment, are rarely homogeneous in terms of other factors important to education. Problems in considering students in categorical terms have already been discussed. The problem of interpretation is even greater with less clearly defined categories such as learning disability or behavioural–emotional disturbance. Definitions of these categories vary from study to study; reports often fail to mention the severity of the disability or other complicating factors, or to specify criteria used for placement in various educational settings. Differences between groups of students with disabilities in integrated and segregated settings are likely to be obscured by variability within a group, resulting in a large overlap between groups on many of the criteria employed to evaluate the outcomes of integration. Under these conditions, statistical tests employed in comparative designs lack the power to detect differences that, although small, may be educationally important.

A second difficulty in comparative studies is the frequent absence of any clear definition about what constitutes a special setting on the one hand, and an integrated setting on the other. Special education may simply be a setting that is not the regular classroom, and may take place in a self-contained class or unit within a regular school, in a segregated school, or in a resource room. Lack of experimenter control over special curriculum, methods of instruction and teacher experience and qualifications adds to the problems of attributing outcomes to settings rather than to what takes place in the setting. Similar difficulties occur in attempting to define integration, which may be viewed as any form of education ranging from mainstreaming one day a week through to full-time integration in a regular class. The setting up of special classes or units in the grounds of a mainstream school has been considered by some educators to constitute integration, and by others to represent another form of segregation. Even placing a student in a regular class does not ensure that the student is fully integrated.

Sociometric ratings, in which students are asked to choose other students in the class with whom they would most like to interact, are particularly subject to misuse in comparative studies of educational settings. In a regular class, choices are made by non-disabled students, whereas in special classes they are made by other students with disabilities. Nor can it be assumed that sociometric ratings are a valid measure of social interaction as it occurs in the classroom.

Lack of control by the researcher over what goes on in a special education setting is compounded by the difficulty of ensuring that intervention is implemented and sustained throughout a defined period (Mann and Kenowitz, 1985). Intervention is often confounded with social and ideological values, and may be regarded with suspicion if it is directed towards achieving educational reforms that are not universally acceptable. Conversely, if there is reason to believe that a certain type of intervention is effective in achieving educational goals, then withholding the intervention from a control group for any extended period is equally unacceptable. Other confounding factors identified by Mann and Kenowitz include personal and interpersonal factors such as teacher skill and dedication, adaptability, previous experience in working with disability, job security and parent–teacher communication. Changes over time in personality, behavioural and cognitive norms as a result of changing cultural and biological influences, and the fact that almost any kind of special educational intervention can be shown to be effective, add to the difficulty of interpreting efficacy studies. The difficulty of equating environmental conditions also makes it virtually impossible to ensure that the same conditions prevail in each type of placement from one study to the next, so that true replication of studies can rarely be carried out.

Is it possible to design a good efficacy study? Center and Curry (1993) matched pairs of students with mild intellectual disability on the basis of academic achievement, social skill development, atypical behaviour, age and gender. One member of each pair was then randomly assigned to a self-contained support class with a special education teacher in charge, and the other to an age-appropriate mainstream class. Another special education teacher supported these students in the mainstream. Important aspects of academic pro- grammes and instructional procedures were kept identical in both settings. Various achievement measures and observations of on-task behaviour and social interaction were applied prior to class assignment and again after sixteen weeks. Gains in academic skills and social interaction were greater for the students in the mainstream classes, and both groups showed gains in on-task behaviour. There were no negative outcomes for the mainstreamed students.

Despite the careful design of this study and efforts to maintain as much experimenter control as possible, the researchers also identified some differences in instructional procedures which could explain the greater improvement of mainstreamed students. For example, the amount of support received in the mainstream allowed more time to be spent in small groups on direct instruction in reading skills. While the purpose of this study — to demonstrate the feasibility of mainstream instruction for students with mild intellectual disability — was achieved, the results cannot be used as an argument in favour of one setting or the other without consideration of what took place in each setting. The small numbers in the study (twenty-six students in all) and its limitation to one support class also mean that the study should be repeated with additional samples and settings before firm conclusions can be made.

Clearly the rigorous control required of a scientific experiment can never be fully replicated in a classroom setting. The question of educational setting for students with disabilities is not, therefore, a good research question. At best, we are limited, as Center and Curry acknowledged, to demonstrating the feasibility of the setting that is most valued on the basis of philosophical principles. As Mann and Kenowitz (1985) indicated, it is the nature, quality and appropriate- ness of opportunities provided for learning, and the skill and knowledge of the teacher, that are more crucial than any adminis- trative arrangement in determining how well a student learns:

The problem with special education interventions is that we *do not know when they work, with whom they work or how well they work.* Nor do we know much about their durability, nor their general applicability. Much less to say that we know which ones are better than others. ... It is time and effort, apart from the vagaries of human activity, that so far as we can tell really make for the differences in the educational results we obtain.

(Mann and Kenowitz, 1985: 9)

A third weakness of many efficacy studies is the frequent use of outcome measures that are inappropriate in both content and normative data for students with disabilities. This weakness is not confined to efficacy studies. Measurement issues are also important in programme evaluations which do not attempt a comparative design. Education for many students with disabilities has emphasised the development of independence and functional skills – skills that are more relevant than academic skills in achieving community integration. Standardised tests of achievement in academic areas do not provide the most appropriate criteria for success, since they do not necessarily cover specialised curricula. The use of both age and grade equivalent scores as the measure for comparison is especially inappropriate, since these scores do not take into account the lack of consistency between grade levels in different settings, differences in growth rates between age or grade levels, or differences in the possible range of variation at these levels. Tests in which students with disabilities are likely to score at relatively low levels may be insensitive to small improvements. Furthermore, as Marston (1988) pointed out, standardised achievement tests are not designed to measure learning or change in student performance, and repeated use that does not take practice effects into account will give a distorted picture of learning.

Some studies have suffered by employing outcome measures that are either too broad or too restricted to be of much use. Storey (1993) distinguished molar assessments from molecular assessments in special education. Molar assessments provide a broad global evaluation of a desired outcome – for example, social adjustment; molecular assessments are concerned with more precisely defined discrete behaviours – for example, the specific behaviours that make up social adjustment. Molar measures are usually not detailed enough to suggest individual programme recommendations; on the other hand, molecular measures may appear relatively trivial if considered in isolation, and it may be difficult to demonstrate exactly how they are related to more global concepts.

The confusion between the levels of assessment employed may be due to a lack of clarity regarding the purpose of many research studies. Olsen (1994) suggested that there are two major purposes for conducting evaluation studies in special education: evaluation for the purpose of improving individual programmes, and evaluation to meet the requirement of accountability for administrative purposes. Olsen questioned the feasibility of using the same measures to serve both functions. Evaluation to identify needed programme improvements is concerned with the student's immediate needs, such as whether the programme meets the objectives of the student's individual educational plan, or whether there are sufficient resources to ensure that a programme can be implemented effectively. For this purpose molecular measures may be most appropriate. Evaluation for accountability, on the other hand, is concerned with the same questions as are asked about education generally, such as broad achievement levels, school retention rates or long-term outcomes such as preparation for employment and adult life. Accountability is more likely to be served by molar measures, even though these measures may not suggest specific actions needed to effect improvement to programmes.

An important requirement of research, then, is that the measures used should be appropriate for the purpose of the research. Both Storey (1993) and Olsen (1994) recommended the use of multiple measures, although it is also important to show how measures used are related to each other, and how they will provide the data needed to meet the specific purpose of the research, whether to inform policy or to monitor and improve programmes (Ysseldyke and Thurlow, 1994). It is also important to show how measures are related to both content and process in educational settings.

ALTERNATIVE APPROACHES

Several alternative approaches have been suggested in an effort to overcome design problems in comparative studies of integration. Mann and Kenowitz (1985) proposed the use of an actuarial approach to evaluation, collecting information over time through various measures, taking into account such factors as the effects of changing social conditions and the availability of resources, as well as interventions, in explaining results.

Meta-analysis has also been employed in an attempt to resolve the integration-versus-segregation debate, using data from numerous efficacy studies. Meta-analysis is a statistical technique that re-analyses data from essentially similar studies, taking into account effect size, or the size of the difference between settings in outcome variables. Carlberg and Kavale (1980) employed meta-analysis to re-analyse data from existing studies to estimate the relative effectiveness of particular kinds of class placement. From 860 efficacy studies located in the literature they selected fifty that met various criteria for re-analysis. The criteria included use of identifiable categories of disability and the comparison of special and regular class groups. Combining data from these studies, the authors found that students with disabilities in special classes were approximately one to two months behind their counterparts in regular classes on achievement tests, and were also significantly behind in social, personality and other measures, although this finding did not apply to students with learning disabilities or behavioural and emotional disturbances, who showed greater improvement in special classes.

Wang and Baker (1985–86) also used meta-analysis to examine four specific questions about integration. The questions concerned academic and social outcomes, contextual variables and student demographic characteristics associated with positive outcomes, type of research design in relation to the results of the research, and characteristics of successful programmes. Of 264 studies published in professional journals in the decade up to 1984, eleven met the specified criteria of consisting of a comparative analysis of outcomes between integrated and segregated environments, including both pre-test and post-test measures of programme effects, and containing sufficient usable data to permit a quantitative analysis. The meta-analysis indicated overall gains in integrated, compared to segregated, settings in performance, attitudinal and process categories, but failed to identify any single independent variable other than mainstreaming that could have been responsible for this finding.

In an effort to find some explanation for the overall lack of support for segregation, Tindal (1985) re-examined both the literature that formed the subject of Carlberg and Kavale's 1980 meta-analysis, and subsequent research. He proposed two possible explanations: firstly, that the tactics and procedures that define special education inter-ventions may indeed be ineffective, and secondly, that the pro-grammes and outcomes may themselves be subject to inadequate measures that are insensitive to the effects of intervention. Several of the methodological concerns identified by Tindal have already been discussed, among them the nature of special education programmes, the variability within disabled populations, the dependence of assignment to intervention on the process of referral and identification rather than on random allocation, absence of experimental control over intervening variables and problems of measurement adequacy. These problems are not removed by meta-analysis. A further limitation of meta-analysis studies in special education noted by Wang and Baker (1985–86) is the small proportion of studies that meet the necessary criteria for inclusion in the analysis.

Many of the design problems in comparative research can be overcome by using time series designs, in which frequent measurements are applied over time to compare intervention phases to a baseline. Participants therefore serve as their own control group. An advantage of the time series design is that evaluation of a programme is concurrent with its implementation, allowing continual revision of the programme as evaluation takes place. Marston (1988) used a time series design to study the reading performance of eleven students with a mild intellectual disability in regular and special education settings. The experiment consisted of two phases. In Phase A, reading performance was monitored over a minimum of ten weeks in a regular classroom. In Phase B, the students were placed in a special setting where their reading performance continued to be monitored over a further minimum ten-week period. Marston was interested not in the absolute difference in performance between the two settings, but in the rate at which students progressed in each setting. The average gain per week was significantly greater in Phase B compared to Phase A for ten of the eleven students, supporting the effectiveness of the special class setting. Marston also identified a number of instructional variables that could account for the greater effectiveness of the special class.

Marston's design did have one serious limitation. Ideally a time series study should incorporate a reversal phase: that is, the participants should be returned to the original phase of the experiment to see if performance – in Marston's study the rate of improvement – reverts to its original level, before returning to the intervention phase, thus strengthening conclusions about the effects of treatment. In effect, the experiment is repeated to confirm that the intervention is responsible for the change in performance. As Marston pointed out, however, it is not ethical to remove a child from a potentially effective treatment – in this case the special class. The time series model therefore lends itself to answering specific questions about aspects of educational programmes rather than global questions about setting. The studies by both Center and Curry (1993) and Marston (1988) suggest that the important factors for student progress are not primarily those concerned with the setting itself, but aspects that are more directly related to instruction. We might conclude that much of the efficacy research has not necessarily posed the right questions:

> What is needed is efficacy research that examines the relationship of the characteristics of different learning environments with methods found relatively effective with mildly handicapped students (e.g. direct instruction, cognitive training, peer tutoring, cooperative learning). This should help to define more specifically the environmental parameters within which these methods are most effective.
>
> (Hallahan, Keller, McKinney, Lloyd and Bryan, 1988: 31)

QUALITATIVE VERSUS QUANTITATIVE APPROACHES

The disillusionment with traditional research methodology in special education, especially in supporting or rejecting different forms of provision, led Schindele (1985: 11) to comment:

> It is increasingly being asked whether the present shortcomings of research in special education may not be caused by the fact that such research is dominated by the *quantitative, experimental research approach*. The basic assumptions and pre-requisites of quantitative–experimental research may be in open conflict with the nature of special education research and with the basic needs and objectives that must be met by such research.

This rejection of quantitative research methods has been accompanied by an increasing trend towards the use of qualitative designs. Simpson (1992) made a useful distinction between the two approaches. Qualitative research involves direct observation of human activity in its natural setting. Methods of data collection can include descriptive case studies, interviews with key people, participant observation and analysis of documents that are not easily translated into numerical measurement, such as diaries or correspondence. In qualitative research, the researcher is an interactive participant in the situation that is being studied. Investigation typically proceeds without preconceptions about research questions or the specific data that are to be recorded: while the researcher may hold tentative ideas about what he or she will discover, and the methods used to make those discoveries, these may change as the research proceeds. Such changes reflect a view that reality itself is constantly changing. In addition, qualitative research is not just concerned with what happens in real life, but with how events and situations are perceived by key participants.

Qualitative research is not concerned with universal laws that govern human behaviour in a variety of situations. Whereas quantitative research yields numerical data that are analysed statistically to give an estimate of the probability of the results being true or valid, qualitative research typically produces a description of a single situation – for example, a class, a school or a family – and the changes that occur in that situation over changing times and circumstances. The advocates of qualitative research argue that quantitative methodology does not acknowledge the values, aspirations and commitments of individuals, as well as the cultural traditions that influence the outcomes of special education (Reid et al., 1995). Qualitative studies, such as those which use narrative descriptions, interviews and participant observation, allow students, teachers, parents and others involved to present their individual reactions to a situation. This rich collection of data gathered through a variety of methods is claimed to provide a more adequate and realistic understanding of students with disabilities and their adaptation to school life.

A risk with qualitative research is that objectivity may be sacrificed in the interests of presenting a particular viewpoint. Case studies of individual students or individual programmes or settings form a common approach in qualitative research. Conclusions are often based on only one participant or a small number of participants. Data from such detailed research based on larger numbers of students become unwieldy to handle without a means of summarising or reducing them, and invite quantitative treatment, whether formally or informally.

A second problem with qualitative research is that studies are almost impossible to replicate because of the subjective, spontaneous and interactive nature of the data collection procedures (Simpson, 1992). Data are applicable to a situation or setting which is unique in terms of context, individuals involved and a multitude of other factors. Difficulties in replication of studies are exacerbated by the fact that data collection procedures, and even the questions posed, may be modified as qualitative research proceeds. In other words, data have a reactive influence, in that information collected at one point in the research may influence the procedures used, and the data sought, at a subsequent point. These procedures provide no guarantee against bias in the interpretation of results.

Related to the problem of non-replicability is a limitation on generalisability of results to other situations. Because of the uniqueness of each situation studied, results may not be relevant to the wider culture from which the case for study has been drawn:

> Qualitative procedures tend not to be confirmatory in a way that allows researchers to be confident about the validity, reliability, or generalisability of their conclusions ... [and] ... could result in 'pseudo-research' that is used in an attempt to validate socially accepted, yet unproven, concepts.
>
> (Simpson, 1992: 237, 241)

By contrast, in quantitative research objectivity is ensured by designing the study, selecting methods of data collection and constructing questionnaires, interview schedules or other measuring instruments before the data collection begins. Specific research questions are posed and procedures set in place to answer those questions. Information that may come to light during a study often raises additional questions that will be addressed in further research, but will not divert immediate attention from answering the original questions posed. The researcher is not an interactive participant in the research, and thus, at least ideally, remains neutral throughout.

The difficulties with the use of quantitative research in special education, particularly in traditional experimental or quasi-experimental designs, have already been discussed. A further disadvantage of quantitative when compared to qualitative research is that procedures can become contrived or artificial. Questions may be studied because they lend themselves to elegant and logically justifiable research designs rather than because of their significance in special education. The use of quantitative research in special education is made more difficult because classroom situations, which essentially involve dynamic interactions between people as teaching and learning take place, are not easily studied under the highly controlled conditions required by scientific research methods.

Simpson (1992) suggested that qualitative and quantitative procedures should be regarded as part of a research continuum, and that meaningful research in special education should include both aspects. Qualitative research should be used for exploratory reasons, for example to identify important, socially relevant questions, or to generate hypotheses for further study. Deriving research questions from initial classroom observations will help to ensure that the research is founded in the real world. Research should move along the continuum beginning with a qualitative approach and moving towards quantitative analysis to answer questions about effectiveness of delivery systems, teaching methods or intervention strategies with the greatest degree of confidence in reliability and validity of the conclusions.

How can problems of reliability and validity be overcome in qualitative research? Reid et al. (1995) identified and described the essential requirements of qualitative research. In practice these requirements do not differ from those required for quantitative research. The first, confirmability or objectivity, involves setting in place procedures for ensuring that research is not biased. Although subjectivity may not be avoided entirely, subjective influences on the outcomes of research need to be acknowledged. To achieve confirmability, all procedures used in the collection of data, the data themselves, and methods for analysing and interpreting data, should be open to scrutiny and subjected to critical evaluation by peers, with appropriate responses to criticism.

A second requirement of qualitative research is credibility, or internal validity. This property refers to the relative 'truth' of the findings. Qualitative research is not subject to the same rigours of sampling and experimental control as traditional quantitative research. The researcher may be exploring only one situation or event. The context in which the situation or event occurs must be fully understood. Internal validity requires all aspects of that situation or event to be explored in depth, using multiple data sources or data collection methods.

Thirdly, external validity, or transferability of the findings, refers to the extent to which the findings of one piece of research are applicable to other situations or events. Many research projects in special education are designed to explore a specific situation and make recommendations about that situation. The constraints of funding often prohibit extension of a study to sample a wider range of situations or events. These studies do not meet the requirements of generalisability in relation to sampling. The evaluation of an integration programme that I described at the beginning of this chapter was a one-off study of this nature. Yet research is of limited value unless we can learn from it information that can usefully be applied to new situations. Careful documentation of relevant factors in a situation helps the consumer of research to judge how applicable results are to other situations.

Fourthly, according to Reid et al. (1995), qualitative research must be reliable or dependable. That is, would someone else doing the same research come up with the same conclusions? Ensuring confirmability and credibility will help to ensure reliability. Research should also be reflexive – that is, the researcher should be able to provide a rationale for choice of the procedures used. Finally, qualitative research must be subject to the rigorous ethical requirements of all human research, with the aim at all times being to protect the interests of the participants.

Quantitative and qualitative methods are not mutually exclusive. Much valuable research makes use of both methods. Carefully designed and analysed quantitative research can provide conclusions that may be accepted with relative confidence, but the meaning of these conclusions can be clarified with illustrations derived from qualitative analysis of case studies, documents or other non-numerical data sources.

Qualitative research is also greatly strengthened when it is based on a range of situations rather than relying on a single event. Typical of this approach was the relatively large-scale survey carried out in the early 1980s by the National Foundation for Educational Research (Hegarty and Pocklington, 1981). This study set the pattern for descriptive research designed to identify important issues in integration. Its aim, prompted by a growing interest in integration and a concern about the capacity of the regular school to cope with large numbers of students with special needs, was simply to document and analyse various existing integration programmes, without any attempt to evaluate their relative efficacy or to establish the superiority of either integration or segregation. However, identification of those factors that make for successful integration was considered an important part of the study, and although the study concentrated on structural and organisational factors, some information on individual students was also collected.

Although theoretical considerations were regarded as important, the dimensions selected for analysis were derived directly from the data as the survey proceeded. A close study of actual examples was used to draw attention to opportunities taken by schools or to clarify possible constraints or problems, and to discuss implications for schools.

The study was based on fourteen integration programmes in the United Kingdom, selected to represent a variety in terms of type of disability catered for, age and number of students involved and organisational structures. The main research technique was the interview, initially loosely structured, but becoming more focused as specific issues and questions emerged. Interviews were conducted with a wide range of people involved in integration, including teachers and ancillary staff, school psychologists, consultants, education officers, therapists and medical officers. Researchers also talked to students, usually informally, although some formal interviews and structured group discussions also took place. In addition, mainstream teachers completed a questionnaire seeking information on the nature and extent of their contact with students with disabilities, attitudes, knowledge of disability and perceived competence in teaching students with disabilities, and relevant information and support received. A further questionnaire sent to special education centres sought factual information on services available. Four integration programmes were selected for structured observation.

Individual student data were obtained from detailed case studies of students selected from the integration programme to represent a range of disabilities, ages and extent of integration. Parents of these students provided information on their attitudes to integration and amount of contact with schools. A social profile of the students, completed twice by teachers over a nine-month interval, covered such aspects as adjustment, independence and social relationships.

The resulting data were considered under six broad headings (Hegarty and Pocklington, 1981): setting up integration programmes; staffing, including mainstream teachers and ancillary and support staff; practical considerations of accommodation, resources and costs; curriculum content and nature of teaching; social considerations; and parents.

The study was thus a mixture of descriptive and in-depth qualitative approaches. Quantitative data were sparse, but a large amount of illustrative detail was provided on how integration was implemented in practice. The survey was thus particularly valuable in identifying possible structural models for integration and the implications of each for school organisation and staffing.

Subsequent studies in the British context have used a similar design. Hodgson, Clunies-Ross and Hegarty (1984) studied integration in seventy schools, focusing on changes in school organisation and the curriculum, staffing and classroom teaching. The study was concerned with practical issues of curriculum modification, classroom organisation and practice, in-service training and the monitoring of students' progress. Dale (1984) examined the individualised integration of students with hearing impairment in some detail in the United Kingdom and New Zealand as well as in other countries. Lynas (1986) also studied the integration of students with hearing impairment in the United Kingdom, giving particular attention to students' self-awareness, to the reactions of normal hearing students and to the day-to-day problems and attitudes of class teachers. Howarth (1987) used a combination of techniques, including use of a comparison group of non-disabled students, in a study of the social structure, emotional climate and educational environment of nine schools in which 50 students with severe physical disabilities were integrated.

FROM RESEARCH TO PRACTICE

Research is of little value unless it influences what ultimately goes on in special education. I have suggested that policy and administrative practices often take little heed of research. Political expediency and economic necessity prevent the implementation of many recommendations that result from research findings. Nevertheless, administrators need to be informed about issues, and many of the surveys and statistical studies commissioned by government or other educational authorities are valuable for planning resources in special education.

A recent discussion suggests that teachers, too, are not greatly influenced in their classroom practices by the findings of research. Malouf and Schiller (1995) identified three groups of factors that may make teachers resistant to adopting new practices or organisational changes. Firstly, teachers will use new knowledge gained through research only if it does not conflict with the knowledge they have gained from their own experience, or with their professional judgment based on that knowledge. Part of the problem in accepting new knowledge is that research findings are rarely straightforward and unambiguous, and do not easily suggest application in any given context. New practices may be appropriate under some conditions but not others. New ideas may be accepted in principle, but appear of doubtful relevance for individual students with specific learning needs.

Secondly, teachers' attitudes and beliefs, not only about disability or in relation to adoption of new practices, but about the value and relevance of research in general, are likely to make them more resistant to change based on the findings of research. Studies reviewed by Malouf and Schiller (1995) suggest that change is more likely to come about as a result of procedures being put in place to help teachers assimilate change into their existing belief systems. Final acceptance of new practices will come only with the accumulation of successful experiences with those practices.

Special education is vulnerable to influence from poorly designed research, not only because of the methodological difficulties reviewed earlier in this chapter, but because those who live and work with disability are always searching for a programme, practice or technique that would seem to solve the problems of students who have difficulty in learning. The proliferation of fads in special education, based on doubtful claims of scientific research, has given research a poor reputation. Teachers may rightly be sceptical of new techniques and procedures that are not in accord with their own knowledge and experience. Further, teachers in special education are usually faced with immediate problems to which they seek immediate solutions. Scientific research is necessarily slow and painstaking, and rarely offers a complete solution.

Thirdly, research findings are only one factor, and a relatively minor one, in the context of teaching and learning. The practical constraints of curriculum requirements, resources and workloads are of more immediate influence in shaping teacher practice.

There is no single approach to research in special education that meets all the requirements of good research and answers the questions that beset administrators, teachers and parents concerned with the education of students with disabilities. The current debate about appropriate research methodology in special education promises to rival that concerning integration itself. Qualitative methods are at present well to the fore as investigators try to tap the human aspects of special education. But there is a danger that an obsession with currently fashionable research methodologies – whether qualitative or quantitative – will mean that the methodology dictates the research question, rather than the research question determining the appropriate methodology. Thus important questions may be overlooked. It is important to ask the right questions – questions which do have answers, and to which the answers will determine the future directions of special education.

Research in special education needs to be more closely guided by a better understanding of special educational practice, and ways in which research can help to improve that practice. In a climate which calls increasingly for accountability of services, special education needs to come to terms with the difficulties surrounding research so that funds are not directed to new programmes and practices without proper evaluation. The challenge of the future is to work out ways of applying the results of carefully controlled research to the complexities of special education practice.

Part II

Models of educational provision

Chapter 6

The special school
A preferred option?

BACKGROUND

The history of special education in both Australia and the United Kingdom evolved largely around the growth of special schools. The advent of universal education in most western countries was no guarantee that schools would provide for all students. Initially, school learning was equated almost exclusively with the acquisition of basic skills of literacy and numeracy. Schools made no provision for students who were for various reasons unable to acquire these skills, or could only acquire them with considerable difficulty. The development of alternative and distinct methods of communication meant not only that students with impairments in vision and hearing would need special instruction in these methods, but that instruction in the rest of the curriculum would also be expected to rely on special communicative techniques. Thus the earliest special schools were set up to serve categories of disability, usually by charitable organisations that would be expected to assume a lifelong support service for the individual with a disability.

Although segregated education has been widely rejected as discriminatory and unjust, it would be wrong to view the introduction of special schools as being motivated by any deliberate intent to exclude people with disabilities from the mainstream of society. Humanitarian motives were equally if not more important. The establishment of special schools needs to be seen within the overall context of education. Individual differences in learning styles and capacity were less well understood than they are today. The classroom teacher had no recourse to instructional and behavioural techniques and technological developments that have enabled many more children with disabilities to be educated in the regular classroom today. The emphasis on basic skills and knowledge left little room for the development of individual educational programmes to serve the needs of one or two students for whom the regular curriculum offered little relevance.

Strict entry requirements were established not to exclude students from the mainstream, but to ensure that students were not placed in special schools unless they were genuinely unlikely to be able to cope in the regular class without extra assistance. The fact that many of the tests and other criteria applied for special school enrolment were not appropriate for the purpose, or were misapplied or misinterpreted, meant that some students were inappropriately placed in special schools, but did not alter the underlying rationale for educating students with disabilities in segregated settings. In most cases a test score was only part of the process in identifying students for special school enrolment: the student would have been referred for testing because problems such as poor academic performance or adaptive skills would have already come to the attention of school authorities.

Much less has been written about special schools and their outcomes for students with disabilities than about special classes or integrated settings. The lack of independent evaluations of special school programmes may reflect the fact that criticisms of special education made by Dunn (1968) and others focused on special classes for students with mild intellectual disability rather than on special schools. In the United States, only about ten per cent of students with disabilities (including learning disabilities) attend special schools, the majority being educated in either special classes or resource rooms (Giangreco and Meyer, 1988). This has not prevented many of the criticisms levelled at special classes being extended to criticism of special schools. However, the thrust towards integration has tended to draw attention away from the special school, and there has been little attempt to evaluate the programmes or curricula they offer.

In Australia and the United Kingdom, special schools are a more common form of provision, with 58 per cent of students with disabilities in England attending special schools (Norwich, 1994b) and 27 per cent in Australia (de Lemos, 1994). Within Australia there is wide variation between states in the proportions of students with disabilities in special schools, reflecting historical differences in special education provision between states, as well as philosophical differences relating to implementation of integration (de Lemos, 1994).

With the worldwide trend towards integration, who are the students remaining in special schools, and why do they remain there?

Most likely, they are students who require a programme that is quite different from that offered in the regular classroom (Lieberman, 1992). Some students need to acquire highly specialised skills taught by specially trained teachers to avoid becoming handicapped by their disability. For example, some educational systems that are strongly in favour of integration have nevertheless retained special schools for students with sensory impairments to acquire fluency in special methods of communication. The more articulate advocacy groups in these areas, particularly in hearing impairment, also see special schools as promoting their own culture.

Other students may be unable to make useful gains in the academic curriculum and need an alternative curriculum, or the amount of teacher time and attention required for academic achievement at a useful level would be to the detriment of other class members. Yet others need to be placed in a situation in which they have opportunities to succeed and so develop self-esteem and confidence. The majority of students catered for by special schools continue to be those who have an intellectual disability.

Despite the trend towards integration, there has not been a corresponding decrease in numbers attending special schools in many areas. In Victoria, for example, following introduction of integration, a tenfold growth in the number of students being supported in integration was accompanied by only a small decrease in students in segregated settings (Auditor-General, Victoria, 1992). Norwich (1994b) noted an upswing in special school enrolments in Great Britain between 1991 and 1992.

However, there have clearly been a number of changes in special school enrolments in the past decade. For example, in Victoria substantial decreases have occurred in the numbers of students with physical and sensory impairments attending special schools. These decreases do not make a substantial difference to the overall number of students attending special schools, because they represent relatively smaller proportions of students with disabilities. There has also been a decrease in the number of students with intellectual disability attending special schools.

There is also a trend to enrolment of more students with severe and multiple disabilities as education authorities assume responsibility for individuals previously served by health authorities. This change reflects a recognition that all students have educational needs that are not served primarily by health care. Another change is the increasing average age of students in special schools. This appears to be due to a number of factors. For example, some primary-aged students are integrated from the start of their schooling and return to special schools for their secondary education. There has been no attempt to relate special school enrolments, or indeed special education generally, to fluctuations in incidence of disabilities, but this is an important question for epidemiologists and educational planners alike to address.

DO SPECIAL SCHOOLS MEAN A DUAL SYSTEM OF EDUCATION?

Until integration gained momentum, special schools tended to operate largely in isolation from the mainstream, leading to a questioning of the necessity for a dual system of education for students with disabilities. Unnecessary duplication of services, lack of reliability of disability categories on which many special schools based their enrolments and the wastefulness of resources are among criticisms directed at the existence of special schools. These criticisms have not always been backed by data. However, special schools have usually been exempt from systems of educational accountability that operate in mainstream schools, and there has been little evaluation of the long-term effectiveness of programmes offered. Part of this lack of evaluation, as well as the separation of many special schools from the mainstream of education, may stem from the historic origin of many special schools in charitable organisations or government health services. Public funding, combined with integration, is now posing a challenge to special schools to provide a more adequate account of their programmes.

In this context, the push to integrate students with disabilities into regular schools, whether in a special class or unit or in a regular class, has often been perceived as a threat to the survival of the special school. Indeed, Collins (1984) foresaw the eventual phasing out of special schools in Victoria as more students became integrated into the mainstream. What was not foreseen in Victoria, or by other authorities which adopted a policy of integration as the primary provision in special education, was the alarm created by this proposal in many parents, who feared the loss of programmes, resources and specialist staff seen as essential to meet the educational needs of their children. As Mittler and Farrell (1987) pointed out, one of the major obstacles to the successful implementation of integration is the high quality of the work being done in many special schools. Many specialised programmes are most effectively implemented in special schools, and without necessarily reducing academic expectations:

> Setting does not eliminate or guarantee the presence of effective instructional practices. After reviewing many programs, it appears that most of the important variables can occur in most settings. However, certain tightly monitored behaviourist programs *may* be easier to accomplish in *self-contained* settings than in mainstream settings. It is also the case that a restrictive setting makes it harder to avoid a certain reduction in valued processes like rapid pacing, high expectation, and cognitive press. We have found examples of these features in restrictive settings, however, and when they are present, the programs are successful.
>
> (Leinhardt and Pallay, 1982: 560)

These examples appeared to be the exception, rather than the rule, however. Leinhardt and Pallay went on to examine the content of a number of special school programmes which were comparatively less effective than those in regular schools. They found that curriculum was often watered down rather than specifically designed to meet the students' needs, that much time and effort were spent in teaching life and leisure skills with little systematic attempt to assess their mastery and that instructional techniques, while more relaxed and less intense than in the regular classroom, were not systematically altered to suit students' learning styles.

However, special schools do not necessarily imply a second system of education. Many are moving to develop closer links with the mainstream, and in turn the mainstream is drawing on the expertise of special schools to support integration.

WHY DO PARENTS CHOOSE SPECIAL SCHOOLS?

Advocates of integration argue that if, on balance, special schools are no more effective than regular schools in meeting the educational needs of students with disabilities, then there can be no case for their continued existence. So why do many parents continue to prefer a special school setting? If special schools offer no more than can potentially be offered in a regular setting, are we not morally obliged to ensure that all students, regardless of disability, receive their education in the mainstream? This question is more complex than might at first be thought. Many parents embrace integration in principle, but 'not for my child'. One parent expressed this view:

My child has high needs and is vulnerable to other children. He would be unable to function in mainstream education. It would not be a positive experience for my child or for the other children. The special school is the only appropriate situation for him.

The arguments put forward in favour of special schools have been concerned with provision of services, cost effectiveness, physical aspects of the environment, curriculum, student–staff ratios and social aspects.

Centralisation of services

Special schools are a way of grouping students with similar educational needs to make maximum use of available resources. This concentration of students with similar needs in a single centre, with a corresponding centralisation of services, is probably the most widely stated advantage of special schools compared to mainstream schools. It is the one factor that is difficult to replicate in a mainstream school. Services include qualified special education teachers, provision of specialist skills such as sign language for students with hearing or other communication difficulties, braille and orientation and mobility training for students with vision impairments, behavioural programmes and social skills building, and independent living programmes. They also include therapies and other health services, which, although not strictly educational, may be necessary to allow students access to an education.

It is impractical for a regular class teacher to develop the degree of expertise needed to teach an individual child with a severe communication difficulty, or a visual or hearing impairment, when the teacher may have the student only for a year. Moreover, for students with severe disabilities there were, and still are, basic issues of survival that need to be dealt with that are beyond the scope and expertise of the regular class teacher. Many of the skills which we take for granted to have been acquired by students in the regular class need to be specifically taught to some students with special needs. Most special school teachers have specialist training beyond the normal preparation for teaching in primary and secondary schools which enables them to understand the educational impact of a disability, and equips them to meet the varying needs of students with disabilities.

In addition to the concentration of teacher expertise and curriculum in a special school, special schools employ full-time or part-time therapists, or have regular visits from medical or paramedical staff. Non-teaching professionals can become familiar with a school's policy and structures if they are in regular attendance. Problems can be dealt with from a multi-professional perspective, with teachers and therapists developing collaborative teams to integrate therapy activities into the student's educational programme.

Cost-effectiveness

An assumption underlying centralisation of services in a special school is that it is more cost-effective than dispersing services across several mainstream schools in which only a few students with disabilities are enrolled. It is difficult to support or reject this assumption, because much depends on what services are actually being provided. A student's support needs may be different in each setting. Indeed, this is recognised in the Victorian context where the major form of support for many students in the mainstream is an integration aide. Students who are integrated part-time are often allocated an integration aide for the time they spend in the mainstream, but not for time spent in the special school. Again, accurate comparative costs are difficult to estimate because of the many factors involved. Cullen and Brown (1992) found that the average costs of educating a student with disabilities in Victoria in either special school or integrated settings were roughly comparable when the provision of integration aides and integration teachers in the mainstream was taken into account. The major source of costs is staff salaries, although special equipment, curriculum materials, transport and modifications to school buildings will add to these costs.

However, comparative costs are very difficult to estimate accurately. Capital costs were not included in Cullen and Brown's estimates. In a study of special education provision in Australia by de Lemos (1994), principals of special schools gave a much lower estimate of average expenditure per student than the Cullen and Brown estimates, partly explained by inaccuracies and inconsistencies in what costs were included.

Although parents may be less concerned than administrators with the average cost of educating students in different settings, a feature of the special school has been the assurance of support once the student is enrolled. Support funding has not been the issue that it has become in integration. Most resources are school-based, and a student enrolled in the special school is entitled to draw on any of those resources without having to demonstrate any additional need (Cullen and Brown, 1992).

We do not know to what extent economies can be achieved if a number of students with disabilities are integrated into a single mainstream school – for example, students may share an integration aide, and modifications made to buildings for one student may very well make the school more attractive to other students with similar needs. Most mainstream schools can achieve economies of scale in other areas because they have large numbers of students who do not have additional needs, an advantage not shared by the smaller special school. There is also some evidence that students remaining in special schools are those with the highest support needs, and the average cost of education in integrated settings might well increase if these students were to move to the mainstream.

These factors make it very difficult to draw any valid conclusions about the relative costs of education in special schools compared to the mainstream.

Physical environment

Most special schools have been built to accommodate students with disabilities and the specialist programmes offered. In many areas, the large growth in special education during the 1960s and 1970s was accompanied by the construction of new, purpose-built schools to provide what was considered an appropriate physical environment for the education of students with disabilities. A cartoon shows a student being integrated from a modern, spacious, single-storey special school into a dilapidated, two-storey mainstream school that gives an impression of having very little space to spare (Bovair, 1993). While the cartoon has obviously been exaggerated to make the point, it helps to draw our attention to some of the physical advantages of the more modern special schools. De Lemos (1994) found that the great majority of special schools in Australia were well equipped with facilities such as ramps for wheelchairs and modified toilets, as well as specialist learning areas. Specialised classrooms for training in vocational competencies and independent living skills, rooms and equipment for therapy, and rooms set aside for consultancy or individual teaching are also more common in special schools.

Curriculum

The special school can develop appropriate adaptations of curriculum materials and teaching techniques to serve the needs of students for whom it caters. Individual programmes can be developed within a total school curriculum. Although this may also happen in mainstream schools, the special school usually has far fewer enrolments than most mainstream schools and staff can work together to develop a coherent and consistent framework for each individual student throughout the course of the student's education.

Student–staff ratios

Special school classes are usually much smaller in size than classes in the regular school. In Australia the overall ratio of teachers to students in government special schools is one teacher to just under five students (de Lemos, 1994). The ratio reflects the need for greater individualisation of educational programmes to cater for the range of student needs in the special school, and for more intensive one-to-one instruction if learning is to be successful. Without this attention, academic learning, if it takes place at all, may be severely limited. As one parent put it:

> My child is able to receive as much attention as is necessary in the special school. The small classes lead to better teacher–student relationships, and ensure that she develops to the best of her abilities. They also allow for a more structured learning environment, which is what my child needs.

Social interaction

Although integration has been promoted as encouraging friendships between students with disabilities and non-disabled students, there is no evidence that this occurs on any firm or widespread basis. Friendships most often form spontaneously between people who share not only goals and interests, but values, aspirations and ways of conceptualising the world. Furthermore, reciprocal communication is vital to the maintenance of friendships. For students with physical and sensory disabilities, many of the barriers to communication may be overcome as students explore and share common goals and interests at a similar level. This is less likely to happen for students with intellectual disabilities, who may be increasingly unable to share many of the pursuits followed by their non-disabled peers at the same conceptual level.

Many students with disabilities may benefit from the support offered by a peer group with whom they share educational and other needs, rather than feel isolated in the mainstream. Teresa is one such student:

> Teresa, a teenager who has Down syndrome, attended a mainstream primary school for six years. The widening social gap between Teresa and her friends during the final years of primary school prompted her parents to enrol her in a special school for her secondary education. Friendships had faded and she had become lonely and depressed. Teresa was also bright enough to realise that she could not participate on an equal footing with the other students. At the special school, she is in a programme which is geared to her ability, and she socialises with others with whom she feels comfortable. Her self-esteem has improved, and her parents describe her now as 'very happy'.

Many parents see the special school as a setting 'where the child is not set up to fail'. Lieberman (1992) suggested that we need to recognise, particularly for people with intellectual disabilities, that quality-of-life aspirations may not be the same as for most students. For example, the range of vocational opportunities is unlikely to include most professions. Quality of life is relative to individual aspirations, and according to Lieberman school failure and the resulting loss of self-esteem are a greater threat to quality of life than simply the lack of academic achievement in itself. Many parents who enrol their children in special schools would agree with Lieberman. Attendance at the child's neighbourhood school and socialisation with non-disabled peers are much less important to these parents than their child's happiness. Would the child be just as happy in the mainstream? Often there is no answer to this question. However, when parents have tried integration and found it detrimental to their child's happiness and self-esteem, the special school has provided the appropriate environment.

DISADVANTAGES OF SPECIAL SCHOOLS

The advantages of special schools are also seen by pro-integrationists as their disadvantages. For example, in concentrating on expertise in dealing with a special population, the special school lacks a standard of comparison, and expectations of what might be achieved by a given age group may be unclear. Curriculum developed in isolation may focus disproportionately on specific educational needs at the expense of a wider range of experiences such as is offered in the mainstream. For example, excessive time may be spent in perfecting communication techniques. The range of curriculum offered may also be limited by the smaller number of staff in the special school and the consequent limited range of subject expertise. The lack of training and experience of most special school teachers in the secondary curriculum is increasingly a cause of concern as more students with disabilities move into adolescence.

Many special schools are category-based. Problems associated with categorisation of disability have already been discussed – students often have secondary disabilities and associated learning problems which may not be recognised by the school, or which may not be adequately catered for in a school that emphasises skills and competencies needed to overcome a specific disability. A small special school set up for one category of disability is likely to have a range of ability and achievement among its students that is as wide as in a large mainstream school. In addition, the age of students within the school is likely to range widely, so that there will be relatively few students at any given age. Given the range of ability and age levels, students may have less in common with each other than might at first be thought. The provision of programmes which both challenge the most able students and cater for those with highest needs will be difficult.

Moreover, the fixed resource levels that apply to special schools can be a disadvantage as well as an advantage (Cullen and Brown, 1992). Fixed resources can mean a lack of flexibility in responding to changes in curriculum, or to changes in the educational needs of the majority of students in the school.

Many parents and educators regard the special school as an artificial environment that is separate from the real world. Students may be sheltered from many situations they will eventually have to face as adults in the community, making transition to adult life more difficult. Chief among these is socialisation with non-disabled peers. This can be a real disadvantage for some students, particularly those with physical and sensory impairments. Lack of appropriate behavioural models, lack of feedback from non-disabled peers and removal from the common culture of childhood and adolescence may contribute to later isolation in the community.

PERCEPTIONS OF SPECIAL SCHOOL PARENTS

How realistic are the views of special school parents about mainstream schools? Teresa had spent time in the mainstream, and we can be sure that her parents, and others in a similar situation, did not make the decision lightly to withdraw their children to a special school. McDonnell (1987), however, showed that many of the fears expressed by parents about integration are not altogether justified. McDonnell questioned four hundred parents of students with moderate to severe disabilities about their perceptions of a range of variables relevant to integration. Parents of students integrated into mainstream schools were asked to respond by reporting the actual occurrence of events in the mainstream; parents of students in special schools were asked to predict what, in their view, was likely to happen if their child were placed in the mainstream.

The parents of students in special schools were generally negative in their perceptions of mainstream placement. They predicted significantly more mistreatment, reduced services, greater isolation and a lower quality of education, compared to reports by mainstream parents of what actually occurred. McDonnell's finding was consistent with other studies that suggest parents are likely to respond positively to the situation they are most familiar with.

How effective are special schools in meeting the educational needs of students with disabilities? Apart from studies that have focused on the views of parents, we have little data to answer this question. Studies of parents indicate a high level of satisfaction with special schools. But we do not necessarily know what criteria parents are using to make this judgment. We should not conclude from the high level of satisfaction that there is little room for change. Some parents also feel forced into choosing a special school that is less than satisfactory because of the negative attitudes of mainstream schools or the inadequate support offered. Alice provides one such example:

Alice has a mild intellectual disability, and transferred to a special school after a change of principal and a minor accident in the school grounds finally convinced her parents that she was not welcome in the local primary school. Since her transfer to the special school, her mother has noticed a decline in Alice's social skills. She is uncertain whether the decline is due to Alice's medical condition, or to the change of school. But Alice's parents have a number of other concerns about the special school.

The absence of any curriculum in academic skills at Alice's age level is a major concern. Alice does not have the opportunity to acquire the skills that her peers in the mainstream are learning. Alice's mother believes that the daily living skills programme offered by the school is a waste of time because Alice is encouraged to develop these skills at home and can cope with daily living at a level consistent with her chronological age. She sees daily living skills and community experiences as a family responsibility, but the school does not seem to welcome her views. To make up for the lack of an academic programme, Alice has a home tutor and has made considerable progress in learning to read.

Alice's future education is uncertain. At secondary level, the special school will maintain the programme of daily living and domestic skills, and will add a strong focus on pre-vocational skills. But academic skills will still be neglected, and Alice's mother is adamant that she should have the opportunity to learn to read.

The school attended by Alice is perhaps no longer a typical example. The school has failed to come to grips with current understanding and knowledge about disability, and with changing attitudes of the community. The school sees parent intervention as a threat to its self-proclaimed expertise. To admit that many of their students are capable of acquiring academic skills would also require an acknowledgment that many could also be educated with little difficulty in the mainstream. Its inflexibility could be its downfall, since it justifies the criticisms that have been levelled at special education by the advocates of inclusive schooling.

THE FUTURE OF SPECIAL SCHOOLS

With the changing population of the special school, and the continuing push to integration, what is the future for special schools?

There is no question that special schools will continue to exist for students who do not fit easily into mainstream education, and whose parents are unwilling to place them in a regular school. In 1984, Fish suggested that the future of special schools would depend on how far the regular school can cater effectively for a wide range of individual differences, rather than on any belief that there is a group of students who can be educated only in a segregated setting. Not all mainstream schools have shown themselves either willing or capable to take on the full range of special educational needs. There has been a swing away from full-scale integration to a recognition that parents cannot make choices about schooling unless options are available to them. Not all parents of students with disabilities see the local neighbourhood school as offering the most appropriate education for their children.

While special schools will undoubtedly continue to fill a role in the education of students with disabilities, there is much to suggest that their role may be changing. Indeed, if it does not change, then special schools, such as the one attended by Alice, may cease to be viable. Further, if they are to continue to provide programmes of excellence for students with disabilities, then special schools need to be seen as offering more than just a location for the education of students whom the mainstream has greatest difficulty in accommodating. The abolition of categories of disability as a basis for special education led to a number of problems both in identifying a statistical basis for planning and in the fair and equitable allocation of funding on a needs basis (Auditor-General, Victoria, 1992). It has also led to a questioning of the retention of category-based special schools. Future special schools may therefore be expected to cater for a much wider range of disabilities and educational needs than they have in the past.

The role of health services and therapies in special schools has also been questioned. It has been suggested that special schools should no longer see themselves as providers of health care, and should focus instead on providing for educational needs. For some students with severe disabilities it may be difficult to separate the two, but clearly there needs to be greater integration between the two services, so that health care does not preclude the provision of an appropriate educational programme. The changing incidence of different disabilities, the geographical nature of the area served and the extent to which primary and secondary schools can accommodate individual differences are also factors to be considered in the future role of the special school.

To a large extent, the survival of the special school will depend on the nature of the programme or programmes it offers. These will need to be flexible, not only catering for individual needs, but also depending on the amount of time a student spends in a special school. Students who are removed from the mainstream on a full-time basis are likely to need a broad curriculum covering all areas of study and competencies (Fish, 1984), regardless of whether they eventually return to the mainstream. Students who are part-time in the special school, whether on a long-term or short-term basis, will require programmes developed in close collaboration between special and regular school teachers. Programmes are likely to be more focused on specific learning problems that cannot readily be catered for in the time the student spends in the regular school setting.

The future is likely to see a much greater similarity between special and regular school curricula. The benefit of emphasising mainstream curriculum in special schools is not only to give students with disabilities opportunities and experiences similar to those of students in regular schools. Links between special and mainstream schools are likely to be strengthened as special schools find they are not well equipped with facilities, resources and subject expertise required for some areas of the curriculum (Fletcher-Campbell and Hall, 1993).

The survival of the special school is thus likely to depend on its willingness to work in closer collaboration with mainstream schools. Warnock (1978) conceived of the special school as a specialist centre which would provide support and resources to mainstream schools to help them in meeting the needs of students with disabilities. These resources and expertise should be made more widely available to provide intensive specialised help on a short-term basis to students in the mainstream.

The call for closer links between special schools and the mainstream has not gone unheeded. Bovair (1993) suggested that special schools should become more proactive in establishing their future role. Both the general public and the educational community will need to be convinced about the value of their programmes, particularly in providing intensive, individualised programmes, or programmes in life skills, which are less readily implemented in the regular school. According to Bovair, this will require a move away from the concept of fixed or indefinite placements of students in special schools to one of transitional placements. This concept would fit readily with Fish's (1984) suggestion that special schools will need to be more flexible in the programmes they offer. Special schools will also need to work collaboratively with regular schools in their neighbourhood, taking a lead in research and development of materials to support students with disabilities in the mainstream, and becoming more involved in teacher training.

Willowdale (not its real name) is an example of how one Local Education Authority in England came to terms with the need for change if special schools were to fulfil a significant role in the future of special education. The outcome has not been simply cosmetic changes to curriculum or to modes of operating in the special school, but a complete reconceptualisation and restructuring of special educational provision in the area. The area in which Willowdale is situated originally had three special schools – two serving moderate and one severe learning difficulties. Special school enrolments were falling, partly owing to population changes, but also because, in a climate which strongly favoured integration, regular schools were becoming increasingly reluctant to refer students to them. The special schools had become over-staffed and over-resourced.

In a bold decision, the two schools for students with moderate learning difficulties were closed down and an entirely new special school was opened on the site of one with provision for half of the former special school students on site. This new school, Willowdale, was to function as a core school, serving cluster schools in the area. The cluster schools, four secondary, two primary and two upper primary or middle schools, joined a scheme for integration of students with moderate learning difficulties, absorbing some of the students from the now closed special schools. Each was given a quota of ten students with a disability spread across age groups, with students carefully selected to ensure that they would fit into the school. Each of the cluster schools was assigned a teacher from Willowdale, absorbing some of the staff from the former special schools. Students who remained enrolled at Willowdale, generally those with serious emotional and behavioural difficulties, could be considered at any time for enrolment in the mainstream either at a cluster school or at any one of the other schools within the area.

Willowdale also set up a support and advisory service which is available to all of these schools. This is backed by a Resource Centre from which teachers may borrow materials to assist in teaching students with specific needs. The support service is staffed by a team co-ordinator and two advisory teachers. It offers direct support to students, for example by observing and preparing a profile of the student's strengths and needs to aid curriculum planning; it also suggests classroom management strategies and teaching methods to enable students to have access to the curriculum. Staff develop materials, advise on school policy in relation to disability and may share teaching with class teachers, either taking a small group which includes the student with a disability or freeing the class teacher to work with this group.

This single centre thus provides a continuum of services under one management for students with moderate learning difficulties through: a core special school for students who, for various reasons, would not be appropriately served in the regular class at a given time; an outreach service to support schools in the mainstream that enrol students with moderate learning difficulties; and a support and advisory service available to all mainstream schools in the area. A student with a moderate learning difficulty could be placed in any one of these settings. The core school follows the National Curriculum, adapted where needed. Willowdale also encourages part-time integration of some of its students into mainstream schools for social interaction and specific activities in which the student can actively participate.

Willowdale works because it is founded on a philosophy of close collaboration and skill-sharing. Participating schools have agreed to allow the core school to take charge of support funding. For this, they receive the services of a teacher qualified in special education, and the support of the resources at the core school. Their willingness to sacrifice autonomy in the administration of these funds is testimony to the quality of the service they receive, and their commitment to supported integration.

Willowdale also works because it provided a solution to a problem of falling enrolments that was compatible with the prevailing philosophy of integration. Rather than seeing integration as a threat to the future existence of the special school, the working party which thought through this structure and its subsequent implementation created a role for the special school that has become indispensable to the provision of special education in the area. In effect, the special school has extended its function far beyond the original concept of a segregated facility for students rejected or excluded by the mainstream. Willowdale has provided a model which many, although perhaps not all, special schools might want to consider for the future.

The eventual breakdown of the dichotomy between special and regular schools was forecast by Cullen and Brown (1992). Special schools with small numbers might eventually combine with a mainstream school to reduce costs, but continue to provide programmes for students who need them. In some cases this is already happening. Cullen and Brown also foresaw a greater need to evaluate the outcomes of special school education. In an era of increasing school autonomy and parent choice, there is no reason why a special school should not develop as one which offers a particular educational programme that is attractive to parents, not because it caters for a specific category of disability, but because it offers appropriate and flexible curricula. Special schools may need to market themselves in a different way as one option among several from which parents may choose. Market forces will ensure that evaluation occurs, and that only those special schools that are prepared to change their underlying philosophy and structure to meet students' educational needs in the future will continue to exist.

Chapter 7

The best of both worlds?
Link schools and partial integration

BACKGROUND

Special schools developed initially as relatively independent units isolated from the mainstream of education. A growing recognition of the need for students with disabilities to have opportunities to socialise with non-disabled peers, even if much of their education is conducted in a segregated setting, has led to a move to establish links between special and mainstream schools. The link school concept involves the establishment of a working relationship between a special school and a mainstream school, usually for mutual benefit. Partial integration usually refers to part-time attendance by special school students at a mainstream school, and may range from attendance for only one or two sessions a week for extra-curricular activities such as music, art or drama, to several days a week in a regular class. Occasionally, partial integration occurs in the reverse direction, with students from mainstream schools attending a special school for part of a week, where they may have the benefit of some of the facilities set up for specialist activities such as independent living or vocational preparation programmes.

Although the establishment of links between schools almost always involves partial integration in some form, partial integration may also take place without the establishment of formal links. Link schools and partial integration are by no means an identical form of provision in special education, but both represent a form of transition between segregated and integrated education. Some special schools, such as Willowdale, described in the previous chapter, have established themselves as an outreach service in which they have links with several mainstream schools, providing advice and expertise, and often staff resources, to support students with disabilities in the mainstream. Most link school arrangements are on a smaller scale, involving one or perhaps two mainstream schools – one primary and one secondary – linked with a special school.

The establishment of link schools was strongly encouraged by Warnock (1978) as a prelude to integration on a larger scale, and has been a significant development in the provision of special education in the United Kingdom (Hegarty, 1988). In a comprehensive survey of special schools by Hegarty, 73 per cent reported having a current link with a mainstream school, and a further 10 per cent were planning one. Although most involved links from the special school to the mainstream school, there were also examples in which mainstream students attended special schools for specific activities. Links involved students and staff sharing resources, with special schools providing information and consultancy to nearby schools and conducting in-service training.

The link school concept has not been as well documented outside the United Kingdom. It is difficult to estimate the extent to which link schools are seen as a means of transition towards integration, and to which they are seen as an end in themselves to encourage social contacts between students with disabilities and their non-disabled peers. Although links often develop informally between schools, more formal arrangements exist as well. In the Netherlands, for example, a focus on administrative, organisational and educational links between mainstream and special schools has been adopted as official policy to encourage transition from special to mainstream schooling (EUR-IDICE Unit, 1993). Although the Netherlands has a strong special school system, the government's policy is to curb the growth of these schools both by reintegrating students from special schools to mainstream schools and by preventing segregated placement in the first place. To this end, a special project has been set up by the Ministry of Education and Science to develop co-operative links between special and mainstream schools. In some cases, 'split placements' (partial integration) are proposed as a prelude to full integration. Special schools will provide help for individual students and advice to mainstream teachers, but will be phased out as the mainstream assumes greater responsibility for all students.

In Australia, most states are able to offer examples of link schools and partial integration, although the concept itself is less formalised than in the United Kingdom or the Netherlands. The most recent Australian survey of special education provision does not include statistics on partial integration or link schools (de Lemos, 1994).

These statistics would be difficult to collect because students in link school schemes or partial integration usually remain enrolled in the special school while attending a mainstream school part-time. Thus enrolment figures are unlikely to provide a true estimate of the extent to which students with disabilities actually participate in educational activities with their non-disabled peers. In Victoria, where partial integration is offered as an option for students with disabilities, one estimate has put the proportion of students in special schools who also attend mainstream schools at around ten per cent (Cullen and Brown, 1992).

Our common perception of schooling envisages a student enrolled in a single school which he or she attends five days a week. The link school concept challenges this perception, and administrative systems have not always caught up with this challenge. Cullen and Brown (1992) found that dual attendance options were restricted by administrative rulings. Their report recommended greater flexibility in the deployment of funds to meet students' needs, as well as closer collaboration between special and mainstream schools so that the dual attendance option could be developed further. The devolution of greater autonomy to individual schools is an unknown factor in the future of the link school concept, although in Victoria changes in funding arrangements for students with disabilities should allow more flexible links to be established. In the United Kingdom, however, Fletcher-Campbell and Hall (1993) saw the move to local management of schools and changes in funding arrangements as posing a possible threat to the continuance of links between the two settings. For example, reductions in class size to accommodate one or two students with a disability could result in a corresponding reduction in funding. Given the relatively high costs of partial integration, link schemes could be the first to suffer in any attempt to cut costs (Fletcher-Campbell and Hall, 1993).

ADVANTAGES OF LINK SCHOOL SCHEMES

The link school concept represents two aspects of special education provision, on the one hand providing a setting for social interaction on a regular basis between students with disabilities and students in the mainstream, and on the other serving as a gradual transition process for students moving from the special school to the mainstream school. The latter arrangement may be extended to the special school providing specialist support for integrated students in the mainstream. Partial integration is often seen as combining the best of both worlds in special education: the student has access to special curriculum and small classes in the special school, while also having the opportunity to socialise and participate with non-disabled peers in extra-curricular activities that are not available in the special school. Matthew is a student whose parents see partial integration as the best solution to meeting both his educational and his social needs:

> Matthew is eleven and has a mild intellectual disability and a number of health problems, including asthma, epilepsy and migraines. At the age of five, Matthew began attending the local primary school, but in his second year it became clear that he would have difficulty learning without a special programme and close one-to-one attention. Hindered by frequent absences from school, Matthew had made little progress in early reading and number skills. Lacking in social skills, he tended to withdraw from his classmates, and was isolated and unhappy.
>
> Assessment by a psychologist revealed that Matthew was eligible to attend a special school, and so he was moved to a special school in a nearby suburb. Matthew has prospered in the small classes and more sheltered environment and his parents feel he is very happy there. He has acquired basic reading and number skills; socially, however, he still seems immature and lacks confidence in social situations. After four years at the special school, Matthew's parents decided that he would benefit from more contact with non-disabled students and he now spends three days a week in the special school and two days in the mainstream. In the mainstream he is fully supported by an integration aide.
>
> Matthew's disability is evident when he communicates, but not in his appearance. It took some time, as well as input from Matthew's integration aide, for other students in the main-stream school to realise that Matthew's behaviour would not benefit from their teasing, but that he could learn if they gave him appropriate feedback. Although he still has difficulty in making friends, Matthew's behaviour has improved consider-ably with exposure to the behaviour of his non-disabled peers. The regular school is supportive, and Matthew is beginning to gain more confidence there. But Matthew will soon reach the end of his primary schooling, and his future in secondary

education is uncertain. His parents would like him to continue in partial integration, and comment:

> The special schools have the time to educate each child and understand their special needs. But the mainstream school is also a must because that is where his peers are. They show him what is acceptable and what is not; they are his role models and we are in the real world – there is no reason to hide him away.

Partial integration also ensures that students can retain access to resources and facilities that may be lacking in the mainstream school. Even though partial integration is successful when judged by positive changes in students' behaviour and in attitudes of mainstream students, parents who strongly support the concept of partial integration may be unwilling to give up the special school setting altogether (Carpenter, Fathers, Lewis and Privett, 1988). Link schools and partial integration may therefore be perceived as serving more than a transition function.

WHAT MAKES A SUCCESSFUL LINK SCHOOL PROJECT?

Superficially, the link school concept, because it is a less radical departure from traditional provisions for special education, poses less of a threat to either special or mainstream schools than full-scale integration. Yet examination of individual link school arrangements reveals some important issues that need to be dealt with if link school projects are to be successful. Many of these issues arise from the fact that such projects do not concern a single administrative or organisational unit, but clearly involve close co-operation between at least two schools. The issues include identification of programme goals, selection of participating students, allocation of responsibilities, preparation and planning, and commitment.

Identification of goals

The first of these issues is the identification of clearly specified goals that are shared between the two schools. A danger with the establishment of link schools is that the arrangement can be seen as an end in itself, paying lip service to pressures to integrate without either threatening the continuing existence of the special school or placing pressure on the mainstream school to accommodate students with disabilities on a full-time basis, with the consequent need for curricular and other adaptations. Without a clear definition of goals, the link school concept may founder for lack of direction. These goals need to be established mutually between the schools concerned, rather than being imposed externally. Ruebain (1987) described a link between a special school for students with physical disabilities and a mainstream school, implemented as a pilot scheme by an educational authority anxious to appear active in integration. The schools concerned were chosen primarily because of their geographical proximity, but also because integration would help to boost falling enrolments in the mainstream school. Neither of these reasons offered specific goals for the project, leading to confusion between schools and among staff within the schools about its aims. Absence of shared goals between the schools also had direct implications for the success of the project. For example, four students from the special school attended the mainstream school for two periods each per week to participate in classes in business studies, computing, biology and design technology. This arrangement led some mainstream teachers to believe that the sole purpose of the programme was to provide students with access to curriculum areas not provided at the special school. Consequently, opportunities for socialisation were neglected. Further, although the mainstream school had some innovative programmes which catered for mixed-ability teaching, including community classes, uncertainty about the goals of partial integration meant that the special school students did not get the full benefit of these innovations.

Student selection

Secondly, there need to be unambiguous and mutually agreed criteria for identifying students for attendance at the mainstream school. In a programme described by Swann (1987), the schools concerned disagreed about whether in the long term integration would be appropriate for all students with disabilities or only for some. Selection of students was carried out by special school staff and was based on their judgments of students' ability to participate in and benefit from the mainstream curriculum with their current level of support. Thus only the most able students were integrated, and this had an impact on both schools. Staff in the mainstream school felt that more students from the special school could be integrated, given appropriate supports. In the special school, the loss of the most able students to the mainstream affected class teaching and staff morale, with teachers feeling they were reverting to being 'special' teachers rather than teachers of academic subjects. The self-esteem of students who were not integrated also suffered.

Swann (1987) identified a number of other issues in relation to student selection. For example, attendance of special school students at mainstream classes may result in numbers beyond the agreed class size. This may be important when a class, such as home economics or science, requires specific resources that are not available for extra students. The issue is not necessarily related to the student's disability, although the disability may compound the problem created by additional numbers. A dilemma is created where a mainstream school has an obligation to provide educational resources for students already enrolled, and then accepts additional students. In such cases, the benefits of a link project may need to be weighed against possible educational disadvantages to students for whom the host school is their local school.

A dilemma also arises in partial integration from the principle that students from the special school should be treated on an equal basis to those in the mainstream school. In practice these students may need to be dealt with differently from other students in either school. Simply the fact of attending a second school, and of having to be transported from one school to another, identifies these students as different.

Shared responsibility

In a number of link school arrangements students integrated from the special school into the mainstream have remained enrolled in the special school. This may occur even when the students are integrated full-time into the mainstream school (Swann, 1987). Initially, special school enrolment may be maintained so that students are able to draw on the resources of the special school. However, in the programme described by Swann, this practice was maintained over a number of years even though staff at the mainstream school now felt themselves to be just as expert in handling physical disability as those in the special school, and believed the obligation to use special school resources was unnecessary and unjustified.

The fact that students remained enrolled in the special school also created confusion regarding responsibility for the student. The principle of shared responsibility meant that one school could not make a decision about a student's educational programme without consulting the other school. The need for constant communication between schools reduced efficiency and added to the workloads of mainstream teachers. The special school staff, on the other hand, felt the continuing existence of their school would be threatened if the integrated students were removed from the roll.

Equally, dual enrolment can create tensions between link schools over responsibility for allocation of integration aide and support teacher time to students enrolled in both special and mainstream schools (Watts, 1987).

Although enrolment may appear to be primarily an administrative concern, these tensions need to be resolved if a programme is to be successful. Furthermore, the concerns are not only administrative. Most of the studies of link school projects have focused on issues of shared enrolment and shared responsibilities in so far as they affect schools. The reactions of students are equally if not more important. Students may appear to be getting the best of both worlds, but some concern has been expressed that students in situations of partial integration find it difficult to identify with any one school (Jenkinson, 1995). This situation will be exacerbated if staff themselves lack a clear identification of their roles and responsibilities when the education of a student is shared between schools.

Preparation and planning

The need for schools to prepare adequately for integration is well recognised, but can be overlooked where link schools are concerned and where responsibilities have not been clearly defined. Warnock (1978) maintained that link school projects require careful planning, not just in preparing mainstream schools to understand and accept disability, but in co-ordinating their day-to-day practices in curriculum development, timetabling, transport and other organisational aspects. From this perspective, planning needs to be undertaken in much greater detail than might at first be thought.

Lack of preparation and planning often reflects failure to establish clear goals for a programme. For example, in the pilot project described by Ruebain (1987) between a special school for students with physical disabilities and a mainstream school, preparation consisted of visits by staff to other link school projects, a video to introduce the special school students to their host school, and a joint school trip over one week, all at a relatively superficial level. Lack of adequate planning also meant that preparation was unco-ordinated, resulting in inappropriate or unnecessary building modifications.

This project is not an isolated example of lack of planning. In a similar link project described by Swann (1987), the mainstream school lacked appropriate facilities for coping with physical disability. For example, there was no privacy for physiotherapy treatment. The schools concerned disagreed on what should be done about the deficiencies and on the extent to which adaptations should be made to the mainstream school. The mainstream school was concerned that adaptations should not disadvantage non-disabled students. In addition, there was some reluctance to allocate a disproportionate amount of funding to school modifications for the small number of students integrated from the special school when there were insufficient funds to meet the special needs of a much larger group of students within the school.

Commitment

Lack of adequate planning and the inability of schools to come to terms with issues of enrolment and shared responsibility may indicate a lack of commitment of staff to the success of the link school programme. Although school staff and administrators may favour the link school concept in principle, many are not adequately prepared for its impact on either special or mainstream school, and are not always willing to make the necessary adjustments for its success. In particular, if a key member of the project is not committed, other staff involved may be discouraged from any effort to make the project work. Incompatibility between power groups, such as unions, education authorities, special needs staff and school governing bodies also prohibits the establishment of agreed-upon goals (Ruebain, 1987).

The situations described by Ruebain (1987) and by Swann (1987) both illustrate a serious breakdown in the link school concept. The problem is not necessarily with the concept itself, however. Both projects had a number of factors in common which could be identified as contributing to the unsatisfactory situation that prevailed. Firstly, in both cases the links were not initiated from within any of the schools involved, but were imposed by authorities outside the schools. The schools had not been chosen for reasons that conform to the principles underlying integration, such as being the students' neighbourhood schools. None of the schools involved could claim 'ownership' of the projects, and although principals and staff appeared to be committed philosophically to integration, in practice the link appeared to pose a threat both to the survival of the special school and to the well-being of students in the mainstream school. It could be said of both these programmes that neither was concerned primarily with meeting the needs of the students involved. Not only were they not child-focused, they were not school-focused either, but were implemented to meet requirements that were primarily administrative.

Secondly, in both cases the goals of the link school concept were not clearly identified. The links appeared to result from a need on the part of education authorities in the area to be seen to be moving towards integration, without any real idea of why they should be moving in this direction, or what outcomes should be expected. There was no expressed policy in relation to integration, so contributing to the uncertainty about the future felt in particular by the special school.

Thirdly, in both cases preparation for integration was at a superficial level. Little forethought was given to the provision of adequate resources within the mainstream school, or to the role of the special school in supporting students in the mainstream. The result was a series of ill-planned, unco-ordinated and often wasteful adaptations to the mainstream school that were implemented on an ad hoc basis. There was little attempt at collaborative effort to ensure that students' needs were being met. In the project described by Swann (1987) this situation was exacerbated by the enrolment issue, which affected funding. Allocation of special school resources to supporting students with disabilities in the mainstream could also have implications for funding for special schools (Fletcher-Campbell and Hall, 1993).

Uncertainty about who should be responsible for deciding on resources, the conflicting views representing different groups involved in the process and indeed the uncertainty of the future of integration in the areas served by the schools contributed to what was undoubtedly a complex and sensitive situation.

CAN LINKS BETWEEN SPECIAL AND MAINSTREAM SCHOOLS WORK?

There is little doubt that link schools will not work unless there is a high level of collaboration and sharing of resources and expertise between schools. Reports of successful link school projects suggest that the first requirement for success is that the impetus for the establishment of the link must come from within the schools themselves, rather than being imposed from outside. Part of this process involves mutual recognition and respect between each of the schools involved in the programme for what the other school has to contribute. Links between Hayford Green Secondary College (not its real name), in an outer suburb of Melbourne, and two special schools, illustrate how this works:

Hayford Green is committed to a policy of integration, although it does not seek to be identified as an 'integration' school and aims to maintain a normal balance across the school between students who do or do not have a disability. The school's integration policy includes among its aims: to ensure that teaching staff work collaboratively with various support services and special school staff in the provision of appropriate programmes for individual students; and to work co-operatively with staff of the special school [for students with physical disability] to develop programmes of benefit to all students from both the mainstream and special school.

After beginning on a small scale to integrate students from a nearby special school, the school now has thirty students who receive support funding, nine of whom are full-time. Twenty-five of the students are from a nearby school for students with severe physical disabilities, some attending the mainstream school full-time and others on a part-time sessional basis. The school has a policy that students will be put only into subject classes in which they have a likelihood of success. As far as possible, students participate alongside mainstream students, but the programme is flexible and if students need extra time to learn a new skill, for example to become familiar with a new computer, they may be withdrawn to allow this. The school also has a life skills programme, which includes any student believed to be in need of such a programme. Staff work closely with the staff of the special school to develop a co-ordinated programme for each student.

The school is fortunate in that it has a range of resources and equipment for subjects such as woodwork, metalwork and textiles, in addition to normal academic subjects. A range of vocational studies leads into further study beyond school, and students with disabilities have now progressed into further education as a result of attending the secondary college. The school has had a special bus built to accommodate nine wheelchairs, and this provides transport between the two schools as needed. In addition to an integration teacher who co-ordinates the programme, integration aides are employed to attend to the physical needs of students. The aides, who have all received in-service training, move around between students so that no one aide is permanently attached to any one student.

The second special school with which Hayford Green has established a link is a school for students with autism. Five of the students integrated full-time are autistic, and the special school provides a teacher for one day a week to work with these students. The project has now become a model programme for other schools who enrol students with autism.

The college is realistic in its expectations. Its goals are to make its resources equally available to all students who attend the school, giving them the best possible preparation for their future life. The staff know that social interactions will not occur of their own accord, and need to be worked on, but have also been pleased to observe some genuine friendships develop. They also know that, for students with autism, excessive social interaction can be stressful. An integration room is provided where students can retreat if they need to be away from other students, and where students who need it can receive individual instruction. At breaks the room is available to any student, although mostly used by the students with autism.

Hayford Green is an example of a link situation where expertise is shared between schools, with special school staff offering support to mainstream staff in dealing with disability and advising mainstream staff about what to expect of students in physical, sensory and behavioural areas. In return, the college offers students opportunities to develop important life skills and to participate in vocational studies that would not be available in the special school.

Low-key projects

The most successful link school projects also appear to be those that proceed on a relatively low-key basis, that are well planned, in which special and mainstream schools work together towards a specified goal and in which staff and students from both schools work together in mutually rewarding and enjoyable activities. Wade and Moore (1992) described one such project in which a special school for students with moderate to severe learning difficulties worked with a mainstream school in a joint production of a musical performance. Students from each school participated in the production, with additional choral support provided from the mainstream school. The successful outcomes of this project were attributed to the fact that it was a collaborative and enjoyable learning experience which posed no threat to either school. Students from the special school displayed hitherto unsuspected skills, participating enthusiastically in singing where previously they had been reluctant to speak, responding appropriately to cues and showing the ability to adapt and take on different roles. Students from the mainstream school, some of whom were asked to partner a student from the special school, learned to behave naturally with the special school students, unobtrusively providing prompts on stage when needed and developing genuine friendships. Teachers from both schools also learned from the experience, with mainstream teachers developing more positive attitudes towards disability and observing the calm but effective ways in which their colleagues from the special school handled difficult behaviour. Teachers from the special school in turn felt less isolated from mainstream teaching.

In its own right this project proved to be a valuable educational experience for all those involved, even if it had had no further outcomes. However, the collaboration and shared experiences between the schools also provided a foundation on which further integration could build.

How might such links be carried further to provide a positive framework for interaction between mainstream and special schools? An important aspect seems to be that each school sees the other as having a positive contribution to make to the project. In some cases this aspect has been extended to mainstream students attending the special school for joint activities, as well as special school students attending the mainstream school. A link scheme described by Carpenter et al. (1988) began with ten children with severe learning difficulties joining in a fortnightly physical education programme in a local primary school. Integration teachers appointed to the special school were responsible for developing the links with mainstream schools. As the project expanded, it included sessions in the special school which had better facilities for some activities such as home economics and soft play.

The willingness of schools to explore opportunities for sharing of resources, combined with the low-key approach to administrative processes, underlies the success of a link scheme undertaken at secondary level in Townsville, a city in northern Queensland (Harker and Hill, 1988). The link between the schools began with an approach by the special school principal to the principal of the high school, followed by consultation within each of the schools and frequent meetings between senior staff to identify areas in which joint programmes could be developed.

A feature of the Townsville project was that, like the link scheme described by Carpenter et al. (1988), it did not simply involve one-way integration into the high school. The special school also offered its resources to a number of low-achieving students who were having difficulties in the mainstream school. These students attended the special school one day a week for a programme of classroom activities, manual arts and excursions.

The main thrust of the Townsville project, however, focused on integration of students from the special school into the high school for development of social skills. A community-based learning pro-gramme already in operation in the mainstream school, which emphasised community service projects, manual arts and basic academic and social skills, provided an appropriate opportunity for participation by fifteen- and sixteen-year-old students from the special school. A pastoral care programme based on vertical grouping enabled younger secondary students to be integrated into a cohesive group that would continue for the remainder of their secondary schooling. With the establishment of a special needs unit in the high school, partial integration was extended to full-time integration. The programme for high school students in the special school was discontinued, and the special needs unit in the mainstream school undertook responsibility for adapting curriculum where necessary and monitoring the progress of all students with special educational needs within the school.

Although Harker and Hill identified some initial concerns about this project, particularly among parents of special school students who feared the loss of intensive academic programmes provided by the special school if students moved to the mainstream school. Few behavioural problems were encountered once students had settled in the school, and problems with the academic programme were addressed by the school's resource teacher. The authors attributed the success of the programme to the receptive attitudes within the mainstream school, as well as to the availability of resources to support integration. This is undoubtedly true, but one of the interesting aspects of this project is that it deliberately set out to minimise both administrative involvement in the programme and changes to provisions in the mainstream school. Integration was a gradual process, beginning with partial integration of a small number of students before progressing to full-time integration of larger numbers. The mainstream school drew upon the resources that it already had in place to support the integrated students in preference to seeking additional special provisions. Teachers involved in the programme were provided with in-service training, and, if problems did occur that they felt unable to handle, informal approaches for assistance could be made to the administration.

A similar process of gradual adjustment was followed by a special developmental school in north-east Victoria which established a link with a large high school in the area (Watts, 1987). The high school, with a declared commitment to integration on the basis of social justice and equality of opportunity, offered a range of programmes selected through collaborative decision making between students, parents and staff of the school. A programme of part-tim3e integration was already in place when availability of funding for an integration aide and an integration teacher enabled this programme to be extended to full-time for a small number of students. This number was limited to five in recognition of the constraints on available support.

Thus partial integration is frequently seen as a form of trial integration, preparing students for full-time placement in the mainstream, or providing an opportunity to assess students for their ability to adapt to the mainstream. Less frequently is it seen as an opportunity to assess the mainstream to see if it can be adapted to meet the needs of the student with a disability. From this perspective, partial integration needs to be seen as a temporary arrangement rather than any permanent solution in special education provision. Indeed, in some arrangements deliberate limits have been set on the length of time a student may spend in partial integration.

SOCIAL INTERACTION IN LINK SCHEMES

From the researcher's point of view, partial integration offers the opportunity to study the social interactions of students with disabilities in both mainstream and segregated settings without the problems involved in comparing different groups of students who are selected non-randomly.

In an extensive study of link school arrangements in the United Kingdom, Lewis (1995) carried out observations of social interactions between mainstream students and special school students with severe learning difficulties. Mainstream students were asked to partner a special school student in a specific task, such as doing a painting or completing a jigsaw puzzle, and their conversations were recorded during these sessions. From an analysis of the conversations, Lewis identified a cluster of characteristics in the conversations of mainstream students when they interacted with the special school students. These characteristics were typical of the way in which children usually address other, younger, children. Their talk to the special school students consisted of frequent repetitions and many direct instructions about what to do or not do. They gave few explanations and asked few genuine questions to which they expected answers. Many of the approaches made by the mainstream students were aimed at getting their partner's attention, or keeping their partner's attention on the task. For young children (aged six to seven years) these approaches were restricted to relatively ineffective methods such as calling the partner by name. Older children were more skilled at getting and maintaining the attention of their partner, for example by nudging or pointing to the materials they were working with.

Many link school schemes have been established in order to encourage social interaction between students with disabilities and non-disabled students. Lewis's studies are extremely valuable for what they tell us about the nature of these interactions. Clearly the interactions are not symmetrical, but more in the nature of a one-way exchange between tutor and tutee. Part of this process may lie in the way in which we tend to prepare students for encounters with people with a disability. The children were told by their teachers that the special school students were just like themselves, but if they tried to interact with the special school students on this assumption, they were unsuccessful. Faced with this puzzling situation, the mainstream students tried the only alternative strategy they knew, and behaved as though the child with a disability were a much younger child.

Furthermore, younger children in the study (seven-year-olds) did not appear to understand the nature of the learning difficulty (intellectual disability) and its implications for social exchanges. After the link project had been operating for a year, Lewis interviewed the children involved about their understanding of disability. When they were asked to describe the special school students, most mainstream students referred to the most obvious aspects of disability – for example, although only one of the special school students wore a hearing aid, many of the mainstream students believed that all of them had hearing and visual impairments. They also tended to over-emphasise what they believed to be 'misbehaviour'. Few mainstream students mentioned speech difficulties, although most of the special school students had a speech problem.

Despite these misunderstandings, the programme had positive results (Lewis, 1995). Achievements of the special school students were also emphasised, in fact over-emphasised, by the mainstream students, and positive attitudes developed early in the peer tutoring project were maintained over the year. Given the misunderstandings about disability that were evident in the younger children, however, Lewis cautions against teachers and others attempting to play down a disability which is likely to have a direct effect on social interactions.

Ware et al. (1992) found that students with severe learning difficulties who were partially integrated initiated fewer interactions and were more likely to be passive recipients of interactions from non-disabled students in the mainstream setting. These findings suggest that we need to be cautious about our expectations that opportunities for interaction will necessarily be greater or more productive in the regular class compared to the segregated setting. They do not mean, however, that link schools cannot be successful in promoting socialisation. What they do indicate is that the nature of social interactions, and the context in which they occur, need to be examined more closely, and ways found of encouraging greater participation by students with disabilities on an equal basis.

THE FUTURE OF LINK SCHEMES

In an ideal world of inclusive education, link school schemes would fade away along with the special schools that form half of the link. This is unlikely to happen in the immediate future, and link schools will have a continuing role to play for some time both as a form of transition to fuller integration and in broadening opportunities for social and academic participation in the mainstream for students with disabilities.

Link school schemes have provided support for students in both full- and part-time integration. Henderson (1988) referred to partial integration as a 'token solution' in a situation in which parents are faced with a choice between special and regular schools, with no continuum of provision in between. Students most likely to be placed in partial integration are, according to Henderson, those who are least likely to be able to adapt to the change between very different school environments – on the one hand involving small classes with a high teacher–student ratio, and on the other relatively large classes and a different set of teachers and students. This is a rather negative view of the benefits that are evident from many examples of link schemes and partial integration. However, it does draw our attention to the problems of uncertainty that students may face in dual attendance.

Further, we need to ensure that link schools, and in particular partial integration, are successfully fulfilling their aims for the students concerned. In Victoria, students who are partially integrated are allocated funds for an integration aide on the days they spend in the regular school. There has been no attempt to evaluate this arrangement in relation to the social objectives of the programme, or indeed to define those objectives. A recent study has shown that not all parents whose children are placed in situations of partial integration are satisfied with the arrangement (Jenkinson, 1995). Not only do students have difficulty in adapting from one situation to the other; they also have problems in identifying the school to which they belong.

In theory, the requirement for special schools to work within a national curriculum framework should enable links between mainstream and special schools to be strengthened and extended to include a greater range of activities in which students can participate together (Mittler, n.d.). Requirements for special schools both in Australia and the United Kingdom to work more closely to mainstream curricula suggest that the exchange of expertise between special and regular schools should no longer be one way, with regular schools drawing on special schools to provide advice and support for integration. In the future, special schools may also have greater need for the expertise of mainstream teachers. Links with mainstream schools offer special school staff the opportunity to work with mainstream subject teachers to develop appropriate programmes in special schools which would be adapted to meet the needs of students with disabilities while also conforming to core curriculum requirements. The existence of link school schemes and partial integration seems assured for the present, but their nature and function are likely to change as changes occur in the role of special schools and as mainstream schools clarify the place of individual differences in a climate that increasingly emphasises the concept of excellence.

Chapter 8

The special class
A changing role?

BACKGROUND

The place of the special class or unit in special education provision is a curious one. On the one hand special classes are criticised, along with special schools, for perpetuating segregated education of students with disabilities. On the other, they are seen as a form of integration, providing more opportunity for interaction with mainstream peers than a segregated special school on a separate site. Even so, the establishment of units or classes for students with disabilities in regular schools has been criticised as paying lip service to integration by allowing the enrolment of students with disabilities in mainstream schools while ensuring minimum disruption to regular classes. Whichever view is taken of the special class depends on structural and organisational arrangements within a school, and the extent to which the mainstream school is prepared to adapt to meet the diverse educational, physical and social needs of students with disabilities.

Traditionally, the special class has been viewed as an alternative provision to special schools, and where special classes have been the predominant provision, especially for students with less severe disabilities, fewer segregated schools have been developed. Special classes, like special schools, were initially set up to cater for students with serious learning problems, but without withdrawing students from the regular school.

In the absence of any evidence favouring either special schools or special classes, special classes became the preferred model for education of students with disabilities in the United States, developing rapidly in the post-war period (Polloway and Smith, 1988). Despite widespread criticism culminating with Dunn's (1968) paper, special classes have remained a significant force in special education.

In 1986 more than half of all students with an intellectual disability were being educated in a special class, with another 29 per cent receiving resource room support and fewer than 5 per cent placed in the regular class (Giangreco and Meyer, 1988). Including students with speech impairments, the resource room and the special class together accounted for more than seventy per cent of enrolments of all students with disabilities in the United States. By 1989–90, this proportion had decreased, but around sixty per cent of students with disabilities continued to be supported in special classes and resource rooms (Hallenbeck and Kauffman, 1994). Polloway and Smith (1988) noted an increasing reluctance of professionals to recommend special class placement, but as the enrolment of students with mild disabilities in special classes declined, there was a corresponding influx of students with moderate intellectual disabilities.

Although a direct causal link between the predominant model for special education provision and moves towards integration cannot be taken for granted, full-time integration into regular classes has proceeded more slowly in education systems that have widespread special class provision. De Lemos (1994) estimated that 24 per cent of students with disabilities in Australia are enrolled in special classes or units attached to mainstream primary or secondary schools. However, there is considerable variation between states, exemplified in the contrast between the two states with the largest populations. New South Wales has a long history of category-based special class provision for students with mild intellectual disability and sensory disabilities. Approximately 46 per cent of students with disabilities were enrolled in special classes in New South Wales in 1993. In Victoria, this form of provision is not common and only about two per cent of students with disabilities were enrolled in special classes or units, primarily in units for students with hearing impairment. As de Lemos pointed out, these differences are important because they may help to explain the different emphases on regular class integration in the two states. In Victoria, where special class enrolment is generally not an option, parents may be reluctant to enrol their child in a special school, and opt instead for an integrated placement with support. This choice is reflected in the 54 per cent of students with disabilities who are enrolled in regular classes in Victoria, compared to 33 per cent in New South Wales, where special class placement provides an option for education in the regular school. A similar, although less marked, trend can be seen in the enrolment statistics for Western Australia, where 34 per cent of students with disabilities are enrolled in special classes, and only 22 per cent in the regular class.

In New South Wales, special classes in regular schools, known as support classes, are maintained as part of a continuum of provision in special education. This policy is based on a belief that the educational and other interests of some students will best be met in a segregated setting. However, the policy is also directed at moving special education from predominantly segregated settings towards provision of services in the student's regular neighbourhood school. The inclusion of support classes in larger primary and secondary schools is seen as one way of achieving this goal by giving students with disabilities appropriate educational support while also allowing participation in the daily activities of their local community peer group. Special classes are maintained for students with mild, moderate or severe intellectual disability, physical impairment, hearing impairment and behaviour disorder or emotional disturbance. In some cases, placement is likely to be on a long-term basis, although placements are regularly reviewed and may be appealed against by parents. In addition, support classes are maintained for short-term placements for students with reading difficulties, severe language disorders, and behavioural problems. To be included in the intensive programme offered by a reading support class, reading performance must lag significantly behind the student's age and ability level, and some attempt must first have been made to deal with the problem in the regular class. The referring school must undertake to support and maintain the programme after the student returns to the regular class. Similarly, language support classes offer an intensive full-day programme with the aim of reintegrating students as soon as possible.

In England and Wales, special classes or units comprising a number of special classes have been widely used to provide for students with sensory impairments, although they are less common than special school provision for students with disabilities overall. In 1992 10 per cent of students in England who had statements relating to special educational needs were placed in special classes in regular schools (Norwich, 1994b), although the proportions varied greatly between local education authorities. The establishment of separate units for students with disabilities on the same site as mainstream schools accelerated after the Warnock (1978) report, primarily to allow students with disabilities supported access to the mainstream and greater opportunities for integration into regular class activities (Wade and Moore, 1992). Hodgson et al. (1984) found this form of provision to be most common where students had moderate learning or communication difficulties or presented behavioural problems.

ADVANTAGES OF SPECIAL CLASSES

Many of the advantages of special classes or units are similar to those described for special schools. Special classes are usually small, ungraded, with high teacher–student ratios, and staffed by teachers with appropriate qualifications and expertise. Classes can be highly structured and teaching geared to individual needs. Concentration of specialist teaching, programmes, equipment and resources, greater one-to-one attention and individualisation of programmes, access to technology, a less threatening environment, suitable physical arrangements and the opportunity to be with peers who have similar needs are usually perceived as benefits of special class placement. Students can progress at their own rate with a teacher who is sensitive to their learning needs, and in a situation where they are protected from frequent experiences of failure. In situations in which extensive specialist services, such as regular therapy programmes, are required, or in which instruction involves specialised methods of communication or cumbersome equipment, the special class or unit may represent the most efficient compromise between full integration into the regular school and the most economical method of providing specialist support. The best units or classes offer a satisfactory learning environment, good physical facilities and a supportive yet stimulating social situation for students with disabilities, with conditions that are at least as good as those offered to students with similar disabilities in special schools (Cope and Anderson, 1977).

But special classes located in regular schools also offer far greater opportunities than special schools for students to participate in mainstream activities. Daily contacts with non-disabled peers may lead, if not to close friendships, at least to a better understanding of disability. Students without disabilities can offer models for behaviour appropriate for their age group, and for students with language and hearing disorders the opportunity to observe normal conversations may be invaluable. As well, the mainstream school offers enriched opportunities in academic curriculum and in extra-curricular activities for students with disabilities. The special class may also provide a wider range of remedial techniques and resources for mainstream students who need assistance beyond that usually available in the regular class. Finally, the special class provides a support base for integration of students with disabilities into the regular class, with special and regular class teachers working together to develop a programme that can be implemented in the regular classroom.

Because of the high level of technology or special equipment required to support many students with physical or sensory disabilities, special classes have often been set up to cater for specific categories of disability.

Wattlefield (not its real name) is a secondary college of about four hundred students which has set up a unit catering for thirty students who have a hearing impairment. The rationale for this unit is that students with hearing impairment have needs in the area of language and communication that are unique, and for which intensive support is necessary if they are to have the same opportunities to achieve as their mainstream peers. The unit is also based on a recognition that students with hearing impairment should be educated as far as possible in their local community, and that curriculum and other educational opportunities should enable them to participate effectively in community life. The unit provides an adapted or supplemented curriculum rather than one that is alternative to the mainstream, and its primary function is to encourage and support integration of students in the regular classroom. Students admitted to the unit must have a severe hearing loss, but must be capable of aural access to the curriculum with the aid of corrective devices and assistance, and of benefiting from placement with normal hearing peers.

The Wattlefield unit has a high teacher–student ratio, with one trained teacher of the deaf for every four students. Its relatively high enrolment means that there are between three and five students with hearing impairment at any year level, so that within the regular class students have peers who are both hearing impaired and normal hearing. Although intensive support is provided by specialist teachers, the regular class teacher is responsible for each student's programme. Working with class teachers, specialist teachers may adapt teaching materials or pre-teach concepts to prepare students with hearing impairment for a class activity. Most teachers have learned to adapt their teaching, giving greater attention to ways of presenting material, for example with increased use of visual aids and rephrasing of language when necessary. There are some withdrawal activities, but generally these are limited to about an hour each day. In addition to reinforcing regular class curriculum, withdrawal includes language sessions and opportunities for students to become acquainted with the deaf community.

The unit has been highly successful and is well accepted within the school. Student interaction is positive and many normal hearing students have learned to use sign language and other communication methods to enhance friendships. The emphasis is not just on students with hearing impairment adapting to the school, but on the school also adapting to meet their needs. Nevertheless, the existence of the unit is vital, ensuring a level of support that would not be present if only one or two students with hearing impairment were integrated into the school. Parents of students in the unit participate in school activities, but have also established their own support group which provides a basis for social interactions with other families and staff of the unit.

Careful and sympathetic planning has ensured that the unit at Wattlefield has not become another form of segregated education. Teachers' roles within the school are clarified, with unit staff participating in the activities of the regular school and frequent contacts between regular and special teachers. The unit is well equipped with appropriate accommodation and adequate material resources.

SOME PROBLEMS IN SPECIAL UNITS

Not all special units have operated as successfully as Wattlefield, particularly in coming to terms with changing views of disability and changing provisions in education. Studies of special units and classes have identified several difficulties in their establishment and organisation. These difficulties include problems arising from the choice of host school for the unit, problems relating to physical location, accommodation and size, selection of students for enrolment in the unit and student composition, organisational problems and staff conflicts.

The mainstream host school

It is vital to the effectiveness of a special class or unit not only that its location is accepted by the mainstream host school, but that it is seen as contributing positively to the life of the school. Host schools are sometimes chosen for the wrong reasons, and this can have negative effects both on the special class and on the mainstream school. Location in a mainstream school on the basis of physical suitability in terms of facilities and accommodation does not ensure acceptance. For example, in one case a host school was chosen because plans for extension of school buildings allowed inclusion of special provisions at the initial building stage. Even this did not guarantee that accommodation would be suitable. In another case, a host school was chosen because it had a declining enrolment, and unused space was available for a special unit. The special class students had no geographical links to the area served by the school, and their presence in the school could be questioned if a new growth in enrolments placed pressure on classroom space.

Another important factor that needs to be considered in relation to the host school is the age level of the students to be served by the unit. For example, the location of classes for adolescent students with severe disabilities in primary level schools carries an implication that these students function at the same level as much younger students without disabilities (Giangreco and Meyer, 1988). This type of location is inappropriate for a number of reasons. Firstly, it does not enable integrated activities to take place with the students' typical age peers. Secondly, it implies that students must reach a certain developmental level in order to benefit from integration. Thirdly, it perpetuates a misguided belief that activities enjoyed by younger children are developmentally appropriate for much older students with disabilities.

Accommodation

The location of a special class or unit within a mainstream school is just as important as the choice of the host school. Even within the mainstream school, there exists a wide range of possibilities for location, all of which have implications for the successful participation of students with disabilities in the life of the school. Some special classes are located on the periphery rather than in the centre of a school campus. Integration, even on a solely physical basis, is hindered by location of special facilities in a separate building from the main school, especially if the unit is some distance from the main school building.

Thomason (1987) advocated a 'side-by-side' model for the location of special classes. According to this model, special classes should be dispersed throughout a school district so that students can attend schools near their homes and have regular contact with their non-disabled peers. Within schools, the model should be extended so that classes are dispersed within the main building, rather than on a separate part of the campus. In an application of this model described by Thomason (1987), special classes for students with severe disabilities were clustered in selected schools, and within each school were dispersed throughout the school building to encourage interaction between students. The clustering of special classes in selected schools overcame the difficulty of co-ordinating the large number and variety of services required by students with severe disabilities. Professional staff could be employed full-time in a school, ensuring that they could have regular meetings and work together as a team to provide an effective programme for each student. The difficulty of co-ordinating an itinerant service, and the loss of time involved in travel between schools were avoided. Clustering of classes also facilitated mutual support for parents and students involved in the programme.

The practical advantages of this approach need to be weighed against the impact it has on the regular school. Schools selected for this programme will inevitably have a disproportionate number of students with disabilities enrolled, and are likely to be identified as such. For example, one school in Thomason's (1987) programme enrolled forty students with severe disabilities in seven classes – many times the proportion that is likely to be found in any community. A limit needs to be imposed on the number of classes and students that can be accepted in any one school if there are to be any advantages from integration.

The dispersal of special classes throughout a mainstream school also needs to be considered in relation to special accommodation require-ments. Extensive physical modifications to buildings may be needed to cater for students with disabilities who are dispersed throughout a school. Other factors to be considered include acoustic and noise factors for students with hearing impairment, lighting and mobility for students with visual impairment, access for wheelchairs, and proximity to rooms and equipment used for therapy.

The students

Although special classes have tended to operate on a category basis, the assumptions underlying category-based provision can be no more justified in special classes than in other types of special provision. The problems associated with a category base may be exacerbated by the relatively small community that exists within a special class. In particular, special classes are likely to have a wide age range of students who are under a single teacher. The number of students at any one age level may not be sufficient to schedule separate age-appropriate activities. A further problem in units for students with sensory or physical impairments may be a wide range of individual differences in intellectual capacity, necessitating almost constant one-to-one attention. In addition, the presence of secondary disabilities may mean that some students are inappropriately placed in a class that focuses on one category of disability. These problems can be diminished, however, if students spend most of their time in an age-appropriate regular class with the unit providing support, as in the Wattlefield arrangement described earlier.

Special classes or units have proved especially useful as a short-term solution for students who have behavioural problems that cannot easily be managed in the regular classroom (Gamble and Palmer, 1989). 'Adjustment' units provide an opportunity for the student to learn in a small group situation, both co-operatively and competitively, allowing time for behaviour to stabilise before the student returns to the mainstream. Once a problem has been assessed, simple behaviour modification programmes designed to motivate the individual student towards more acceptable behaviour can be introduced, and close liaison with parents will help to ensure that they are maintained.

The unit described by Gamble and Palmer (1989) also provided a base from which to integrate the student back into the mainstream, once the student achieved control over his or her behaviour. Several criteria were used for deciding whether a student was ready for reintegration. The student should have shown a considerable period of settling behaviour in the school, accept the ordinary behavioural norms of the classroom, respond favourably to approaches from staff and other students and to normal controls on behaviour, and have enough confidence to cope with minor setbacks. In addition, the student should be able to fit into the relevant curricular area without too much difficulty. If necessary, the student could be supported by a teacher aide while in the regular class. The aim was to integrate the students for about seventy to eighty per cent of the time, with the remaining time spent in the unit for further counselling. Once students were well integrated, they could return to their original school or to a new school. Those unable to integrate would be placed on a longer-term basis in a special school.

Although a student might have shown stable behaviour in the unit and appear ready for integration, problems were identified that could arise in the regular class. For example, staff could perceive the student as threatening, or feel inadequate and be unwilling to report problems. Staff also needed to be sensitive to the problems of the student without appearing to excuse them. The less structured environment of the regular class sometimes made it more difficult for the student to observe behavioural norms and some students were unwilling to co-operate with unfamiliar staff. Other problems also occurred in adjusting to mainstream curriculum.

It would be easy to overestimate the needs of many students with disabilities for the security provided by the special class or unit. Students do not necessarily want special concessions in relation to school rules and disciplinary action if it makes them appear different from other students in the school (Wade and Moore, 1992). In addition, they want to be able to enjoy the same privileges of freedom to move independently around the school, and to travel to and from school in the same way as other students. Students may also object to mainstream students being brought into the unit to provide help with academic work or mobility, if this makes the special unit students seem more dependent or somehow different in status.

Staff and organisational aspects

The special class or unit offers a variety of forms of provision within the mainstream school. In its most segregated form, students may receive virtually all of their education in the unit, without any structured opportunities for socialisation with mainstream peers. Although students may share school grounds and facilities, and even participate in some joint activities such as school assemblies, there is no assurance that productive contacts will take place.

Separate administrative structures for special and regular educa-tion, with the aims of integration confined to joint use of physical resources within the school, have been detrimental to close co-operation. Some schools have restricted joint participation between special and regular class students to non-routine activities, for example end-of-term celebrations. Under these conditions staff in one setting learn little about the role of staff in the other setting. In some schools, special class teachers have been excluded from main-stream activities. Differences in status or workload between regular and special class teachers can create resentment. On the one hand, the special class may be perceived as inferior to the rest of the school, or a place to send students who are disruptive in the regular class. On the other, it may be perceived as the focus of too much attention, placing a drain on already limited resources within the school. Lack of clear definition of roles and responsibilities, especially when students are spending part of their time in a special class and part in the regular class, is a further source of friction. Special teachers may be unfamiliar with the regular class curriculum, or may be inexperienced in teaching students without disabilities, and so be poorly equipped to prepare a student with a disability for placement in the regular class.

The most successful special classes and units have involved close co-operation between special and regular class staff. The best arrange-ments involve strong links between mainstream and unit staff on a day-to-day basis. Co-operation is more easily achieved where aims and organisational structures allow staff to work closely together so that they can develop mutual respect for the contribution each has to make within the school. Regular class teachers can advise special class teachers on general curriculum matters, and special education staff can provide expertise to regular class teachers both in integrating students with disabilities and in helping to design programmes for any student who might be experiencing difficulties.

The problems experienced in establishing close working relation-ships between special and regular class teachers highlight the need for careful preparation of a host school. Bell and Colbeck (1989) described a programme in which preparation of the school community took place over a period of two years following construction and opening of the school before students with disabilities were enrolled. The host school was built with the intention of including a special needs unit for students with behavioural problems, as well as units for students with a variety of other handicaps. The purpose of the lengthy period of preparation was to enable regular school staff and staff of special schools who would become part of the proposed units to each become familiar with the other's educational philosophy, organisation and methods of teaching. This goal was achieved through an intensive in-service programme. Consensus on the aims and policies of the programme was targeted before admission of students to the unit. It was expected that students with behavioural problems would spend most of their time in the units, but would be integrated individually into regular classes according to their needs. An important principle to be followed in integration was that it should not interfere with the normal running of the classroom.

Despite the lengthy preparation, the introduction of the unit had a considerable impact on the school. A major impact was the increase in size and diversity of student and staff populations within the school. Communication was not always smooth, although no major problems were identified. For example, integration of students into some mainstream classes meant that timetabling by individual class teachers could no longer be flexible, because work had to be agreed in advance with the unit. The appropriateness of the teaching styles of mainstream teachers for students from the unit was initially questioned, although once regular class teachers gained experience with these students they ceased to regard the special education teachers as necessarily the sole experts.

The problems that occur with special units are not all insuperable and many have relatively simple practical or organisational remedies. Several positive features have also been reported, especially when there has been careful preparation of the host school, where students have been carefully assessed for their suitability for placement in the unit, where appropriate caution has been accompanied by a determination to succeed and where there has been a high level of co-operation between regular and unit staff. The Warnock report (1978) recommended that, for full integration to be successful, special classes or units should function as part of the regular school, and be answerable to the school principal rather than organised separately or attached to another establishment. In addition, the proportion of students in special classes or units should not be so high as to change substantially the nature of the school.

There is little evidence that special classes continue to exist without some form of contact with the host school, although in a climate which strongly favours integration it is doubtful if descriptions of purely locational arrangements would be published. Warnock (1978) identified three broad types of special class provision, all of which included some contacts between special class and regular class students. In the first type, students considered unable to benefit from formal education in the regular class would be enrolled full-time in a special class or unit, and social contacts with regular class students implemented with careful planning. Contacts could include students from regular classes coming into the special class for specific activities if mobility or other problems made it difficult for special class students to move away from their home base.

In the second type, students would receive most of their formal education in the special class, which would provide a base for partial integration into the regular class so that the student could benefit not only from the social contacts but from the wider range of extra-curricular activities offered. In some cases students might also attend the regular class for selected academic subjects, but the special class would continue to provide some teaching.

Both of these arrangements imply that the student's educational needs could not readily be met within the regular class, and both recognise that even limited periods of contact with mainstream students are likely to be beneficial. However, such arrangements have been criticised for their continuing restrictiveness, and indeed they appear to be motivated more by administrative convenience than by a willingness to maximise opportunities for students with disabilities to participate in the daily life of a mainstream school.

The third type of special class arrangement more closely resembles the resource room model, with students enrolled in the regular class being withdrawn to the special class for specific educational activities. These students would include those who needed a modified or supplemented curriculum, specialist teaching techniques, access to special equipment or occasional participation in smaller instructional groups.

RESOURCE ROOM PROVISION

The resource room model has been most popular in the United States, where in 1986 61 per cent of students with learning disabilities were receiving resource room support (Giangreco and Meyer, 1988). The combination of resource room and regular classroom is also the most common model for special education provision in Canada (Winzer, 1994), although differences in provision exist not just between provinces but also between school districts and individual schools. It is not possible to estimate the extent to which resource rooms are used in countries in which learning disability (in a specific area of academic performance rather than a pervasive learning difficulty) is not included in special education for funding or statistical purposes.

Warnock (1978) favoured the establishment of resource rooms or units in all large schools, particularly secondary schools, to provide additional help for students with learning difficulties integrated into the mainstream. The resource room would perform a number of functions, for example as a clinic providing intensive support through assessment, providing one-to-one specialist teaching or carrying out behavioural observation. Resource rooms should be well provided with material resources such as technical equipment and materials for individualised programmes, and should be adequately staffed and located in an easily accessible part of the school:

> We see a resource centre as a room, or suite of rooms in a large school, where special materials and equipment are kept and to which groups of children may be withdrawn for special help. In some instances, it may also be the class base for children from which they join ordinary classes for a considerable part of the normal school day. We also see it as a base in which visiting specialist teachers may work with children with special needs and where the school's special education teachers can prepare their work when they teach children elsewhere.
>
> (Warnock, 1978: 111)

The resource unit model has suffered from a lack of agreement on exactly what function it serves in the overall context of special education. Resource units often begin on an informal basis in an attempt to provide for students experiencing difficulties in basic academic skills. These provisions have a tendency to grow without adequate planning, and as they grow problems surface which need to be resolved if the unit is to fulfil its aims. Bryanston College (not its real name) provides an example of a resource unit which started in this way, developed largely on an ad hoc basis to meet individual needs as they arose. The unit is now undergoing a review to more clearly define its future role and resource needs.

> Bryanston College is a co-educational secondary school of about eleven hundred students, situated in a relatively new housing area close to an industrial estate. When the school opened some ten years ago, it made no formal provision for assisting students with special needs, although occasionally curriculum modifications were introduced for individual students who were failing in the normal curriculum. It soon became obvious that more needed to be done, especially for students entering the school with poor literacy and numeracy skills.

The idea of a resource unit began with one of the English teachers allocated regular time each week to assist students in Years 7 and 8 who were having difficulties on a withdrawal basis. Over the ten years since it began, the amount of time devoted to specialist teaching has grown sixfold, with three teachers each working half-time in the resource unit. Two of these, both qualified in special education, continue to support students in English and mathematics in Years 7 and 8, also providing some assistance to students in Years 9 and 10. Support is provided both on a withdrawal basis and through team teaching in the regular class. The third teacher conducts remedial English classes for senior students. Specialised individual programmes, for example to deal with behavioural problems, are also developed when necessary.

The Bryanston College unit employs a pastoral care approach to special education, with an emphasis on individual support and building self-esteem. Its approach has evolved through the long experience of the two special education teachers: the unit has no stated policy or formalised objectives. Herein lies its difficulty – although unit staff are perceived as having expertise and commitment to their work, there is much uncertainty and misunderstanding about the aims and functions of the unit, what it can be expected to achieve and the effectiveness of its programme. Part of the problem seems to be a lack of clarity about who is ultimately responsible for the work of the unit, and part a lack of communication between unit staff and class teachers, so that individual programmes conducted in the unit are not co-ordinated with what is happening in the regular classroom. Subject teachers believe that too much attention is given to remedial English, and that instead students' problems should be approached through the total curriculum. Team teaching and withdrawal programmes are seen as only moderately effective in supporting teaching within the regular class.

The school recognises these problems and written policy and guidelines currently being formulated promise the development of a much more effective unit.

Despite the major role that resource units have played in special education, and their potential role in supporting integration, the resource room model has been rejected by the inclusive schools movement which envisages all services being provided in the regular classroom. In the United States, students with learning disabilities who are enrolled in resource rooms appear to be the most likely candidates for full integration. Hallahan and Kauffman (1995) confirmed this trend, noting that the proportion of students with disabilities who were being served in resource rooms decreased between 1987–88 and 1990–91. However, the number being served in special classes actually showed a small increase. The increase in special class enrolments could be explained by the increasing movement of students with severe disabilities from segregated schools to self-contained classes in regular schools. Notwithstanding these trends, Hallahan and Kauffman (1995) viewed the reduction in resource room placement and the corresponding growth in special class enrolments with some concern, given that the resource room model represents a less segregated form of education than the self-contained special class. They suggested that many students currently enrolled in special classes might be adequately accommodated in a regular class with appropriate resource room support.

Hallahan and Kauffman (1995) may be unduly pessimistic in predicting the possible demise of the resource room while special classes continue to flourish. Although the major use of resource units has been to provide support for mainstream students with learning disabilities, some schools have found it useful to set up resource units within the school, rather than rely on an external source, to support students with more severe disabilities integrated into regular classes. At a school I visited in Richmond, on the outskirts of Vancouver, four or five students with varying educational needs – some, but not all, associated with an identified disability – had been withdrawn from their classes for a resource room session with the special education teacher. Here they received the intensive instruction that a class teacher, especially one in a class that contained a large proportion of non-English-speaking students as well as a wide range of other individual needs, could not hope to provide. Although withdrawal programmes have often been blamed for negative attitudes towards disability, they would appear to focus less attention on a disability than either intensive individual instruction within the regular class or the constant presence of a teacher aide supporting an individual student. In this school, the presence of individual differences and individual needs was so taken for granted that withdrawal for some sessions during the day invited little comment from other students.

SPECIAL CLASSES – A MAINSTREAM RESOURCE?

Like special schools, the continuance of special classes seems assured at least for the near future. But like special schools the role of the special class is also changing, becoming less distinct from resource room provision. Special classes are becoming more flexible in their approach, often taking on the functions of a resource unit in addition to their normal teaching role. Indeed, this appears to be occurring successfully in many cases. Support for students in the mainstream, whether as a base for integration of students with identified disabilities, or as a resource to assist regular class teachers in catering for all students with additional educational needs, will be an increasingly important function of the special class.

Chapter 9

Inclusive schooling
The regular class

WHAT IS INCLUSIVE SCHOOLING?

It is something of a paradox that the advocates of inclusive schooling would question the place of a chapter on this topic in a book on special education, for inclusive schooling sees no role for special education either as a separate system of education or as a system for supporting the education of students with disabilities in any setting. Inclusive schooling, as has already been suggested, implies that all children, no matter how severe their disability or how intensive their needs, can be accommodated in the regular class in their neighbourhood school – the school they would attend if they did not have a disability. Inclusive schooling is not synonymous with integration or mainstreaming (Mittler, 1995), nor is it concerned only with the education of students with disabilities. The philosophy underlying inclusive education is that schools have a responsibility to meet the needs of all children, and that teachers should be able to differentiate and adapt curriculum and instructional strategies to suit the differing needs and abilities of each child in the classroom. Also referred to as a 'whole school approach', inclusive schooling requires the utilisation of full school resources to provide an appropriate education for each student.

Equally paradoxically, much of the thrust of inclusive schooling, at least in the United States, has come from a group concerned with students with severe intellectual disability – students who might be thought least likely to benefit from learning experiences in the regular class. The primary aim of inclusive schooling is to eliminate altogether any continuum of service, including special education and special educators as a system of provision. This is not to suggest that the expert skills and knowledge of special teachers no longer have a role in education. Implementation of inclusive schooling requires the redeployment of special education staff and resources to mainstream schools where they would be employed not only for the benefit of students with disabilities, but in a supportive and advisory role across the whole curriculum. Supports and services currently used by students with disabilities would be relocated into the regular classroom to provide support to all students in need.

A second aim of the inclusive schools movement is to enhance the social skills and community participation of people with severe disabilities, and in so doing to change the attitudes of both teachers and students towards disability. In this aim, it differs from the regular education initiative, which had as its prime goal the improvement of academic skills among people with mild to moderate disabilities (Fuchs and Fuchs, 1994), and advocated the continuing placement of students with severe disabilities in segregated classes or units.

Inclusive schooling thus brings together several fundamental aspects of education. Firstly, it is rights-focused. Inclusive schooling can be considered the ultimate educational outcome of the principle of normalisation. It begins with the premise that every individual has the right to participate in the mainstream of society and enjoy the same privileges, benefits and opportunities as his or her age peers. Participation in mainstream schooling is a recognition of the fact that students with disabilities have more in common with their peers than they have differences. Enrolment of a student with a disability in an age-appropriate regular class in the school which the student would attend if he or she did not have a disability is a logical outcome of normalisation. It represents an extension to education of other generic services and entitlements in the community. Special classes or cluster schools in which resources are concentrated for economic or other practical reasons and resource rooms to which students can be withdrawn for specific purposes are all rejected by the most extreme advocates of inclusive schooling. Inclusive schools should have natural or normal proportions, rather than a cluster, of students with disabilities, if they are to avoid being seen as a centre for any one group of students, or to avoid the creation of subgroups of students within any one classroom (Stainback and Stainback, 1989).

Secondly, inclusive schooling claims to be child-focused. It is founded on the premise that all children, regardless of disability, are capable of learning and should be given the same opportunities to achieve, through learning, to the best of their ability. Judgments of individual achievement should not be limited to expectations based on what is 'normal' for a given age cohort, but should be considered in the context of the child's individual capacity. All children have different styles and rates of learning, and teaching must be adaptable to suit these differences. Thus all children, including those who are academically gifted as well as those who have learning difficulties, should be catered for in the regular class. If for any reason the standard curriculum is not appropriate for a student, then that curriculum should be adapted for the student rather than attempting to fit the student to the curriculum.

Further, inclusive schooling claims to recognise the needs of all children to gain feelings of self-worth and self-respect through their own efforts and achievements, no matter how small those achievements might seem. Children should not be set up to fail by being required to follow a set programme that is not related to their individual needs and capabilities. Schools should not aim to teach a set of predetermined curriculum objectives, but to ensure that each individual student develops to their fullest potential. In a climate in which diversity is valued, the goal is interdependence rather than independence, with support networks for students with disabilities being fostered among staff and students in their natural setting – the regular classroom (Stainback and Stainback, 1990).

The concept of inclusive schooling thus requires a breakaway from traditional concepts of teaching and learning to embrace programmes that enable children with differing needs and abilities to work together. This concept implies two important requirements (Lipsky and Gartner, 1989): firstly, the acceptance by class teachers of responsibility for a diverse range of students; and secondly, a classroom perspective that sees this diversity, including the presence of students with disabilities, as providing positive opportunities for learning through the development of new organisational and instructional approaches.

Inclusive schooling also requires a breakaway from traditional concepts of disability and special education, in which programmes have been based on categories of disability rather than on providing individual students with the means of gaining access to mainstream curriculum. Inclusive schooling avoids problems associated with misplacement of students in special category-based schools or classes which serve the primary disability without regard for either the student's capacity for learning or additional needs that might be quite separate from the disability. Individual needs, rather than patterns of service provision, become the focus of educational services.

An assumption underlying inclusive schooling is that resources and services hitherto made available in segregated settings can be applied with equal, if not greater, effectiveness in the regular classroom. If inclusive schooling proceeds without acknowledging this as fact, or proceeds on the assumption that it is sufficient to place a student with a disability in a mainstream class without additional resources, then it will undoubtedly fail. Inclusion of students with disabilities into regular classes does not mean that these students no longer have special educational needs. What is does mean is a need to identify those needs and investigate ways of providing for them in the regular class so that students may fulfil the main purpose of schooling – learning.

The advocates of inclusive schooling have endeavoured to show that their proposals will not just benefit students with disabilities by including them in the mainstream, but will create schools that are more effective for all students because of the greater emphasis placed on diversity. The role of the class teacher will be to provide all students with educational experiences that are both challenging and appropriate for each child's capabilities and needs (Stainback and Stainback, 1989). If the range of individual needs within a class is such that additional support and assistance are required to meet those needs, then all students, including students with learning or physical and sensory disabilities, students considered to be 'at risk' and students who are academically gifted, are entitled to additional support.

SUPPORT IN THE REGULAR CLASSROOM

Inclusive schooling also emphasises the provision of support in its 'natural setting' – within the regular classroom. Special needs would be supported in the regular class through a partnership between regular and special education. Special educators would work with regular class teachers to develop programmes and instructional strategies for individual students on a regular basis, for example through collaborative teaching within the classroom setting. The special teacher would act as a resource within the mainstream school, providing advice and programmes for students with special needs, or occasional individual teaching for students needing extra tuition to enable them to participate in the normal curriculum with other students.

The concept of a partnership between the regular class teacher and the special educator would seem to place at least part of the responsibility for a student with a disability on the special educator. There are, of course, a number of ways of maintaining the class teacher's primary responsibility for each student while also providing necessary specialist advice and resources within the classroom setting. Stainback and Stainback (1989) suggested the formation of teacher assistance teams, comprising the class teacher as the leader supported by others involved in the student's education such as parents, school administrators, guidance and support staff and therapists. The prime function of such teams would be to support the teacher with both advice and suggestions on any matter in which the student requires assistance. However, these teams should not be seen as part of a referral system, or as being involved in evaluation or placement of students. The Programme Support Groups which operate in Victoria to support individual students with disabilities in the regular classroom are similar to the teacher assistance teams advocated by Stainback and Stainback (1989). These groups are usually led by the school principal or a nominee of the principal, and would include the integration teacher or special needs co-ordinator, the student's regular class teacher, support staff, and, if appropriate, the student. Such groups are responsible for preparing an individual programme for a student and identifying the supports needed to implement the programme in the regular class. In some cases, support groups have included the class peers of the student with a disability.

In a class of thirty or so students, how might teaching be differentiated to meet the wide range of individual needs proposed in inclusive schooling? Among instructional strategies proposed by Stainback and Stainback (1989) are co-operative learning activities, individualised programming, and adaptive learning environments. According to Putnam (1993), co-operative learning, in which students work together to achieve common goals, is the key to successful inclusion. Co-operative learning in small groups requires positive interdependence: activities are co-ordinated so that students share their resources and provide mutual assistance. Each student is responsible for his or her contribution to the group. Ideally, groups are composed of students with different cognitive and social competencies, so that each student contributes according to his or her ability, to achieving the common goal or learning target. All students must be given the opportunity to contribute to the group: for some students with disabilities this may mean adapting some tasks, but all contributions are valued and acknowledged, so that learning becomes a positive experience for all students. Learning necessarily involves face-to-face interactions, so that social skills as well as academic skills are developed. Co-operative learning has been demonstrated to promote greater interpersonal attraction between students with disabilities and their non-disabled peers, more positive interactions, greater self-esteem and greater cohesiveness of students within classes, compared to competitive, individualistic learning situations (Johnson and Johnson, 1986). Social benefits extend beyond the classroom and are long-term (Putnam, 1993), although there is no evidence of academic gains for students with disabilities as a result of co-operative learning.

Individualised programming entails setting specific objectives based on an individual student's needs, and targeting the student's learning towards the achievement of those objectives rather than towards the achievement of a common class learning goal. Inclusive schooling advocates have not made clear how individualised pro-grammes can be made compatible with co-operative group learning.

Opportunities for inclusive schooling have been greatly enhanced by the increased use of technology in the classroom. Technology has helped to provide access to curriculum by giving many students a means of communication that compensates for the loss of a sensory or physical function, for example speech synthesisers for students with visual impairments, or speech recognition devices for students with hearing impairments, and a range of other adaptive devices for students with motor impairments that have affected speech and limited the use of a pencil or keyboard. But technology has also allowed greater individualisation of educational programmes. Curriculum material, integrated with other teaching materials used in the classroom, can be presented at a pace suited to the student's rate of progress. Male (1994) identified a number of trends in the use 'of computer technology which would favour students with special needs, for example greater use of small group instruction and co-operative goal structures, more attention by teachers to weaker students, more active involvement in a task and greater differentiation of learning. Against these advantages, Male cautioned that use of technology could diminish interaction between students and between students and class teacher, and could impose control over the student's learning rather than the student controlling his or her own progress. A further danger is that use of technology can become an end in itself if its purpose – to enhance learning – is forgotten.

The processes suggested for implementation of inclusive schooling are, on the surface, attractive. They also represent an ideal that may not be as easy to achieve as their advocates suggest. Inclusive schooling has not proceeded without controversy – indeed, the radical changes proposed by the concept make its universal acceptance unlikely without radical reforms to the whole of education itself. This has been well recognised by its proponents who see the enrolment of students with a wide range of disabilities in regular classes as the catalyst for change by forcing schools to deal with the problems raised by special educational needs (Fuchs and Fuchs, 1994).

IMPLEMENTATION OF INCLUSIVE SCHOOLING

Given the radical changes implied for both special and regular education systems, how might inclusive schooling be implemented? Policy changes are of little consequence unless they are supported by action. In Victoria, a policy of inclusion was recommended by Collins (1984), but the absence of supportive legislation and failure to come to grips with opposition to integration from all sides resulted in a subsequent reversal of the decision to phase out segregated educational provision for students with disabilities. Integration proceeded on an individual basis, but problems associated with redeployment of special education staff, resistance to integration by regular schools where resources were perceived to be inadequate, inequitable distribution of funds to support students in inclusive settings and substantial numbers of parents continuing to choose enrolments in special schools worked against full-scale implementation of inclusive schooling.

Clearly such a radical change to special education requires bold decisions that are enacted, not overnight, but with a period of careful planning and preparation. A comprehensive review of practices in the Yellowhead School Division in Alberta, Canada, provides us with a detailed picture of how inclusive schooling was gradually introduced to this rural area over a five-year period (Alberta Education Response Centre, 1992). The review also shows that even careful planning and thorough consultation with all those involved do not necessarily ensure success.

The Yellowhead programme began with an initial phase of raising awareness, and proceeded through the gradual introduction of students with disabilities into mainstream settings, to adjustments and refinements of the programme as problems and concerns were identified and dealt with. Only in the fifth year of the programme was the division's special needs policy replaced by a new policy of inclusive education. The most significant feature of the programme was that it encouraged integration at a natural pace, monitoring problems as they occurred and deferring development of a final policy statement until more was known about the process of integration (Alberta Education Response Centre, 1992). Practice therefore preceded policy, and although with hindsight this created some problems, policy was able to benefit both from a knowledge of what could be achieved and from an understanding of the problems that were likely to occur.

The Yellowhead Division, serving over five thousand students in seventeen schools, was the first in Alberta to implement full integration. A firm belief in inclusive schooling led to a decision to dismantle special education services and to reassign responsibility for the education of special needs students to regular classroom teachers. The first year of the project entailed clarification of the detailed decisions involved in this process, and communication of those decisions to school principals, special and regular education teachers, and parent groups through meetings, discussion groups and staff in-service sessions. The major aims at this stage were to raise awareness of the integration plan among those concerned and to clarify and define the goals of the programme. This was not a simple process, since some of the proposed measures, for example the abolition of special classes and the contracting out of specialist support services, could be seen as cost-cutting exercises rather than as part of a process of movement towards the long-term goal of full inclusion.

In the second year of the programme, students with disabilities were gradually moved into regular classrooms. At first emphasis was on socialisation and development of friendships. Class teachers were supported with in-service training, teacher support groups and redeployment of special teachers following closure of special classes. Assistance was provided to develop teaching strategies, modify curriculum and develop new models for individual educational programmes, including alternative forms of assessment.

The third year of the programme was described as one of adjustment and refinement as inclusion gained wider acceptance among school administrators. It now became possible to deal with specific problems, such as development of models for classroom support. At the same time, a decrease in referrals for external assistance was noted as regular class teachers became more comfortable in teaching students with disabilities.

In the fourth year, integration audits were conducted in each of the schools in the division. The result was generally positive, with all schools found to be operating in accordance with the philosophy of inclusion; that is, based on a model of classroom support rather than use of a resource room. The change had entailed a redefinition of roles in many cases, with classroom support coming from teacher aides, counsellors, librarians, outside consultants, parents and peers as well as from support teachers. Nevertheless, support teachers retained the primary role of preparing individual educational plans and delivered modified programmes more often than regular class teachers.

The inclusive education policy introduced in the fifth year of the programme was concerned with the inclusion of all students, not only those with disabilities (Alberta Education Response Centre, 1992). Its guidelines included the principle that all students were to receive their education in an age-appropriate regular class, and with a programme that was suited to their educational needs. The class teacher would have responsibility for all students in the class, and classroom support should be directed both to teachers and to individual students. All students were to have the opportunity for successful participation in all aspects of school life. Additional guidelines were included for students with special educational needs which emphasised the adaptation or modification of regular class programmes set down for the student's grade level, rather than the development of a separate programme. It was also recognised that some students may require specific objectives to be met outside the regular classroom, for example in community settings.

Although by the end of five years it was felt that considerable progress had been made towards achievement of inclusive schooling, some problems still remained to be addressed. Foremost among these was the question of attitudes. Inclusion was accepted in principle as consistent with community values, but in practice concerns remained, for example about the extra burden placed on class teachers. There was a high resignation rate among special education staff. Withdrawal from class was still practised in some schools as an option for supporting students with disabilities. Children who were at the borderline of special needs often did not receive appropriate services. There were problems with the use of consultants who were external to the school. Finally, there was no measure of the impact of the changes on students without disabilities.

In the overall evaluation of the five-year programme, a number of general criticisms emerged. Firstly, although the process of integration itself had been a gradual one, the initial decision to close special education facilities had come from the top, and was announced without warning. This created some resentment which had not dissipated even three years into the programme. Secondly, there was neither a clear model nor a clearly outlined policy to guide the implementation of inclusion; thus much time was wasted early in the programme in developing procedures on an ad hoc basis. The lack of policy guidelines contributed to teacher anxiety, exacerbated by the fact that for many teaching staff the process involved significant relocation. In particular, there was little focus or support for the needs of teachers at secondary level. Case studies of individual schools in the programme suggested that there was clearer direction, although not necessarily greater acceptance of inclusion, in schools which had devised policies before putting the programme into practice.

Despite these problems, commitment to inclusion remained high (Alberta Education Response Centre, 1992). There were positive changes in the attitudes of all those involved in the regular school, but particularly of teachers. Students with disabilities were judged to have improved their socialisation and communication skills, but showed little change in their academic performance. The impact on students without disabilities was judged to be minimal.

The Yellowhead review provides an overall perspective on the introduction of inclusive schooling. How does inclusion work in individual schools? Two schools, one in Canada and one in Australia, help to throw light on this question.

Fairview School, in a provincial city in Alberta, enrols three hundred and fifty students ranging from a beginners grade to Year 10. In line with official policy in Alberta, the school has a policy of inclusiveness, and about forty-three students, or twelve per cent of all enrolments, have been identified as having special educational needs. These students are enrolled in their age-appropriate grade. The policy of inclusion extends to a mix of grade levels throughout the school: Year 2 children happily share a corridor with Year 9 children from the classroom next door. The school buildings are new and well equipped to cater for students with a wide range of disabilities. Each classroom has its own computer terminal linked to a central computer room. There is a large computer laboratory with thirty terminals. A centralised video system is operated through the school library. There is a large gymnasium, and two time-out rooms for students with behaviour problems. Wide corridors and ramps allow easy movement of wheelchairs around the spacious school, which is all on one level.

The approach within the school is flexible. An individual student may work at the classroom computer terminal at his or her own pace, with an individual programme or with an adaptation of the programme being followed by the rest of the class. A peer tutor may support the student at the terminal. The school employs a qualified special education teacher who acts as a consultant and is occasionally involved in team teaching or withdrawal of a student to the well-equipped resource room. Four classroom assistants are employed to assist students whose needs are greatest.

This beautifully designed, well-equipped school, with the expertise of a special educator to draw on, would seem to have all the ingredients necessary for successful inclusion. But physical environment, although important, is no substitute for a climate of acceptance. The commitment of the principal and teaching staff is reflected in the attitudes and behaviour of students: students with disabilities mingle in the playground and in the corridors and their presence in the school is taken for granted. Support is given when needed – pushing a wheelchair, opening a door, or helping to read a notice, but students with disabilities are regarded as a normal part of the school.

Eastern Hills Primary School (not its real name), in Melbourne, is physically very different from Fairview School, but shares with it a policy of inclusion. Eastern Hills is built of the drab concrete blocks typical of schools that were constructed in the late 1950s to accommodate the baby boomers. When I visited the school on a wet winter afternoon, the only external clue to its renown as one of the state's successes in inclusive schooling was the series of ramps leading to each building. The school is a large one, and of the more than six hundred students enrolled thirty-three have funding for special educational needs. School policy is unequivocal: any child may enrol, and if the school does not have the needed resources to support a student, it will take action to ensure that they are obtained and in place before the student begins. Some students arrive after several unsuccessful experiences both in the mainstream and in special schools. There are no geographical boundaries: one family arranged for their child to board in the area during the week, finally moving from the country so that their child could attend the school.

Inclusion at Eastern Hills is not new. Long before integration was state policy, a small number of students with disabilities was enrolled as part of the school community, the numbers increasing as more funding became available for support. The Ministry of Education provided funds for ramps and a hygiene centre; other resources, including computers, standing frames and other technological supports, are purchased as they are needed from special needs funding. The level of satisfaction with inclusive schooling at Eastern Hills is high among all those involved, including parents, teachers, integration aides and students. Some parents I talked to expressed concerns, but generally these were about issues that could potentially be resolved with extra support, such as additional speech therapy or more assistance to an individual class teacher in adapting curriculum for a specific student. The school's emphasis on acceptance of individual differences, social behaviour, self-esteem and intolerance of bullying or disrespect has also helped to create a positive attitude to integration in teachers. Students are not perceived as different simply because they have an integration aide or follow a different programme. Class sizes vary, but are smaller if they include students with disabilities.

What aspects contribute to the success of integration in these schools? It is tempting to conclude that the positive feelings about inclusion in both schools can be attributed to a committed and dynamic principal. As one parent put it: 'The principal determines the culture of the school. If the principal is for it [integration], the teachers will follow.' The principal of Eastern Hills disputes this view, maintaining that inclusion cannot be regarded as successful if it depends on one person; what is important is creating a positive climate in the school that will survive any individual staff member.

Firstly, both schools have embraced all aspects of inclusive schooling. Each student works at his or her own level. Indeed, Eastern Hills school has a programme for students who are academically gifted as well as supports for students with disabilities. Age groupings are flexible. Students are not labelled by their disability: the absurdity of labelling is illustrated by one student who has cerebral palsy and no speech, and is also gifted in mathematics and working well above his class level. The schools are also flexible in their age groupings. Withdrawal of students from classes is kept to a minimum, and is usually only for therapy programmes which cannot be implemented satisfactorily in the classroom. At Eastern Hills, students who are withdrawn are allowed to select a partner to take with them to therapy. This helps to remove any mystique or misperception of therapy as a soft option by non-disabled students, and satisfies their natural curiosity about what goes on in these sessions. Some non-disabled students have benefited indirectly from their attendance at these sessions.

Secondly, there is a high level of support for students with disabilities. The regular class teacher has primary responsibility for each student's curriculum, which is determined by collaborative teams that meet regularly. Both schools employ support teachers who are qualified in special education to co-ordinate the various services available and to prepare budgets and submissions for special needs funding, as well as providing support to regular class teachers through consultation and team teaching. Teacher aides are considered an essential part of the programme: at Eastern Hills at least two aides are allocated to work with a student to cover different sessions, so that a back-up person with whom the student is familiar is always available to cover breaks or absences. Both schools are self-contained in the support they provide, except for specialist therapy services, which must be brought in from outside, or, for students with sensory impairments, consultation with visiting teachers.

Thirdly, and of crucial importance, the roles and functions of various staff concerned with the education of students with disabilities are clearly defined. The qualified support teacher is available to provide advice on curriculum modifications appropriate for the student's needs, but implementation of curriculum for each student is the responsibility of the class teacher. The teacher aide does not initiate any curriculum directions – her role is to act as the child's 'eyes and ears', facilitating access to the curriculum by whatever means necessary, and providing assistance with mobility, hygiene and eating. Thus staff members fulfil the roles for which they are best equipped as members of a team.

Fourthly, classroom teaching is structured on small group learning, and each student must be a member of a group. This ensures that the student participates with his or her classmates, and is not left to work in isolation in a corner of the classroom with a teacher aide.

Fifthly, inclusion is extended to parents of students with disabilities, who are encouraged to be actively involved in their child's education. At Eastern Hills, a parents' support group meets regularly. But the parents themselves realise that inclusion also depends on their

responding to opportunities within the school, and many make a point
of attending social gatherings arranged for class groups. This is not
always easy – as one parent pointed out, having a student with a
disability in a mainstream school brings home to her the fact that her
child is indeed different in many ways.

SOME COMMON CONCERNS

I have described these schools in some detail to show that inclusive
schooling can work, given the dedication and commitment of all those
involved. But even within successful programmes, questions remain
unresolved.

At Fairview School, for example, there were some difficulties in
obtaining adequate therapy services for the students with disabilities
enrolled there. The policy in Alberta is that specialist health services,
such as speech therapy, are not made available within a school setting.
Waiting lists for the regional health service mean that many students
miss out altogether. There are no staff at the school with expertise in
communication skills for students with vision or hearing impairments, and these students must be referred to residential schools
within the province.

In the face of such resource limitations, the school has some concern
about the high cost of one-to-one attention needed by students with
severe disabilities. Although the school is committed to full inclusion,
the possibility of introducing a small resource room has been
considered to cater for about four students with severe disabilities at
one time, spreading the financial burden by sharing staff and
resources, while still ensuring that these students receive the
individual attention that they require.

The insufficiency of resources to serve students with mild
intellectual or learning disabilities is a common criticism of inclusive
schooling. The case of Jason shows that in practice the needs of
students who do not receive support funding may be neglected:

Jason has just started secondary school, and has learning
problems associated with moderate sensory impairments. Severe
long-sightedness is corrected with glasses, but Jason has no
three-dimensional vision and problems with depth perception
and spatial processing. Although his hearing has been assessed as
normal, auditory processing, especially memory for auditory
information, is poor. Jason knows he does not perform as well as

his classmates, and his learning difficulties led to behaviour problems in the primary school. For a time he was placed in a special class, where efforts to help him with reading met with limited success. On return to the regular class, Jason was supported by an outreach programme and a teacher aide for two mornings each week.

Jason's learning problems have not been overcome, but he does not have an intellectual disability and his sensory problems are not severe enough for him to qualify for a teacher aide in the secondary school. The school claims to have a policy of inclusion, and several students whose disabilities are much more severe are enrolled. However, these students receive funding for additional support. Jason participates in a special literacy programme three times a week, and has the use of a typewriter in the classroom, but the school does not have sufficient resources to provide him with an adapted curriculum or extra teaching in all his subject areas. Jason often feels overwhelmed by the demands of the regular classroom – he cannot follow many instructions and does not understand what is expected of him. He has not been helped by the staff's tendency to label him as 'hyperactive', as if that explains his low achievement. He needs one-to-one teaching, but his teachers either do not understand his needs or feel that priority must be given to teaching the majority of students in the class. Efforts to include Jason are frustrated by thinly spread resources in the school.

Anxiety about secondary schooling is common among parents of students with disabilities integrated into the mainstream. Teachers are subject experts rather than class teachers, and may not get to know individual students and their needs to the same extent as at primary level. Frequent room changes, larger numbers of students, a more competitive atmosphere and greater emphasis on independent work provide a challenge that many students with disabilities are not well equipped to meet without intensive support.

IMPACT OF FULL INCLUSION

To what extent does inclusive schooling affect a school community in terms of benefits for all students? The responses of a focus group set up in the Richmond (Vancouver, Canada) School District suggested that the impact on a school can be both positive and negative (Holborn and

McPhie, 1994). Positive aspects included the additional resources that were now available for all students, such as speech and language programmes, improved parent–teacher communication, greater use of group work and more student participation in class discussions, and increased community acceptance of people with disabilities. Against these benefits, inclusion also brought its share of challenges. Some focus group participants felt that students with disabilities received too much attention and the concern with adequate resource provision for these students meant that students without disabilities were missing out on the attention and encouragement that they also needed. Catering for a range of needs in a single class was difficult for some teachers.

A further concern about inclusive education is implicit in some of the stories told by parents of students who have 'shopped around' for a mainstream school that will accept their child. To what extent do some school administrators see their schools absolved from the radical changes implied by inclusive education by the very existence of schools such as Eastern Hills? It may be too easy for the principal of a school to refer a student on to another school that they know will be more accepting of disability. There is then a risk that a school that is well known for its inclusive policy becomes a type of cluster school, attracting a disproportionate number of students with disabilities and defeating the broader purpose of inclusive schooling that would see every student attending their neighbourhood school.

It is tempting to suggest that these are transitory concerns associated with the radical changes that are required for implementation of inclusive education, and that they will disappear once inclusive schooling is accepted as the norm. A difficulty with evaluating inclusive schooling both as a concept and as a practice is that it is heavily charged with emotive appeal on both sides. Inclusiveness signifies warmth and belongingness and numerous other positive feelings that few of us would want to reject. Movements which promote such concepts are hard to resist; thus Kauffman and Hallahan (1995) have referred to full inclusion as 'an illusion' and 'a bandwagon' – language that also has emotional connotations – and warn of the dangers that are inherent in its unquestioning acceptance.

The greatest danger for the inclusive schools movement is that it may founder in its own zeal. Undoubtedly inclusive schooling can work – numerous examples in the literature show that it is not entirely an illusion, even though it may not be perfect. The real danger is that we may expect too much of it. The model assumes that the reason for a student's failure lies with the school, not with the student (Gallagher, 1995), and that radical changes to school structure and climate will ensure that experiences of school failure are a thing of the past for students with disabilities. A problem with this assumption is that it has not been carried through to empirical verification. We have very little knowledge of the real impact of inclusive schooling on outcomes for schools themselves, particularly in a climate that is increasingly placing schools in a managerial–industrial context and demanding outcomes in return for expenditure. In such a climate, the high cost of intensive support to maintain all students with disabilities in inclusive schools will need to be justified. Studies carried out by Semmel et al. (1995) showed that mainstream schools which produce the best outcomes for the majority of students in terms of academic achievement do not necessarily produce the best results for students with disabilities, even when criteria based on specially designed measures of academic performance, self-esteem and school adjustment are considered.

Strong opposition from members of the deaf community to full inclusion as the only option for students with disabilities was expressed by several writers in a special issue of the journal *American Annals of the Deaf* in 1994. The thrust of their argument was that inclusion does not represent normalisation for students who are deaf and who lack oral communication skills. As Innes (1994) pointed out, many of the supports provided to give these students access to curriculum in the regular classroom create a situation that is not normal for any individual. A retrospective view of a student who had been educated in the mainstream supports this claim (Kyle, 1993). All students need to be able to communicate directly with the class teacher and with their peers, not through the intermediary of an interpreter. Normal social and emotional development requires direct interaction with peers without the intervention of support personnel. Without a peer group that communicates in the same language, students who are deaf lack normal opportunities for peer group participation. Co-operative group work that has been so strongly advocated as a foundation for inclusive classroom practice will create further difficulties. Moreover, students who are deaf do not have the same access as other students to aspects of common culture such as television, radio and peer and adult conversations from which social codes are implicitly acquired. Innes (1994) argued further that students who are deaf need to be exposed to role models who are deaf, just as other students are exposed to role models with normal hearing.

The argument for a separate deaf culture is a controversial one, but one that ought not to go unheeded in the debate about inclusive schooling. Bunch (1994), while acknowledging the generally superior academic performance of students who are deaf in regular classes compared to special classes, also pointed out that a policy of full inclusion does not allow any more choice than a policy of complete segregation in special education. Positive attitudes to students with disabilities in the mainstream, acceptance by peers, opportunities for participation and the availability of resources and support staff may not be enough for many students to develop as fully as possible. We need to consider whether this argument also applies to some students who are not deaf but who have other disabilities that limit communication with regular class peers.

The numerous studies of social outcomes of integration have indicated that, without actively structuring situations to facilitate social interaction, attempts at inclusive schooling are more likely to result in rejection, or at best isolation and indifference towards students with disabilities who lack the skills to initiate positive contacts on their own. The effects of strategies such as co-operative learning experiences on the academic performance of students in the mainstream have yet to be established. Nor do we have any sound evidence of the ways in which collaborative team teaching or a consultative model of specialist support in the regular classroom can facilitate learning. The success of these practices is likely to depend on the interpersonal skills and compatibility of individual teachers. While training may contribute to their effectiveness, entrenched habits of working are difficult to change, and it may take a full generation of teachers before inclusive schools become the norm rather than the exception in providing for students with disabilities.

Part III

Providing for special needs

Curriculum and resources

Chapter 10

Teaching and learning
Curriculum, resources and support

CURRICULUM AS AN ISSUE IN SPECIAL EDUCATION

Curriculum refers to what students should learn, and, by implication, what schools should teach. Underlying inclusive schooling is a belief that students with disabilities should share the same curriculum as the majority of their age peers. This issue is beginning to dominate the debate about schooling for students with disabilities. For these students, debate about curriculum cannot be considered without also considering the additional resources required for delivering curriculum and the supports to enable students to gain access to curriculum.

Two of the major arguments for the existence of segregated special education have centred on curriculum. Firstly, segregated provision has been justified by a belief that the curriculum requirements of students with disabilities are very different from those of students in the mainstream. Secondly, students with disabilities – especially those with intellectual disabilities – have been perceived as incapable of benefiting from the standard academic curriculum that is offered to the majority of students. What, then, are the options for curriculum for students with disabilities?

DOES SPECIAL EDUCATION MEAN A DIFFERENT CURRICULUM?

The belief that students with disabilities had different educational needs led to the development of specialised curricula for implementation in special schools and classes. In the 1960s and 1970s, special education programmes emphasised a developmental approach. These programmes assumed that skills develop in a set sequence, and that more simple skills typical of early development must be mastered before more complex skills are taught. Given that many disabilities were assumed to involve a developmental delay, it seemed logical to implement teaching at a level commensurate with the developmental level of the student. Thus many programmes emphasised perceptual and motor activities as a basis for acquiring later cognitive skills. Activities such as bead threading, copying designs, assembling formboards or tracing patterns were assumed to develop eye–hand co-ordination skills necessary for mastering writing and other complex manipulative skills. Perceptual exercises such as matching and discrimination of shapes were believed to assist recognition of letters and words as a prerequisite for learning to read. The philosophy underlying this approach was explained by Johnson (1975: 218):

> The curriculum [for students with mild intellectual disability] . . . should be developmental in nature. . . . By developmental is meant that specific skills and concepts are introduced and taught when the child has achieved the maturity and had the experiences necessary for their acquisition. . . . It is necessary to organise more than a sequence of cores or experiences, skills and concepts; they must be presented at the time the child is developmentally ready and not according to a specific time schedule based solely upon such factors as chronological or mental age.

The developmental approach contained several flaws. Firstly, there was no scientific evidence that perceptual–motor or similar programmes actually enhanced the subsequent learning of academic skills. Secondly, if the developmental approach were followed to its logical conclusion, students who failed to master the earlier elements of a programme would have no opportunity to move to more advanced levels, remaining locked into a programme of 'readiness' skills that was not only inappropriate for their chronological age, but also risked frustration, boredom and loss of self-esteem. Thirdly, many of the activities included in developmental programmes had no immediate relevance to daily life. Fourthly, the approach was based on a remedial model which implied that there was a deficiency in the learning of academic skills for which there was some potential 'cure', and failed to consider individual characteristics and needs.

For students with disabilities who did progress to the traditional academic curriculum, Wade and Moore (1992) painted a bleak picture. Instruction assumed that students with learning difficulties were capable of learning only a greatly reduced curriculum. The result was a 'watered down' version of basic skills, divided into small steps and with much repetition. Since curriculum focused on basic skills at the expense of more educationally rewarding areas, it held little intrinsic interest. There was an expectation that literacy (defined as reading at the level of a nine- or ten-year-old) would be acquired by about the fourth year of secondary schooling. According to Wade and Moore, once literacy was acquired much time would be spent in practical tasks such as writing letters, filling forms and completing job applications, rather than on the more pleasurable aspects of reading.

The differences between special and mainstream curriculum were increased by the isolation of many special schools from the regular school system, and the lack of familiarity of many special school teachers with mainstream subject areas. Special schools therefore tended to devise their own curricula, rather than attempt to adapt core curriculum, but in some cases with limited success:

> As a result of the prevailing practice of teaching basic skills in special education classes, the curriculum is clearly differentiated from that of general education; there is less of it, fewer subjects are valued as important to study, and consequently, children's educational experience is severely limited.
>
> (Pugach and Warger, 1993: 134)

Pugach and Warger also pointed to a conflict between the expectation that many students with disabilities would be unlikely to follow an academic career, and the excessive time spent in teaching literacy and numeracy skills outside a functional context.

As disenchantment with the developmental approach grew and special education began to take responsibility for students with more severe disabilities, greater emphasis was given to design and implementation of a curriculum that was more truly functional. A functional curriculum emphasises the learning of skills that have a high probability of being used regularly in daily life, and that would have to be performed by someone else if students did not learn the skills themselves. For students without disabilities these skills would not necessarily be formally taught, but would be acquired through incidental learning in the home environment or community. Skills in areas such as self-care, personal hygiene, banking, travel, cooking, shopping, social skills, including sex and human relationships, and more intensive language development are included (Elkins, 1994). To learn these skills in an integrated setting alongside the mainstream curriculum, Elkins suggested that students would either have to attend school for a greater length of time than their peers, or some of the content of the regular curriculum would have to be eliminated. Difficulties with generalisation of learning meant that, in contrast to traditional curriculum, functional skills should be taught in the setting in which they would be used, for example the home or work environment rather than the classroom.

The functional approach gained ready acceptance. For example, Pickering and Dickens (1991) had teachers and parents of students in special schools rate various areas of the curriculum for their importance. Highest ratings were given to communication and survival skills, including self-care, daily living skills, independent travel, work preparation, and recreation and leisure. Priorities in basic skills remained at a functional level.

The need to teach students specific daily life functions conformed well with an individualised approach to education and the provision of a continuum of educational services. In the United States the provision of individualised educational programmes based on comprehensive assessment and diagnosis was mandated for students with special educational needs, and specified procedures were laid down for devising and implementing these programmes. A programme would identify an individual's strengths and weaknesses, and target areas for learning with the setting of precise objectives. Neither the individualised programme nor the emphasis on functional skills precluded a developmental approach, however, and specific functions were often broken down into a sequence of subskills that lead towards mastery of a function, with the sequence assumed to be developmental in the sense that earlier skills in a sequence were less complex and therefore easier to master than later skills.

Despite its wide acceptance as the basis of special education programmes and its focus on preparation for life as an independent adult, the functional approach to curriculum has also been subject to criticism. Some of these criticisms are based on a belief that people are not independent, isolated individuals, but are interdependent, social beings who rely on others as well as themselves to meet their daily needs. This means recognising and accepting the fact that for many people with disabilities true independence may not be achievable. Spending large amounts of time attempting to teach skills in which full functional independence may never be achieved may be more detrimental to a person's quality of life than providing unobtrusive support. Mittler (1995) questioned the value of many areas that have formed the content of special education curricula, and pointed out that little time is spent in helping students with disabilities to anticipate and deal with the harassment and discrimination they will encounter in the real world, or to develop greater assertiveness. Mittler also suggested that greater attention should be given to enabling students with disabilities to obtain the supports they need, for example by teaching them how to understand welfare entitlements, and how to obtain assistance.

For students with physical and sensory disabilities, the curriculum itself has presented less of an issue: the key issue has been how to provide these students with access to the regular curriculum (Elkins, 1994). Segregated special education for these students has been justified by the need to acquire specialist skills that are additional, rather than alternative, to the regular curriculum. In addition, the need to learn alternative communication methods, to work through an aide or interpreter, or to use adaptive technologies to gain access to curriculum materials could mean that learning is at a slower pace than for the majority of students. The risk with special education is that the teaching of specialist skills such as sign language, braille or compic may come to be seen as an end in itself, rather than serving a functional need. Looking back on their education, some students with sensory impairments have been critical of programmes in which too much time was spent in perfecting communication skills at the expense of progress in academic skills or socialisation.

CORE CURRICULUM AND SPECIAL EDUCATIONAL NEEDS

Inclusive schooling takes the view that special educational needs are actually created by a mainstream curriculum that is inappropriate for the full range of individual differences likely to be encountered in any one classroom: as Dessent (1987: 120) noted, 'The curriculum is seen as both the main cause and the potential cure of many learning difficulties'. An emphasis on academic grades and standards as proof of learning is not compatible with the designing of programmes to meet students' individual educational needs. The problem is not solved with extra remedial work: curriculum must be adapted and modified to make it appropriate for a wider range of needs. The inclusive schools movement has called for a broadening of curriculum to take in all of a student's needs: thus curriculum would not be confined to academic skills, but would be seen as including preparation for life as an independent adult.

Curriculum adaptation will largely involve an attempt to compromise between the special needs of the student with a disability and his or her normal educational needs. Wade and Moore (1992) suggested a number of principles that should guide individual programming in mainstream settings. These included basing individual programmes on the mainstream curriculum as well as on the needs of the individual, adapting curriculum where necessary to meet students' needs, and emphasising the same learning skills and outcomes as for other students. Resources should be adapted and modified to give students with disabilities access to common curriculum opportunities and environmental experiences.

Some consideration needs to be given as to how differentiation of curriculum can be achieved without sacrificing programmes that have been devised to meet the specific needs of many students with disabilities. Flexibility is essential. For example, one way in which curriculum may be differentiated is through multilevel curriculum selection (Snell and Drake, 1994), with a student working at different levels in different curriculum areas according to his or her individual needs. Hegarty and Pocklington (1981) proposed a continuum of curriculum provision ranging from a full special curriculum through various reductions or modifications of the normal curriculum to the full normal curriculum unchanged. In practice, a special curriculum on its own – that is, one that has little or no reference to work done by age peers – would be unlikely to have a place in integration except on an intensive short-term basis to facilitate eventual placement in the regular class. However, students with disabilities in special classes or units in the regular school may follow a special curriculum supplemented by participation in some parts of the normal curriculum. Others may follow the normal curriculum, but with reductions of varying degrees to allow inclusion of specialist work, for example auditory training for students with hearing impairment. Modifications to the normal curriculum may be made to take account of specific impairments, to allow the student to take part in alternative activities in which the impairment is not a handicap, or to provide more intensive work in basic skills.

The problem with a continuum of curriculum provision is that some areas are seen as more difficult to adapt for students with disabilities, and this, rather than individual needs, may determine the areas in which they are able to participate. Studies of partial integration suggest that participation is often limited to non-academic areas of the curriculum. Agar et al. (1989) asked teachers about the suitability of mainstream curriculum for students with disabilities integrated into regular classes part-time. Participation tended to be limited to 'safe' areas in which academic standards were less formal, such as library and dictionary skills, and extra-curricular areas such as music, art and craft and physical education. A limitation of safe areas was that teachers often had less opportunity to get to know the integrated student. In addition, if the student lacked the maturity to perform well, the so-called safe areas could be detrimental to the student's self-esteem. For students with behaviour disorders who needed the reassurance of feedback there was a tendency to avoid areas that involved reasoning and problem solving, or areas in which there might be ambiguity (no right or wrong answers). For students with visual impairments, the requirement to prepare materials in advance, for example with print enlargement, preparation of tactile materials and ensuring availability of low vision aids placed some restrictions on spontaneity in teaching. Physical education could pose hazards if not carefully planned and supervised. Areas regarded as inappropriate for students with hearing impairment included drama and discussion groups, or other activities that depended largely on oral language with no visual cues.

Perhaps no aspect of curriculum has raised more anxiety in the education of students with disabilities than the introduction of compulsory core curriculum into mainstream education. The Education Reform Act of 1988 in the United Kingdom stipulated that all students were entitled to access to a 'broad and balanced' curriculum, which should be available in all schools, including special schools. The National Curriculum and uniform processes for assessment which it incorporated reflected a move away from a child-centred approach to education to a concern for standards of academic excellence. It challenged both functional and behavioural approaches to the education of students with disabilities, placing a greater emphasis on participation in subject areas studied in the mainstream. The implication was that subjects such as history, science and modern languages were appropriate areas of learning for these students, and could be suitably adapted for learning at this level. 'Entitlement' became something of a catchword: in principle, the requirement for all students to follow the same curriculum was seen as benefiting students with disabilities by minimising differences between students. However, although by implication all students were entitled to access to the

National Curriculum, the Act did not indicate how students with disabilities might exercise their entitlement. To many special educators, this provision appeared to contradict the existing requirement for programmes to meet the individual educational needs of students with disabilities (Wedell, 1990).

The Act thus created several dilemmas. Many students with disabilities would be unable to reach Level 1 of the curriculum, yet if exempted from the provisions would not only forgo their entitlement to 'a broad and balanced' curriculum, but could risk exclusion from education altogether (Ware, 1990). If instruction were limited to essential skills or a highly watered down version of the core curriculum, access might be seen as narrowing rather than broadening the range of experiences of these students. For students with severe learning difficulties, time spent attempting to master even the most basic elements of the National Curriculum might be more usefully spent in intensive programmes to develop self-care skills or to address challenging behaviour that restricted full community participation. Some attempts were made to modify the curriculum to meet the needs of individual students, but clear guidelines for modification were lacking. Subsequent provisions were introduced to allow 'disapplication' of the National Curriculum for students with a formal statement of educational needs. Because disapplication could also potentially lead to segregated education, there was some dissatisfaction with this provision. Greater competition between schools led to a fear that some schools would apply temporary exemptions from the curriculum to students who were unlikely to do well in assessment in order to boost the school's overall performance, although this fear appeared to be unjustified (Audit Commission, UK, 1992). To overcome problems with assessment, Level W was introduced to indicate that a student was 'working towards' Level 1. In turn, Level W has been broken down into smaller steps that would be more sensitive to limited progress made by students with disabilities.

In Victoria, the introduction of a core curriculum has been followed by a document setting out guidelines and suggestions for implementation for students with disabilities and impairments (Directorate of School Education, 1995). This is being followed by supplementary course advice and support materials in specific subject areas, beginning with English. Interpretation of curriculum is flexible: for example, AUSLAN (Australian sign language) is considered alongside other modern languages as a language other than English; physical education may include the most basic motor skills.

The move to a core curriculum has raised questions not only about the content of the curriculum for students with disabilities, but about adaptation of the methods by which it is implemented. Students with disabilities may require special methods of instruction to compensate for their disability, or they may need special equipment or communications technology to enable them to benefit from an otherwise unmodified curriculum. Many subject area teachers are unfamiliar with the nature of learning difficulties experienced by students with disabilities. Case studies by Lee (1991) showed that modern language learning was feasible and could provide positive experiences for students with quite severe disabilities. However, language teachers began on the assumption that students could read and write in their own language, and had to modify their expectations and instructional approaches significantly to cater for students without these skills.

Implementation of core curriculum for students with disabilities in the mainstream requires considerable planning and organisation. Montgomery (1987) described the processes involved in one school district. A committee of teachers for each subject area was formed to develop a curriculum outline. All of the skills taught in a subject were organised according to the scope and sequence to be covered at each grade level. Each subject committee developed a list of skills that included only those necessary for the student to move to the next grade level – an Essential Skills Curriculum. Teachers could vary instructional strategies to suit individual students, but the content and sequence of material would be the same for all students. Although teaching might be limited to essential skills, common textbooks could be used and the progress of atypical students could be evaluated by the same bench marks as their peers.

It is debatable whether curriculum that has been developed by special educators to cater for the very real needs of individual students should be so readily discarded. It is important to achieve a balance between special and core curriculum. There is a growing pressure for special schools to follow a core curriculum similar to that followed in the mainstream, although modified to suit students enrolled in the school. These changes also have implications for the future deployment of resources.

SUPPORTING CURRICULUM WITH RESOURCES

In Chapter 1 I referred to special education as involving provision that is in some way additional to the education that is provided for the majority of students. Students with disabilities who have special educational needs require additional resources to meet those needs. During the 1960s and 1970s, a growing recognition of the needs of students with disabilities led to substantial increases in funding for segregated provision. These increases were reflected in the establishment of many new special schools, the upgrading of teacher training courses concerned with various categories of disability, and the provision of programmes, materials and equipment designed specifically for special education. Resources included programmes for the development of independent living skills, requiring domestic and vocational equipment often not found in the regular school, academic programmes for teaching basic skills at a level and pace believed to be appropriate for students with disabilities, equipment for encouraging motor development, and technological aids to support students with sensory, physical and communication difficulties. Above all, the highly favourable teacher–student ratios in special schools enabled students to receive more intensive teacher support and one-to-one attention than regular school staffing could allow. Many special schools were equipped with rooms for specialist therapy and other services.

A persistent concern with integration has centred on ways in which resources can be provided and curriculum adapted or modified in the regular classroom without penalising individual students by reducing the level of resources considered necessary to meet their needs in the special school. Resistance to integration has centred on the potential loss of many of these benefits if students with disabilities are dispersed in neighbourhood schools. It is the provision of additional resources that imposes a heavy cost burden on the education of students with disabilities, regardless of the setting in which education takes place.

Integration, and indeed participation in core curriculum, may be seen, perhaps not without some justification, as an economy measure, with the closure of special schools and classes implying an end to many of the resources, expertise and other benefits. The outcome will be not only to withdraw many of the resources needed by students with disabilities if they are to take their place alongside their non-disabled peers in regular school activities, but also to place an unfair burden on regular class teachers who already face changes implied by the restructuring of education as a whole.

STAFF RESOURCES

The change in thinking about what is appropriate curriculum for students with disabilities has also involved changes in the nature of support requirements. A higher teacher–student ratio generally distinguishes special education provision from that found in most regular classrooms. However, teachers are not the only staff resources that are available: staff specialising in therapy and counselling as well as teacher aides are usually found in special education settings. Not surprisingly, salaries for additional staff form the largest single expenditure on resources for students with disabilities in both primary and secondary schools (de Lemos, 1994). Although principals, parents, administrators, therapists and school psychologists all form a part of the resources available to students with disabilities, the key players in providing a student with access to the curriculum are the class teacher, the special education teacher (including the visiting teacher), and the teacher aide (also referred to as ancillary staff, or integration aides).

The class teacher

Although the class teacher is not an 'additional' resource in the regular education setting, the role of the class teacher is such a crucial one in the success of integration that it needs to be considered in its own right. Early studies of integration programmes found a high level of anxiety among class teachers arising from lack of familiarity with disability and its implications for learning, feelings of inadequacy, uncertainty about appropriate educational programmes, instructional methods and expectations of performance, and difficulties in providing needed attention without depriving other students in the class (Anderson, 1973; Hegarty and Pocklington, 1981; Jenkinson, 1982). Although these studies also suggested that much anxiety was dispelled as teachers became more familiar with individual students, concern has persisted about the provision of individualised programmes in large classes. Adding to this concern are changes in the roles and functions of the regular class teacher implied by inclusive schooling.

A change in instructional role is implied by the need to differentiate curriculum to a much wider range of ability than has previously been encountered in the regular class. The normal range of variation within a class is unlikely to include the special needs of many students with disabilities. Indeed, segregation of students with disabilities in special classes and schools meant that regular class teachers rarely had to deal with the more exceptional needs. Many pre-service teacher training courses introduced elements dealing with exceptional students to prepare teachers for integration, but these were often elective rather than core units. The majority of regular class teachers in Australia who teach students with disabilities have not completed any units in special education in their initial teacher training (de Lemos, 1994). Rationalisation of training courses could also mean the abolition of elective units in special needs (Mittler, 1993). As education moves back towards a core curriculum with standardised assessment, a focus on differentiation of curriculum to take account of individual needs seems unlikely.

In-service training has been seen as having a significant contribution in the preparation of class teachers for integration. Many descriptions of integration programmes include in-service preparation for the teachers involved, but often such courses are designed to meet immediate needs rather than reflecting long-term plans to change the attitudes and beliefs of teachers to cope with a greater range of individual differences in the classroom.

Inclusive schooling also implies a change in the level of responsibility assumed by class teachers. Direct instruction is only one aspect; the class teacher must also take on the role of programme manager (White, 1984). The class teacher administers and directs the contribution of teacher aides, volunteers and other helpers such as peer tutors to meet the needs of the student. Moreover, the increasing use of teacher aides to support students with disabilities means that the teacher, accustomed to instructing children, must be competent in giving instructions to another adult. Teachers are not trained to act as managers and may not necessarily feel comfortable in this role.

Teachers in the regular class must not only learn to accept a new role themselves, but also need to realise that they are responsible for bringing about change in the education of students with disabilities. Teachers provide behavioural models for students to follow in their interactions with each other, and their acceptance of a child with a disability in a class is likely to be reflected in acceptance by other students. Unfortunately we do not have any direct data on the relationship between teachers' behaviour towards a student with a disability and that of other students in the class, although it seems highly likely that students will pick up cues to behaviour from their teachers which may have a lasting influence on their attitudes to disability. The extent to which pre-service training can adequately prepare regular class teachers to influence attitudes to disability is doubtful. Studies suggest that experience in working with students who have disabilities is most effective in removing initial teacher anxiety and opposition to integration. Mittler (1993) argued that preparation of teachers to work with students with special needs might be better achieved through a 'permeation' process rather than through separate elective units. Permeation would ensure that teacher training in all aspects would focus on differentiation of curriculum and ensuring that individual needs were being met.

Nor will training regular class teachers to deal with exceptionality remove the need for specialist trained teachers. Even with careful preparation and adequate provision of information about individual students, the presence of a student with a disability in the class can make demands on a teacher beyond those of the regular class. The burden of such demands in terms of extra time, knowledge and skill required to prepare adapted curriculum materials and implement special instructional techniques is difficult to estimate because of the varying needs of students with disabilities. Mittler (1993) argued that if some students require educational provision beyond that available to the majority of students, then some teachers might also require additional training. Inclusive schooling does not dispense with the expertise of the special teacher, but does imply a further change in which the traditional focus of special education teachers on assessment and remediation of special needs will be extended to include support and advisory roles across the whole curriculum.

Support teaching

Traditionally, the provision of special educational needs in the regular school has been viewed as the sole domain of the special education teacher in a special class or unit, or in a resource or remedial centre separate from the rest of the school. Inclusive schooling has changed this role to one of classroom support, although there is disagreement about what that support entails (Hart, 1992). What is agreed is that support teaching involves the provision of special education in the regular classroom setting, rather than on a withdrawal basis, that it is concerned with access to the regular curriculum, and that it involves close consultation with the regular class teacher, or, at secondary level, with subject teachers.

Hart (1992) distinguished two major approaches to support

teaching. The individual approach emphasises assessment of an individual student's needs and the provision of additional or different instructional strategies to ensure that those needs are met. The role of the special education teacher is to work in partnership with the class teacher, providing whatever additional resources are needed for a student to participate in activities undertaken by the rest of the class. These resources may include one-to-one teaching, or provision of supplementary materials or specialist equipment. The focus of support is on the progress of the individual student. Hart argued that this approach is divisive because it perpetuates an image of the student with a disability as different and is not consistent with the aim of a differentiated curriculum that is available to all students. From a practical perspective, it is less effective than withdrawal because individual instruction must compete against noise and other distractions in the regular classroom.

The whole curriculum approach favoured by Hart differs from the individual approach. The focus is on adapting curriculum materials and strategies to meet the needs of all students. The role of the special education teacher is to examine the curriculum from the perspective of all students in a class, to identify any likely difficulties and to develop teaching methods and materials to avoid those difficulties. Difficulties experienced by students with disabilities are seen as highlighting problem areas of the curriculum, rather than as problems inherent in the student. The support teacher works with the class teacher to plan and organise instruction, helps the class teacher to adapt teaching practices to accommodate the learning styles and strategies of all students, and participates in class teaching. Rather than focus on student progress, support teaching focuses on the development of teacher awareness and skill in curriculum development.

Much has been written in recent texts about the need for collaboration between regular and special teachers in inclusive classrooms. Collaboration means working co-operatively on an equal basis, rather than one person being regarded as more expert than another. The class teacher is presumed to have expertise in curriculum and in knowledge of individual students in a class; the special education teacher is presumed to have expertise in curriculum adaptation and differentiation. Close communication and mutual respect for what each has to contribute to a class are essential to effective collaboration. Successful collaboration depends on consensus regarding the roles and responsibilities of the class teacher and the support teacher, on agreement regarding teaching goals and activities for learning, and on procedures for evaluating students' strengths and weaknesses (Ireson, 1992). Planning of activities, monitoring of student progress and evaluation of teaching must therefore be shared.

Not all educators see the involvement of the special education teacher in teaching a whole class as appropriate. Ireson (1992) described support teaching as a continuum of provision rather than embodying two separate models, ranging from student withdrawal, with the class teacher having no say in the child's programme, to the special educator performing an advisory or consultative role and providing in-service training for class teachers. In between, Ireson suggested that there could be several arrangements involving collaboration with the regular class teacher in planning and teaching. However, Ireson supported Hart's (1992) view that collaboration is likely to be more successful if support is directed to the class or subject teacher rather than to the individual child. The class teacher's knowledge of the individual student, rather than that of the support teacher, would be an integral part of the support service.

How do class teachers perceive the role of support teachers? Richmond and Smith (1990) found that the most valued support was practical help in providing for students with special needs such as withdrawal teaching (provided the class teacher was consulted about it first), provision of materials and programmes, diagnosis of a learning difficulty and in-service training, particularly if this helped to modify school organisation, classroom practices, and curriculum and teaching. Co-operative teaching was generally favourably regarded, but mainly for help with weaker students rather than adapting or modifying curriculum.

For classes with students who have low-incidence disabilities that require highly specialised resources, support for the class teacher is most likely to be linked to the needs of an individual student. Hass (1994) investigated the activities of forty itinerant teachers of students with visual impairment in British Columbia. Consistent with a need to provide support to the regular class teacher, much of the time of the specialist teacher was spent in adapting curriculum or instructional methods for low vision access. Less time was spent in specialist skills such as braille or mobility, although increased time on the use of technology was predicted as more programmes became available to support students with low vision. Common problems experienced by visiting teachers are isolation from colleagues and the time spent in travelling.

These studies suggest that support teachers are specifically linked by class teachers with the needs of specific students, rather than providing curriculum differentiation within a whole class, even though support may be directed to the class teacher rather than to the student. There is little evidence available to support the effectiveness of either model in determining student outcomes. Although mainstream schools are increasingly allocating a staff position to take responsibility for special needs, these positions continue to focus on the needs of individual students rather than on whole school or whole class curriculum implementation. In England, partly as a result of lobbying in reaction to the neglect of special education in the 1988 Education Reform Act, the Education Act passed in 1993 specifically addressed the needs of students with disabilities with a Code of Practice on the Identification and Assessment of Special Educational Needs. The requirements of the Code included appointment of a special needs co-ordinator by all schools. In Victoria, the role description of the integration teacher emphasises implementation of a school's integration policy through co-ordination of services and support for teachers who have students with disabilities integrated into their classes (Directorate of School Education, Victoria, 1991). Although these roles do not preclude support for students who do not receive additional funding for special needs, support is still more likely to be on an individual basis rather than through overall curriculum policy.

Training of special education teachers

Changes in special education provision have had important implications for training of special education teachers. There has been a significant trend away from courses dealing with a single area of educational need, and a move towards generic courses dealing with a range of disabilities. This trend is consistent with rejection of a categorical approach to disability and the appointment of special education teachers to mainstream schools where they are likely to encounter several kinds of disabilities. Other arguments against categorical approaches to training have suggested that categories are educationally irrelevant – that teaching of students with learning difficulties requires the same approaches and strategies regardless of the cause of the difficulty (Blackhurst, Bott and Cross, 1987). Further, training in a specific category, particularly one of low-incidence disability, restricts professional opportunities, and does not adequately prepare teachers to deal with secondary disabilities. Arguments which have continued to favour a categorical approach to training have pointed to the different techniques and range of skills needed to deal with physical, sensory and intellectual disabilities. Indeed, some courses that have attempted a generic approach through an emphasis on curriculum differentiation have provided little specific information on the nature of disability and its implications.

There has also been a trend towards competency-based training in special education (Hegarty, 1993), although studies reviewed by Blackhurst et al. (1987) indicate a lack of agreement on competencies required in special education, or indeed whether these differ in any significant way from those required in the mainstream. Zabel (1987) claimed that some specific competencies are required for teaching students with behaviour disorders, and clearly teachers of students with hearing and visual impairments could identify specific skills needed to give students access to the curriculum. Disagreement on definition of a competency, problems in actually observing and measuring some competencies and the absence of data on the relationship between teacher competencies and student performance make this a difficult area to interpret.

The changing role of special education teachers in both mainstream and special schools suggests that a better balance needs to be achieved between generalist skills relating to educational provision for students with disabilities and the specialist skills that will continue to be required to meet specific needs for curriculum adaptation and modification. There may be less need for knowledge about medical aspects of a disorder, and more for an understanding of its educational implications (Freeze and Rampaul, 1991). Skills for direct teaching of students with disabilities will need to be supplemented by the interpersonal skills needed for collaboration and consultation with class teachers, other professionals and teacher aides, and greater familiarity with core curriculum. Training should also give more attention to preparing graduates to take a lead in discussion about policy, and about various options for provision of special education.

Teacher aides and classroom assistants

The provision of teacher aides and classroom assistants has been seen as a major way of supporting regular classroom teachers and compensating for the reduced teacher–student ratio in the regular class compared to the special class or school (White, 1984). In Victoria the teacher aide has played a major role in the provision of support for students with disabilities integrated into regular schools, and was the support most frequently mentioned by parents in a recent study (Jenkinson, 1995). The ratio of teacher aides to students with disabilities in Victoria greatly exceeds that in Australia overall – with approximately one teacher aide for every four students with a disability at primary level, and one for every five students at secondary level. This compares with a nationwide average of one teacher aide for every eleven students with a disability at primary level, and one for every fifteen students at secondary level (de Lemos, 1994).

The role of the teacher aide is perhaps the least clearly defined of all in special education, and varies widely depending on individual student needs and teacher preferences (Fletcher-Campbell, 1992). The major emphasis has been on the provision of physical care, especially of students with both physical disabilities and severe learning difficulties, and students with severe sensory impairments. This role is usually extended to promoting independence and facilitating social contacts between students with disabilities and their non-disabled peers. The aide can take the role of an understanding adult and provide a source of security, especially in the early stages of integration.

However, as Fletcher-Campbell (1992) pointed out, it is important that assistants do not work full-time with one student if the student is not to be perceived by the rest of the class as different. Too much support can emphasise a student's disability and hinder the development of independence and group participation. The case of Paul illustrates this point.

Paul is confined to a wheelchair and has learning problems that make it difficult for him to keep up with the class. Since he started school three years ago, Paul has had the same teacher aide full-time. Joanne, the aide, is devoted to Paul and has been happy to move to a new class with him each year. She has got to know Paul's family well, she understands his needs, and although Paul has a severe speech problem she always seems to know just what he wants and what he is capable of. Each year, the class teacher has found Joanne's knowledge and support of Paul invaluable in the classroom. Joanne encourages other students to interact with Paul and there is never a shortage of volunteers to push his wheelchair in the playground. Joanne is always there to keep a watchful eye on things to ensure there is no risk to Paul.

Recently, Joanne became ill and another aide was found to support Paul. Paul could not get used to the new aide. He has become unhappy at school and refuses to co-operate with the aide. His behaviour has become disruptive and the other students are less willing to talk to him in the playground.

Fortunately, Paul's situation may not be common. Although some assistants have been appointed to work with a particular child, many find themselves taking on other duties to assist the class teacher. Clayton (1989) interviewed one hundred welfare assistants appointed to work with specific students. Only four indicated that they spent all their time with the 'named' child – half worked with other children who had special needs, and many also worked with non-disabled students in the class.

More effective use of teacher aides can be made if careful note is taken of the tasks needed to enable a student to function in the regular school. In a survey by Fletcher-Campbell (1992), one school allocated assistance on the basis of an audit of the specific needs of students within the context of the school routine by 'shadowing' a new student admitted to the mainstream. The student's practical skills and ability to cope with classroom work were observed, and any areas in which assistance might be required were noted.

The role of the teacher aide is not limited to physical care, or even to facilitating socialisation. The aide can be used to facilitate small group activities, to liaise between the teacher and other programmes or professionals, and to provide relief for the teacher from time-consuming activities that do not require professional training. Aides can help in instruction by providing one-to-one attention under supervision of the class teacher. They may also contribute strengths and talents the teacher does not have. In one school, the teacher aide in a Grade Six classroom is something of an expert in international cookery. The class teacher draws on her expertise to conduct regular cookery sessions for the class.

Even when the role of the teacher aide is limited to physical care, it is still quite complex and demands a degree of specialised knowledge of disability, as well as a high level of interpersonal skills. The aide may experience many of the difficulties of the class teacher in lack of appropriate training and inadequacy of information about individual students, with possible negative consequences if, for example, equipment is mishandled or a student's need for adequate exercise is not realised.

Extension of the role of teacher aide beyond a purely caring one to an educational one depends on individual teachers, but studies of the functions performed by teacher aides reveal several useful contributions that can free teachers from routine tasks and allow them to make better use of their professional skills. These include preparation of teaching materials, help with individual reading and language work and assistance with practical activities like craft work and domestic skills. Conversations between aides and students who have communication difficulties are an important part of language development. Some aides may also take responsibility, under professional supervision, for day-to-day therapy programmes.

In Victoria, although the use that is made of an integration aide will depend very much on the individual teacher, the needs of the student concerned and the amount of time the aide is employed, integration aides are seen as providing more than physical and social support for the student. A much more central role in teaching is implied in the State's Curriculum Guidelines (Ministry of Education, Victoria, 1986: 8):

> Integration aides will have responsibilities in areas of student mobility, personal hygiene and communication, as well as lesson preparation and classroom involvement, assisting in paramedical and physical education sessions and intensive supervision. Assistance with program implementation is an important aspect of the integration aide's role.

To some extent, this expanded role of the integration aide may justify the greater use of aides in Victoria. But surveys of teacher aides have consistently shown that most lack formal training or qualifications that are relevant to their work. There is a high demand from aides for in-service training, and some formal training courses exist, but it is usually up to the individual aide to take advantage of these opportunities. Training is made more difficult by the fact that aides are often employed on an hourly basis, and training must be undertaken in their own time. Further, there is usually no career structure for aides, so no rewards other than personal satisfaction for such training.

The diversity of functions performed by teacher aides in physical care, socialisation and educational support implies a need for training if the job is to be carried out effectively. Studies indicate that most teacher aides lack training that is relevant to the task. Many have had voluntary experience working with children in schools, but few have either experience with disability or an appropriate qualification before they take up their duties (Clayton, 1989). On-the-job training is often limited, usually consisting of a briefing by the principal or class teacher, and often also by parents. Other professionals are rarely involved in briefing or training the aide.

If training for teacher aides is implemented, what should it include? Surveys suggest that aides would like to have more practical skills in areas such as first aid and behaviour management as well as understanding of specific disabilities and their implications for the problems and management of individual students. Balshaw (1991) followed up four hundred teacher aides who had completed a two-level training course totalling eighty-five hours. The aides generally reported an increase in confidence, greater assertiveness about their working conditions and expectations, new skills developed, and feeling better prepared to work in specific areas such as supporting teachers in secondary curriculum, or working with students who had language difficulties. They benefited from the opportunity to interact with other teacher aides. The course was also useful in identifying other areas that needed to be addressed, such as management issues.

A significant issue in the effective use of teacher aides is the ability of teachers to make use of the help provided. This is part of the change that is expected in the role of the class teacher. Clear definitions of responsibilities and absence of conflict between the teacher and teacher aide are also necessary to ensure that a student has clear direction.

In this chapter I have focused primarily on the issue of curriculum for students with disabilities and the people who are most closely involved in ensuring the student's access to curriculum, particularly in the regular classroom. I have not considered the issue of physical environment in any detail. This is not because physical environment and modifications and adaptations to regular school buildings are not important. However, the design of buildings so that students can move freely around a school in the same way as other students, the provision of ramps, lifts, wide doorways and wheelchair access to toilets, and the need for special classroom furniture or aids, are less controversial than many of the other issues surrounding curriculum and staffing. Physical resources require funding, but, perhaps because of their more tangible nature, they are less subject to controversy and resistance to change than new teacher roles or new curriculum directions.

In the next chapter, I explore some of the issues of curriculum and resourcing for students with severe and multiple disabilities.

Chapter 11

Students with severe and multiple disabilities

Robert has a severe intellectual disability resulting from a comparatively rare genetic disorder. He lives in a country town where there is a well-established special school that he could attend. The paediatrician who looks after Robert suggested to his parents that this school would offer an excellent programme that would recognise his needs and help Robert develop his limited skills to the full. The special school could also offer regular speech therapy which would help Robert in learning to talk. But Robert's parents also belong to a parent support group which strongly advocates the integration of all students into their local school. Other members of the group encouraged them to enrol Robert in his neighbourhood school. The school is a large one, and the principal was reluctant to take him, feeling that even with the support of an aide Robert would be isolated by his inability to communicate with his peers and to participate in the mainstream curriculum. Robert, although mobile, is small for his age and has a visual impairment, and the principal was also concerned about the possibility of an accident in the school ground or that Robert might wander away from the school if not watched for the whole time. Robert also has epilepsy, and, although this is controlled, someone in the school would have to take responsibility for administering his medication. At times, he exhibits bizarre behaviour – rhythmic rocking movements and flapping his hand in front of his face. Robert is toilet-trained, but at times needs reminding if an accident is to be avoided.

Robert's parents did not push the issue – they did not want to send him to a school where he was not welcome. Then through their parent group they heard about a small school in a rural area outside their town. The school had two composite grades, each with twelve students. Since the grades cover a range of ages, each student has an individual programme, and this would enable Robert to fit easily into one of the grades. The principal, who also takes one of the classes, agreed to take Robert provided that funding was available for an integration aide. Robert's disability had been assessed as severe and his support needs high, and an aide was provided for twenty hours a week.

Robert has no special programme. The main aim in integrating him into the mainstream is to encourage socialisation with his non-disabled age peers, and for him to learn acceptable behaviour. Integration appears to be working well in achieving this aim. Robert has settled happily into the school. He is not aggressive and the other students have learned to accept his unusual behaviour when it occurs. A favourite free time occupation is to seat Robert in a bean bag and read him a story — the aide has noticed that this is an especially popular activity with the girls in the class. This has the added benefit of giving the teacher aide time to assist the class teacher with the other students. For the rest of the time, Robert is given crayons and paper to draw, or the aide attempts to get him to talk. A speech therapist visits once a fortnight and the aide tries to implement the exercises that have been suggested. She thinks he is trying to copy words, but his articulation is so poor she cannot be certain. She tries to get him to match pictures with words, but getting and maintaining his attention for long enough is a problem.

The speech therapist sees Robert's attendance at the school as 'marking time'. She is frustrated with Robert's lack of progress in communication. She would like to implement a more intensive programme, trying alternative methods of communication, but her schedule does not allow more frequent visits to the school. The class teacher sees his role as one of facilitating socialisation, but does not feel qualified to attempt any formal instruction with Robert. The teacher aide does her best, but neither she nor the class teacher has the training in instructional techniques needed for teaching students with severe learning problems.

The principal is also concerned about Robert's apparent lack of progress, but a more pressing problem looms. The school has falling enrolments and is likely to be closed. Students will be absorbed into one of the larger schools in the nearby town. Robert is almost ten, and will most likely transfer to the special school, where he will be given a more structured programme to teach him many of the skills he lacks. What will happen to the friends he has formed?

Attendance at the small mainstream school has undoubtedly had benefits for Robert in exposing him to the more normal environment of his non-disabled age peers. In turn, his classmates have learned to accept his disability. But Robert is slow to learn, his attention is not easily engaged, and clearly he cannot participate in much of the regular class curriculum. He needs skills to help him fit into the community – skills that have already been acquired by his classmates and are not part of their curriculum.

BACKGROUND

For students such as Robert who have severe disabilities, the dilemmas of special education are intensified. The debate about inclusion of students with severe and multiple disabilities in regular schools is of much more recent origin than the integration debate generally. Until the 1970s, the prevailing belief was that students with severe intellectual disabilities were incapable of learning and would gain little from attempts at formal education. Care usually focused on health needs in an institutional setting. In advocating an end to segregated special classes, Dunn (1968) was not concerned with students who had moderate or severe disabilities who had never been a part of public education.

With the development of instructional technologies derived from behavioural psychology, the outlook for students with severe disabilities became brighter. Programmes were developed for implementation in day centres and later, as education authorities assumed responsibility for education of all students, in special schools, although the education of students with severe and multiple disabilities remained outside the mainstream education system. While students with mild learning or behavioural difficulties often began their education in a regular class, only to be excluded as their learning difficulties became apparent, the regular school system had no experience with the problems faced by students with severe disabilities until pressure for integration of all students gained impetus.

Who are the students with severe disabilities? Students with severe disabilities form a heterogeneous group with widely differing needs. Typically, they have severe impairments in a number of areas, with a level of intellectual functioning that is significantly below that of their age peers. The inappropriateness of most measures of intelligence for these students makes any definition in terms of an intelligence quotient meaningless, and their level of functioning is usually defined in behavioural terms rather than through direct testing. Usually their impairments are traceable to some form of brain damage, and the pervasive nature of the injury often means that the student also has impairments that may be quite severe in sensory functioning, motor skills and behaviour. Health problems, in some cases life threatening, are often also present. Students with severe disabilities may be unable to communicate, they may lack basic self-care skills, and they may, especially if mobile, exhibit behaviour that is injurious to themselves or to others, that is destructive to property or that is in other ways socially unacceptable. Or they may simply withdraw into a world of passive acceptance showing little interest in their surroundings.

Yet the needs of these students for companionship, achievement and a sense of belonging and self-respect are no less than those of others of their age. In providing for their needs, the educator must come to terms with the many problems that are associated with a severe disability. The claim that integration into the regular class is the right of all students including those with severe and multiple disabilities, and that the necessary supports should be provided to enable this to happen, has not met with universal support. Unlike programmes for students with sensory impairments or mild learning difficulties, educational programmes for students with severe disabilities do not necessarily ensure access to the mainstream curriculum. We do not at present have the technology to compensate for a severe intellectual disability in the same way that we can use technology to provide alternative methods of communication for students with hearing or vision impairments. At best we can work at developing limited capacities to their maximum potential, but no amount of support can guarantee the conceptual level needed to follow an academic curriculum with any degree of success. Moreover, as Stieler (1994) pointed out, the provision of resources is only one factor; effective application of resources is crucial to ensure that learning takes place.

In terms of numbers, students with severe and multiple disabilities form a minority among those with special educational needs. The abolition of categories of disability by some educational authorities has made it difficult to estimate the true prevalence of any type of disability. Moreover, some estimates include students with moderate as well as severe disabilities; others do not. One estimate placed the number of students with severe intellectual disability in New South Wales at about 14 per cent of all students enrolled in special schools or classes (de Lemos, 1994), and 0.14 per cent of all students. Sailor (1989: 54) refers to the 'lowest one per cent on any measure of intellectual functioning', but the fact that so many of these students cannot be directly tested by conventional tests makes this figure no more than a rough estimate. The small proportion of students involved belies both the wide variation in patterns of individual functioning and the intensity of their support needs.

The relatively small numbers of students with severe disabilities means that there is not a great deal of evidence about outcomes of educational programmes. Research is usually limited to case studies of three or four students and their responses to specific programmes or instructional techniques. The enormous variation between students with severe disabilities, and likely bias in the selection of students for inclusion in experimental programmes (Mittler and Farrell, 1987), make it difficult to generalise the findings of these studies: at best they suggest avenues for further exploration, but are not proof that a programme that has succeeded with some students will succeed with others. Failure to describe specific functional levels of students participating in research studies adds to the difficulty of interpretation. Further, evaluations of large-scale programmes have generally been carried out by those with a vested interest in demonstrating the value of the programme, rather than by independent evaluators. Although bias in these studies may not be deliberate, complete impartiality cannot be guaranteed.

Reports of successful programmes for integration of students with severe disabilities have been promoted as evidence that integration is feasible, given appropriate resources and commitment. Others have greeted proposals for integration into the regular school system with considerable scepticism. Gent and Mulhauser (1988) pointed to an unexplained discrepancy between reports of successful integration of students with severe disabilities and the failure of students with mild disabilities in similar settings. Although this discrepancy may be due to differences both in expectations and in the criteria used for evaluating outcomes for students with mild or severe disabilities, it does raise questions about the validity of published evaluations. Gent and Mulhauser also claimed that the predominance of qualitative research in this area had contributed to the paucity of objective data on the effectiveness of programmes for students with severe disabilities.

Despite disagreement about what is an appropriate curriculum for students with severe disabilities, the changes that have occurred in educational provision over the past twenty years have been in a positive direction. Ware (1989) suggested that these changes had their source in two main motives. The first derived from the ethical viewpoint that all students, simply by virtue of their being human, are entitled to an education. This principle underpinned the concern of the Warnock (1978) Committee that students with severe learning difficulties should be included in special education. This entitlement was also reflected in the transfer of educational responsibility for students with severe disabilities from health authorities to education authorities in many western countries in the 1970s. The principle was taken further in the United States by the advocates of inclusive schooling, in particular by The Association for Persons with Severe Handicaps (TASH), which called for the inclusion of all students in regular age-appropriate classrooms, and access to 'campuses and classrooms, including co-curricular and extracurricular activities, that are free from prejudice and other physical and psychological barriers' (TASH, 1993, repr. in Kauffman and Hallahan, 1995: 315). Inclusion was succinctly referred to by Sailor (1989: 54) as 'zero rejection' – that is, no child was to be rejected from the regular school except in the most exceptional circumstances, such as need for a cumbersome life-support system or behaviour that could be considered life-threatening.

The second motive referred to by Ware (1989) was an optimistic belief that all students, no matter how severe their disability, are capable of learning and can progress. Although this statement has often been expressed as a principle rather than as a statement of fact, it had its origins in theories of behavioural psychology and has been supported by carefully designed experiments. The development of instructional strategies such as task analysis and precision teaching allowed instruction and progress in learning to be measured in more detailed and precisely defined steps. Changes in behaviour could be observed even in students with the most severe disabilities. These technologies, by breaking down tasks into discrete sequences of component behaviours, offered a means of teaching students more complex skills than had hitherto been thought possible. Teaching involved the systematic analysis of behaviour and the setting of precise objectives for mastery by the student. It was assumed that students could learn to perform a complex task if they first mastered the discrete components of the task. This procedure fitted well with legislative requirements for individual educational programmes in which specific objectives related to skills already mastered and those still to be learned were precisely defined for each student. Other behaviourally oriented strategies based on operant conditioning also contributed to a general optimism regarding the learning potential of students with severe disabilities. The way was open for development of an educational curriculum for these students.

CURRICULUM FOR STUDENTS WITH SEVERE AND MULTIPLE DISABILITIES

The transition from a developmental approach to education for students with severe disabilities to an age-appropriate functional approach proceeded smoothly because instructional techniques developed within a behavioural framework could be used equally well with both approaches (Billingsley and Kelley, 1994). Reasons for rejecting a developmental curriculum were discussed in the previous chapter, but were complemented by a growing awareness of the importance of social development and the benefits that could be derived from social interaction between disabled and non-disabled students (Sailor, 1989). More recently, debate about curriculum has become more heated with a shift to controversy about functional curriculum versus participation in core curriculum, and a lack of agreement on instructional approaches as well as curriculum content (Ware, 1990).

Billingsley and Kelley (1994) questioned the effectiveness of traditional mainstream classroom methods for students with severe disabilities who depend heavily on intensive teaching in a one-to-one situation. They suggested that advocates of inclusive curriculum were more concerned with structural arrangements such as small-group co-operative learning, and had given little attention to appropriate instructional techniques for these students in the regular classroom. Ware (1990) claimed that an objectives approach to curriculum for students with severe disabilities was too restrictive, and pointed to the difficulties of defining a set sequence in which any task is learned by all students. Despite the value of objectives in indicating a starting point for teaching, and in providing criteria for assessing progress, Ware considered that the emphasis on teaching to specific objectives could lead to a narrow view of curriculum. A task analysis approach could also result in undue emphasis on relatively trivial components and place a brake on progress in performance of the task until all its separate components are mastered.

Further, the curricular goals and needs of students with severe disabilities may differ from those of students with mild disabilities (Pugach and Warger, 1993). The proponents of inclusive education have maintained that the goals of education are the same for all students. In a climate in which the ultimate goal of education is viewed as the student becoming a 'responsible contributor' to society, this claim has to be questioned (Ware, 1989). According to Ware this goal implies that an individual is valued only for his or her part in the economic life of society. For many students with severe disability, neither economic productivity nor full independence as adults is a reasonable expectation except in a very limited way, and therefore they should not be considered as the goals of education. However, different goals or expectations should not exclude students from participation in either educational or community activities alongside their peers. Activities can be shared even though objectives may be different. For example, in one link school arrangement, special school students with severe disabilities attended a local secondary school to participate in a class in international cookery with mainstream students. Their objectives were not related to the mainstream curriculum in the sense of gaining expertise in complicated cookery, but were primarily addressed at encouraging conversation and social interaction with non-disabled peers in a co-operative group situation.

Thus the goals of education need to be considered realistically: independent living and open employment may be unrealistic for many students with severe disabilities, but satisfying occupation and the ability to perform at least some essential self-maintenance tasks independently, in so far as these enhance an individual's dignity and quality of life, are goals to strive for. The move to a broad and balanced curriculum for students with severe disabilities seems long overdue: an over-emphasis on development of independence may be at the expense of enjoyment of a wider range of experiences.

A further dispute concerns the content of curriculum for students with disabilities. Strong arguments have been made in favour of a curriculum that is truly functional, with the focus on skills that are likely to be needed in the student's daily life. Stieler (1994) maintained that curriculum should not be based on hypothetical sequences of normal development, but should focus instead on functional skills as they will be used in real life – taking into account the context in which the skills will be used. Generic skills may be less important than skills that are applied in a specific context. For example, Stieler suggested that for a student with a severe disability learning to count may be of less value than learning one-to-one correspondence, needed for example in setting a table for a given number of people. Telling the time may be less important than learning to function within time constraints.

The learning characteristics of students with severe disabilities mean that their instructional needs are different from those of their non-disabled peers. Albright, Brown, Vandeventer and Jorgensen (1989) identified differences in learning characteristics that also raise doubts about common curriculum goals and content. Students with severe disabilities will be slower at acquiring skills and therefore need more time for learning; in addition they will lack the conceptual ability to grasp many of the skills acquired by their non-disabled peers. Other skills that are not formally taught to non-disabled students but are acquired incidentally in the home and community will need to be specifically taught to students with severe disabilities. These include domestic, vocational and recreational skills which are critical to an integrated lifestyle – if they are not taught, then the student's potential for independent functioning and community participation will not be maximised and the goals of education will not be achieved. Since students with severe disabilities are more likely to forget skills if they do not have continual practice, there is a need to teach skills that will have frequent use.

Despite these limitations, acceptance of a functional curriculum has been questioned by those who advocate access to a common curriculum by all students. Certainly it is difficult to dispute the entitlement of every student to a 'broad and balanced' curriculum, as the Education Reform Act of 1988 required in Britain. The danger with a functional curriculum is that it will become just that, emphasising skills that are needed to function in the community rather than learning for its own sake or simply to satisfy natural curiosity. A focus on functional skills may also mean that too much time is spent teaching complex skills that are difficult to master and require disproportionate amounts of time at the expense of skills that might be more easily mastered and provide the learner with a greater sense of achievement.

Access to a common curriculum opens up opportunities for a far wider range of experiences for students with disabilities. It also allows more opportunities for interaction with non-disabled peers through the sharing of common learning experiences. At a policy level, Visser (1993) maintained that it was important for students with severe disabilities to remain in the National Curriculum – if not, they risked segregation from the education system altogether. However, curriculum needs to be made more flexible so that expectations are not dependent on age or grade level. Because students with severe disabilities need a greater amount of instructional time or practice trials to master a new skill or understand a concept, the number of skills that can be acquired in any given time will be only a fraction of those acquired by their non-disabled peers. Because fewer skills will be mastered, the skills taught need to be more stringently selected than for the majority of students. These considerations have been expressed in curriculum guidelines prepared for students with disabilities by the Directorate of School Education in Victoria (1995: 13):

> Organisational strategies need to address the questions of when, where, by whom and with whom the curriculum is to be delivered. For example the appropriateness of the environment for the student's learning, the amount of time necessary to teach an activity and how much time will require to be assigned for practice will need to be considered. Other factors such as the need for intensive teaching times to coincide with the times of the day when the student learns best and the maximising of the time spent in active student engagement also need to be considered.

Thus catering for the needs of a single student with a severe disability in a classroom of non-disabled students is not simply a question of resources. A major question is whether some or all students with disabilities have distinct curricular needs (Dessent, 1987). Moreover, for students with severe disabilities, the gap between their educational needs and those of the majority of students will increase as secondary level is reached to the extent that the academic curriculum followed by their non-disabled peers may have little to offer that is useful. At secondary level, opportunities for group teaching and social interaction are likely to be reduced, and for academic areas it becomes more feasible to group students with similar curricular needs. This does not necessarily mean a narrowing of the curriculum. In Victoria, curriculum is organised into eight key learning areas, and all students are required to participate in these areas (Directorate of School Education, Victoria, 1995). A flexible interpretation of content ensures that a wide range of functional skills may be included: for example, health and physical education includes hydrotherapy and physiotherapy, road safety, sex education and personal hygiene, as well as leisure activities such as camps and riding for the disabled. Mathematics may include skills with money and time. Work experience and legal rights may be included in studies of society and environment. English may include augmentative communication or receptive language skills. Similarly, other key areas include activities that are appropriate at all levels of ability.

The advantage of this framework is that it ensures that students with severe disabilities, along with their non-disabled peers, have access to a 'broad and comprehensive' curriculum that is relevant to their needs and capacities, rather than focusing on a narrow range of skills.

LEARNING ENVIRONMENT

A further issue concerns the school and classroom environment as it relates to approaches to learning. Advocating the comprehensive local school as the appropriate setting for all students, Sailor (1989) identified six minimal requirements for successful inclusion of students with severe disabilities. Firstly, the school should be age-appropriate. That is, if a student is of secondary school age, then he or she should attend a school for secondary students. Placement in a school or class at a younger age level simply because the work is easier, the student is smaller than average for the age group, or the school is more conveniently situated, does not constitute full integration. Secondly, the school should be close enough to the student's home that excessive time is not spent in travel, and, unless there are exceptional circumstances, transport can be shared with other students. Thirdly, if the school includes special classes that provide programmes for students with severe disabilities, these should be located centrally so that students have the opportunity to interact within the school building, rather than being in an isolated part of the school. Fourthly, deliberate procedures should be implemented to encourage interaction between students with disabilities and non-disabled students. Fifthly, the proportion of students in a school who have severe disabilities should be no greater than the proportion that occurs naturally in the wider community. Thus while about ten per cent of students might be expected to have special educational needs, no more than one per cent of students in any one school should have a severe disability. Opinions about ideal proportions of students with disabilities have differed, however (Jenkinson, 1993), with some educators recognising that the provision of adequate support staff may be economically feasible only if a school accepts a larger proportion of students with severe disabilities. Finally, Sailor (1989) indicated that the school should encourage inclusion of students with severe disabilities in all activities in which they are able to participate.

These conditions are designed to ensure maximum interaction between students with severe disabilities and their chronological age peers, at a level that should also occur in the wider community. However, the appropriateness of the regular classroom environment for optimal learning by students with severe disabilities has been questioned. For maximum learning to take place, both structured environments and structured curriculum are needed (Marozas and May, 1988). Lacey (1991) pointed out that the ideal classroom in the regular school is designed to encourage student independence in learning, with students able to retrieve their own resources from open shelves or cupboards and return them when they have finished. The range of individual differences within a regular class may require a large variety of curriculum materials to be accessible. Students with severe disabilities, however, may be unable to retrieve their own resources. More important, difficulty in focusing attention means that a limit is needed on the number of items they are working with at any one time. The stimulation provided in the regular classroom is likely to be distracting. Further, independent behaviour displayed by students with severe disabilities is often not helpful for learning, so that an organisational structure that is designed to encourage independence in the majority of students may be less appropriate for their needs.

Sailor (1989) also acknowledged that as students with severe disabilities move through the school system, there is a decreasing likelihood that their educational needs will be met in the classroom context, whether in a regular or special class. Because of the difficulties people with severe disabilities have in transfer and generalisation, skills need to be learned in the setting in which they will be used. This could be the student's home, the community or the work environment. For example, skills involved in dressing might best be taught in the locker room after physical education, after washing in the privacy of the individual's home, or when removing and putting on outer clothes when the student arrives or departs from school. Practice in motor skills or eye–hand co-ordination might be gained through the performance of relevant tasks such as putting coins in a slot machine to buy a drink, operating a washing machine, dialling a telephone, putting a card in a letter box, using a key to lock and unlock a door or opening a food can. Clearly not all of these skills can be taught in a classroom. Nor are they skills that are likely to be taught to the majority of students.

With most core curriculum taught within the confinement of a regular classroom or specialised area such as a school laboratory, it is difficult to reconcile the concept of inclusive schooling for students with severe disabilities with the need for teaching in a community context. For many students with severe disabilities fully inclusive schooling is not feasible. There are aspects of the core curriculum from which they cannot be expected to derive benefit, and there are other experiences that they need that are simply not available in the regular school, not only because they are not required by the majority of students, but because they take place in a specific environment other than the school. If we are honest about catering for individual differences, then we must accept that groups of students sometimes need to be segregated for some aspects of their education.

EDUCATION FOR COMMUNITY LIVING

Recent curriculum for students with severe disabilities has emphasised the acquisition of skills needed in the wider community. Numerous studies cited by Falvey (1989) provide instances of successful teaching of community skills, including use of public transport, crossing the road, making purchases and using a laundromat. However, setting up a community training programme requires considerable planning and effort, and raises concerns that are additional to the operation of regular school programmes. Among the concerns identified by Falvey (1989) were funding for community activities, including use of public transport, making purchases and using community facilities; staff resources to ensure that individual programmes are followed in the community; legal liability for any injury or property damage that may occur during community programmes; dealing with physical and attitudinal barriers to access to appropriate community environments; support from administrators, teachers and families; procedures for ensuring student safety; and student mobility. Falvey also stressed the importance of providing opportunities for interacting in context with individuals occupying a variety of roles in the community, such as sales people or transport workers.

Not all education can take place in the community. Students with

severe disabilities need intensive training and practice in some skills
that may not be available in some community settings. They also need
the opportunity to mix with non-disabled peers in their day-to-day
activities in the regular school. Henbury Avenue School is an example
of a school that meets these needs by providing a successful blend of
special curriculum, community experiences and access to the mainstream.

Situated in Darwin, in the Northern Territory of Australia,
Henbury Avenue School provides programmes for students with
moderate, severe and multiple disabilities aged from twelve to
eighteen years. Its students are drawn from the Darwin urban
area and outer suburbs, surrounding rural areas and Aboriginal
communities. Each student has an individual programme that is
developed in consultation with parents, senior staff, teachers and
therapists. The framework for each programme is provided by a
school-based curriculum that is divided into three major
domains. Skills such as communication and personal management are developed across all these domains.

A Daily Living Skills domain includes self-care and a range of
domestic and budgetary skills. To ensure that skills are mastered
in the context of home living, the school has acquired the use of a
house in a nearby street. This forms the base for a House
Programme. In the first part of the three-stage programme,
students learn a range of independent living skills in the real-life
environment provided by the house. This forms part of their
normal school programme. In the second stage, these experiences are extended and students gain experience in independent
living over two or three days and nights each term. In a third
stage, yet to be phased in, students in their final year at the
school will spend a full school week in independent living.

The House Programme has a number of other benefits besides
the opportunity to learn and experience independent living.
Most important, it provides an opportunity for students to
interact with peers with whom they share similar needs,
developing friendship and peer support groups in the informal
and relaxed setting of a home. The programme includes
shopping and a variety of social activities that are a part of
normal daily living. These activities also provide students with
opportunities to learn to make choices. Successful achievement
through the acquisition of skills that are within their capacity,

and which clearly have practical value, develops students' self-confidence.

The Vocational Domain provides a range of vocational experiences and training both within the school and in outside work. Within the school, the curriculum includes grounds maintenance, food preparation, screen printing and office skills. Work attitude skills are also introduced. Outside work experience begins at a nearby high school, where students work in the school canteen on food preparation and packing for half an hour each day. Older students gain experience in open employment situations where they are supported on a one-to-one basis by school staff. The school also recognises that for some students voluntary work is the most likely option when they leave school, and encourages this option for the value it places on the contribution made by the student.

The third domain in the curriculum is Recreation and Leisure, with a wide range of age-appropriate activities available. This domain allows students to develop skills in choice as they select their activities, as well as encouraging their integration into the community.

These areas focus on the special needs of students with severe disabilities for preparation for community living, emphasising learning through experience in a real-life context. A further important element of the programme involves two secondary schools with which Henbury Avenue School has established an integration programme. Students attend classes in each of these schools either on their own or in pairs, with the support of a staff member from Henbury Avenue School. They participate in classes such as art, drama, health and fitness, recreational studies, sewing, science, automotive studies and developing employment potential. In some cases they follow the same objectives as the mainstream students; in others objectives may be modified to allow work at a different level, or alternative objectives may be set. Each of the secondary schools has also allocated a classroom for use by students from Henbury Avenue School, which provides them with a base and allows them to experience the environment of the larger mainstream school even though they may not attend classes within the school.

TEACHING STUDENTS WITH SEVERE DISABILITIES

Teaching is generally believed to be a stressful occupation, but for teachers of students with severe disabilities stress is exacerbated by additional demands, combined with outcomes that may be less valued by society than the outcomes of regular education (Tilstone, 1991). Teacher aides are equally vulnerable to the stresses created by working with students who have severe disabilities. Tilstone suggested a number of specific factors that contribute to stress, particularly for teachers who lack training or experience in teaching students with severe disabilities.

The challenging behaviour that is often displayed by students with severe disabilities is usually outside the range of experience of the regular class teacher. Tilstone (1991) pointed out that teachers who are not aware that behaviour problems are relatively common in people with severe disabilities, and are unsure or do not have the necessary techniques to handle the problems, will lack confidence, feel inadequate and become anxious about the occurrence of the behaviour. Tilstone suggested that schools should develop a policy for dealing with challenging behaviour and provide teachers with appropriate techniques through in-service training. However, although problem behaviour is undoubtedly an important concern, studies have suggested that seriously disruptive behaviour is generally not a major problem in integrated settings – possibly because students with severe behaviour problems are not usually enrolled in the regular class, or because they learn to model the behaviour of the majority of students in the class.

A second concern is the teacher's relationships with colleagues and other professionals, especially where ultimate responsibility for a student's programme has not been defined (Tilstone, 1991). Conflict can arise, for example through disagreement about the extent to which core curriculum can be adapted, or the necessity to teach core curriculum. Specialist teachers who have worked hard to develop individual programmes for students with severe disabilities may feel that their skills are threatened by a need to follow core curriculum. Regular class teachers may feel threatened by the more expert knowledge of both special education teachers and parents. Where community- or home-based training is being implemented, teachers may have to yield their instructional responsibilities to staff of community organisations or to families.

The additional work load of teaching students with severe disabilities, not only in the individual attention required for the student to learn, but also in the administrative tasks required to co-ordinate services and curriculum, and possible conflicts between different aspects of the job, can add to teacher stress.

Compounding the difficulties that teachers face in defining and assuming new professional roles are the health needs of many students with severe disabilities. Coping with health problems that may impinge either directly or indirectly on a student's educational programme requires collaboration between educational and health professionals at a level that has not occurred in the past (Wolraich, 1986). Health authorities may have only a limited understanding of the goals of educational programmes for students with severe disabilities, and may fail to recognise the contribution that teachers can make in assisting in the management of health problems. In turn, teachers may have a limited understanding of therapy programmes and their role in facilitating and maintaining a student's access to an educational programme. The Alberta Education Response Centre (1990) also referred to the possible legal implications of staff without an appropriate medical background providing health care. Teachers or teacher aides carrying out therapy exercises in the classroom or giving medication may need to seek clarification of this issue.

Tilstone (1991) suggested that reduced morale may be a problem for teachers working over a long period of time with students who have severe disabilities, and nominated two years as an optimal period. The limited response from students and generally poor motivation to learn mean that for many students achievement may be minimal despite teacher efforts. Teachers may have to learn to come to terms with failure with children who learn very little or even regress. However, studies have suggested that perception of change in students with severe disabilities may depend on the qualifications and experience of the teacher. York et al. (1992) found that special educators were more likely than regular class teachers to identify positive changes in students with severe disabilities integrated into regular classes. Training in observational skills and an understanding of the importance of even minute changes in behaviour are clearly impor-tant. In addition, regular class teachers are likely to use a different frame of reference in judging behavioural change in students with disabilities (York et al. 1992), comparing rate of learning with that of non-disabled students rather than other students with severe disabilities.

Other factors that may affect teacher well-being but are less frequently mentioned include the significant physical demands if students have physical disabilities and require frequent lifting and positioning (Tilstone, 1991). Tilstone also pointed out that regular class teachers are often inadequately prepared for the emotional demands created by the death of a student with a severe disability – death of a student is rare in a mainstream school, but is more likely to occur with integration of students with severe disabilities who often have reduced life expectancy.

Tilstone may have over-estimated the extent to which these factors create stress in teachers. Numerous studies suggest that much stress is dispelled after teachers have become accustomed to students with severe disabilities, and provided that they have the support of other staff in the school, particularly the principal. Grbich and Sykes (1992), for example, found that the major concerns of educators involved in integration of students with severe disabilities centred on curriculum modification, the need for specialist support, lack of evidence of student progress, timetabling, lack of time and lack of resources.

However, where it does exist, low morale is likely to be compounded by the fact that education of students with disabilities is currently receiving less attention than it has over the past two decades. Recognition of the contribution made by teachers of students with severe disabilities is not commensurate with the amount of specialist training they need to perform their job adequately.

CONCLUSION

Although significant progress has been made in the education of students with severe disabilities over the past twenty years, there are still many issues to be resolved. Warnock in 1978 did not foresee the inclusion of students with severe disabilities into regular schools, assuming that the programmes required for these students, involving therapy and health care as well as educational goals, could be implemented only in special settings. As Hegarty (1993) pointed out, neither is the case for integration self-evident nor does it have universal support. This is particularly true for students with severe and multiple disabilities, the majority of whom continue to be catered for in special programmes either in segregated classes or schools.

There are undoubtedly benefits to be gained both from integration and from a broadening of the curriculum for students with disabilities, but a policy of full inclusion is not compatible with needs for specific learning approaches and community-based experiences, especially at secondary level. The most successful programmes require extensive resources and planning that ensure a blend of functional skills, community experience and access to a range of curriculum opportunities with non-disabled peers in which the student with a severe disability may have some useful participation. There are other long-term issues to be resolved: Warnock (1978) pointed out that students with severe disabilities may continue to learn useful skills well beyond the minimum school leaving age, and indicated a need for continuing education, especially in social and vocational training, into the early twenties. The possibility of an extended school year also needs to be considered to ensure that skills do not decline over long school breaks through lack of practice (Rapport and Thomas, 1993; Stieler, 1994). Any extension to the school year must be considered in relation to students' normal needs for recreation and leisure.

The future of education for students with disabilities may well change as technology continues to play an increasingly important part in providing students with alternative forms of communication and with access to a wider range of experiences. Computer-assisted learning, with students working individually or in small groups at their own pace, has offered a way of differentiating instruction to meet individual needs in the regular classroom, but may have less value for students with severe disabilities who need to learn skills in the context in which they will be performed. The potential for use of computer programs to perform many of the cognitive functions involved in problem solving and decision making which students with severe disabilities find difficult to perform is an issue for the future (Holmeister and Friedman, 1986), and offers a further unknown element in their future education.

Part IV

Conclusion

Chapter 12

Trends and practices
The future of special education

There is much to be learned from the many changes that have taken place in special education. But to what extent can we generalise policy, practice and the findings of research from one country to another? There are many differences between countries in history, size, population, culture, systems of government and legislative procedures that influence education. In this chapter, I will explore some of these differences as they relate to special education and then look at some of the common trends in special education that have occurred over the past two decades.

AN INTERNATIONAL PERSPECTIVE

Many of the changes that have occurred in the education of students with disabilities reflect the exchange of new ideas about policy and practice in special education, both within and between countries. The proliferation of publications in special education has ensured that ideas have spread internationally, especially among English-speaking countries, often with little consideration of the context in which they have been developed. There has been much uncritical adoption of models of provision, often with little modification to accommodate cultural differences. Even within developed countries, many local differences occur in educational practices and policies, in legislative provisions and in definitions and prevalence of disability.

Educational policies and practice in Australia have depended heavily on overseas influences, especially from the United States and the United Kingdom. Although Australia is not unique in this respect – Canada, for example, draws heavily on the United States – a major difference between Australia and the United States is that educational policies and practice in the United States are rarely, if at all, influenced by other cultures (Safran, 1989). Indeed, there are a number of factors that have influenced special education in the United States that seem to have had far less of an influence in other countries.

Australia, unlike the United States, does not have legislation guaranteeing civil rights, including the right to public education. Anti-discrimination legislation guarantees the rights of people with disabilities to equal access to services, but has not had the impact on special education that rights legislation has had in the United States. The Canadian Charter of Rights and Freedoms appears to have had little influence on special education practice in that country. Nor do Australia or Canada have federal legislation guaranteeing special education. Identification and placement procedures are not formalised in legislation in many countries and in Australia at least are more dependent on professional judgment than in the United States (Safran, 1989). While this has helped Australia to avoid the excessive costs and pressures associated with legal action, it has not avoided the inequities in policy, practice and resources that exist throughout the country, not only between states, but within states as well. In the absence of central legislation for special education, policy and practice may vary widely within a country, especially in countries in which greater autonomy is being given to local districts and even to schools in policy implementation. In Australia, the federal system of government has made it very difficult to gain an overall picture of special education. School education is a state matter, and while governments at both state and federal levels have declared a commitment to integration, and the federal government has allocated funding to support special education (de Lemos, 1994), there are wide differences in the way in which integration is interpreted and implemented. These differences occur in criteria for determining eligibility to receive special education, and in alternative forms of provision. Canada, too, has no federal legislation governing special education as the United States has. Each province or territory has its own legislation and related regulations for education, and there are differences between provinces in definitions and approaches to service delivery in special education (Winzer, 1994).

In the United Kingdom, where Local Educational Authorities have responsibility for implementation of legislation, there have also been wide differences in interpretation and practice. For example, Norwich (1994b) noted differences in the proportions of students being served in special schools in different areas. These differences may well lessen as each school implements the Code of Practice (Department for Further Education, 1994), developed in the United Kingdom to define the duties and responsibilities of schools and authorities towards students with special educational needs.

The United Kingdom, however, is now a part of the European Community, and there may be important ideological differences between member countries that impinge on special education (O'Hanlon, 1993). Differences in traditions, culture and social structure are reflected in variations in years of compulsory schooling, legislative and policy-making practices, procedures for identifying disability, proportions of students identified as having special needs, and approaches to special education ranging from segregated category-based schools to a more general concept of special educational need. Italy, for example, and more recently Spain, have abolished special schools altogether, ensuring that all students with disabilities are integrated into regular classes.

Another problem in interpreting research and other literature from the United States has been the disproportionate numbers of minority group students in special education. Studies in the United States of students with mild disabilities include students whose real problems may arise from cultural differences. Many of the risk factors for placement in special classes apply especially to minority groups (Chinn and Selma, 1987): for example, negative attitudes, low expectations, inappropriate classroom practices including monocultural textbooks and curricula, and a narrow range of instructional techniques. Ford (1992) claimed that many teachers in special education lack the appropriate knowledge, attitudes and skills to provide a truly multi-cultural education. Under these circumstances, problems that are at least partly due to cultural differences are not likely to be redressed by special class placement. It was within this context, prompted by the Civil Rights movement, that special classes were judged to be of little benefit to students with disabilities in the United States.

Like the United States, Australia is a multi-cultural country, but, although grappling with issues of past injustices to its Aboriginal population, has not experienced the same degree of racial protest that has characterised the United States. No statistics are available in Australia on ethnic minority representation in special education, although the United States provides a timely warning for all multi-cultural countries of the risk factors linking special education with minority groups. New Zealand, however, has a disproportionate number of minority group students in special education. In Australia, generic issues of equity and social justice, rather than specific issues relating to minority groups, were prominent in the thrust towards integration of students with disabilities. Furthermore, disability advocacy groups tend to be less vocal in Australia than in the United States in promoting any one viewpoint. There is, for example, no equivalent of The Association for Persons with Severe Handicaps pushing for full inclusion of students with severe disabilities. Advocacy groups are active but tend to be more concerned with day-to-day issues such as the provision of funding and resources than with rigid enforcement of ideology.

Underlying philosophical differences are likely to have subtle, but important, consequences for special education provision. In the United Kingdom, changes in special education in the 1981 Education Act were seen as part of a broader policy move away from a selective system of education towards a comprehensive system in which all students, regardless of ability, received their education together (Croll and Moses, 1994). Further important distinctions between the United Kingdom and the United States were reflected in the fact that the Warnock (1978) Committee was made up of experts in education and disability, whereas organised interest groups and legislative bodies were most involved in policy development in the United States (Croll and Moses, 1994). Although neither the Warnock Committee nor United States legislation provided for the elimination of segregated education altogether, there were differences in the conceptual frameworks underlying recommended provisions in the two countries. Warnock, by identifying three levels of integration – locational, social and functional – was concerned with maximum possible participation of all students with disabilities with their non-disabled peers. The continuum of provision embodied in United States legislation, although variously interpreted (see Chapter 2), was based on an assumption that each of its levels necessarily represented increasing participation in mainstream education. In practice the continuum did not guarantee that any provision other than full-time or part-time integration into the regular class would ensure interaction with non-disabled students. Although there is no way of determining the practical outcomes of this distinction, the success of link school schemes in the United Kingdom is one indication of the influence of Warnock's focus on integration.

COMMON TRENDS

Despite apparent differences between countries, and between education systems and organisations within countries, it is possible to
discern common trends that characterise special education in most
developed countries. Many of these trends reflect a wider move
towards normalisation of services for people with disabilities: as Croll
and Moses (1994: 283) also suggested, they reflect a 'shift away from a
purely humanitarian concern for handicapped children to an emphasis
on the rights of all children in education'. These trends include an
increase in the number of students receiving special education in some
form, widespread acceptance of integration in principle, but also
resistance that has in some cases led to the abandonment of plans to
phase out segregated provision, greater involvement of parents in
decisions that affect students with disabilities, and a general realisation that integration cannot work effectively without adequate and
equitable funding of resources for all students who have special needs.

Increase in students served by special education

Paradoxically, and in spite of differences both between and within
countries in proportions of students identified as having special
educational needs, the move to inclusive schooling has been accompanied by an overall increase in the number of students seeking
support for special needs. In many countries the number has increased
significantly and in greater proportion than general population
increases. According to Fuchs and Fuchs (1994), between 1976–77,
when the Education for All Handicapped Children Act in the United
States was replaced by the Individuals with Disabilities Education
Act, and 1989–90 there was an increase of 23 per cent in the number of
students with disabilities receiving special services.

The increase is at least partly due to the extension of special
education policies to embrace a larger proportion of the student
population, including students in regular classes who for various
reasons had special educational needs not associated with a specific
disability. Education systems which minimised segregation often did
not keep statistical records of students with special needs who
remained in the regular class, particularly if additional funding was
tied to placement in a special school or class. An increased awareness of
disability and the availability of funding and resources has encouraged
submissions for support from these students who hitherto would not

have been considered for enrolment in special education. A view that learning problems are the fault of the school for not providing appropriate programmes for students with disabilities, rather than of any problems inherent in the student, is also likely to lead to greater demand for services.

The result is that a significant proportion of the increased numbers receiving special needs support can be accounted for by students receiving support in regular classes, either full-time or part-time, without a corresponding decrease in the numbers being served in special schools. In Victoria, for example, the number of students receiving support in integrated settings increased tenfold between 1984 and 1992, with only a minor reduction in numbers enrolled in special schools (Auditor-General, Victoria, 1992). Some of this increase was explained by inclusion in more recent figures of students supported in the regular class by the visiting teacher service (Cullen and Brown, 1992). But the elimination of categories of disability as a basis of funding also meant that students with learning problems but without an identified disability could apply for assistance.

The consequences of this situation in the New Zealand context were described by Wilton (1994). Although the special class in a regular school has been the major provision for students with a mild intellectual disability in New Zealand, Wilton estimated that in 1988 fewer than 25 per cent of eligible students were actually in special classes, the remainder being placed in regular classes. A number of policy proposals imply significant changes in this situation. These proposals include the replacement of special classes by individualised programmes in regular classes and replacement of an IQ-determined definition of mild intellectual disability by curriculum-based assessment and observation. These changes could mean a large increase in the number of students seeking special support, not only from the 75 per cent of students with a mild intellectual disability who had remained in regular classes, but also from students with specific learning disabilities. Since many special classes had also functioned as resource rooms, the proposed changes would mean not only a significant reduction in the resources available to any one student, but an end to resource room support. Elimination of categories of disability cannot be blamed entirely for the increase in numbers of students receiving support. The United States has continued to maintain a category-based system at least for administrative purposes to determine those qualifying for special services. Categories include learning disability, serious emotional disturbance, mental retardation (intellectual disability), speech and language disorders, visual impairment, hearing impairment, physical disability and other health impairments. The IDEA Act of 1989–90 added categories of traumatic brain injury and autism (Hallenbeck and Kauffman, 1994), and there is continuing controversy over the inclusion of attention deficit (hyperactivity) disorder.

Efforts to reduce the proportion of ethnic minority students classified as having an intellectual disability by lowering the IQ cut-off did not reduce either the numbers of minority group students or the overall numbers receiving special education in the United States. One outcome of the change was a larger number of students classified as having a learning disability. Inclusion of learning disability as a category of disability significantly inflates the proportion of students considered to have special educational needs. In the United States, its inclusion is claimed by Safran (1989) to be associated with a recognition by parents and professionals of the legal advantages of a defined category of disability in securing funding.

The overall increase in numbers receiving special education in a number of countries is also partly explained by education systems accepting responsibility for education of students with severe disabilities who had previously been the responsibility of health authorities. Increased survival rates of infants with severe disability may also contribute to an increase in the number of students served in special settings.

Integration – universally accepted?

The second common trend to be noted is, of course, the wide acceptance, at least in principle, of inclusion of students with disabilities into regular education. Acceptance of this principle has been accompanied by moves to replace categories of disability with a greater emphasis on educational need as a basis for support, a focus on adapting the school environment to cater for a wide range of exceptionality, greater involvement of parents in decision making about educational settings and programmes, rationalisation of resources and related funding mechanisms, and the scaling down, although not phasing out altogether, of segregated provision. These trends, however, are by no means universal, and integration has also met with opposition from a number of sources.

It would be true to say that integration was introduced into many educational systems without a full realisation that the changes proposed in special education would also require changes in the mainstream. Indeed, the mainstream was often ill-prepared for the introduction of students with disabilities. Some schools accepted integration in principle provided it did not mean substantial changes to either organisational structures or to curriculum. Resources were obtained and adaptations made to the physical environment where necessary, but in general these entailed minimal disruption to the life of the school. The employment of teacher aides minimised the responsibility of the class teacher. In the worst situations, the teacher aide was often the major person with whom the student interacted. As long as the student was receiving adequate care, had some kind of educational programme and did not place an undue burden on resources or disrupt the smooth working of the class, students with disabilities were accepted in a school. In Victoria, as a result of union pressure, mainstream teachers could refuse to accept a student with a disability in their class. Often the condition for acceptance of a student with a disability was the employment of a teacher aide, thus relieving the teacher of the responsibility of caring aspects, if not instructional programmes, for students with disabilities. Since the primary aim of integration was often perceived as socialisation rather than academic learning, instructional responsibility was not given high priority.

Other schools rejected the concept of integration altogether, seeing their school as providing a programme to encourage academic excellence, a goal that would be made more difficult to achieve by inclusion of students who for various reasons did not meet the standards set by other students in the school. Some schools may have seen themselves as absolved of responsibility for integration by the existence of nearby schools that made a point of accommodating the needs of all students, including those with disabilities.

Yet other schools wholeheartedly embraced a policy of inclusion, seeing benefits to all students in the acceptance of a wide range of individual differences in their school. It would be unrealistic to suggest that they have not encountered problems along the way. It is also difficult to attribute the success of many of these changes to anything other than commitment and strong leadership of individuals who are able to convince others of the benefits of inclusive schooling.

It would also be true to say that special education was equally unprepared for the changes brought about by integration. Many special schools and classes saw their existence threatened and resisted moves to support relocation of their students in the mainstream. Some special education teachers also resisted redeployment in mainstream schools. In fairness, their concerns were not only for their own survival, but for the survival of expertise, programmes and support structures that had worked well for students with disabilities in segregated settings, but were not easily translated into regular schools. Some special schools maintained programmes and services with little change for students they saw as incapable of benefiting from education in the mainstream. Others acknowledged the benefits their students could derive from social contacts with their non-disabled peers and supported link activities or partial integration for non-academic activities. Still others have accommodated a radical change in their role, actively encouraging inclusive schooling and providing an outreach service supporting regular class teachers in a variety of ways.

In this context, special schools and classes have continued to remain viable even in educational systems which have abandoned categories of disability. Further, statistics from a number of sources suggest an inflow of students from regular schools to special schools. For example, in the United Kingdom, Norwich (1994b) identified a small overall increase in the proportion of students in special schools. Not all of the increases can be explained by enrolment of students with severe disabilities. In the United States, McLeskey and Pacchiano (1994) claimed that between 1979 and 1989 there was an increase of more than 4 per cent of students with learning disabilities spending various amounts of time in special classes, and a corresponding drop in the numbers placed full-time in regular classes. There is also evidence that some students move from the mainstream to special schools as they reach secondary level and require alternatives to mainstream curriculum, or to restore self-esteem after negative experiences in the regular school (Jenkinson, 1995). The introduction of vocational preparation classes and transition programmes has also contributed to a higher retention rate in special schools, adding further to the student population.

Where integration might once have been seen as inevitably resulting in the demise of special schools and classes, there seems to have been a swing back to retaining a range of options for the provision of special education. For example, in Victoria proposals to phase out special schools have now been abandoned, although Cullen and Brown (1992) recognised that special schools must establish stronger links with the mainstream and must become more accountable than they have been in the past for the effectiveness of their programmes. In Canada there has been a substantial move of students with disabilities into the public school system, where the most common model of service delivery is the combination of resource room and regular class (Winzer, 1994). The future viability of special schools and classes may lie as much in the provision of an outreach service to students integrated into the mainstream as it does in maintaining a base for students with more severe disabilities who continue to require a curriculum that is more closely tied to their individual needs.

Parent involvement

Virtually without exception developed countries that have embraced inclusive schooling have given greater recognition to the role of parents in the education of students with disabilities, at least in principle. Professional judgment regarding the most appropriate educational environment for a student is now widely seen as only one part of what should be a collaborative decision-making process. In giving a greater say to parents, many education authorities assumed, wrongly, that parents would unanimously endorse integration. Many parents felt more secure with special schools and were not confident that resources would be reallocated adequately to support their children in the mainstream.

In practice, education authorities continue to have a strong influence on placement decisions (OECD, 1994). There are still a number of reasons why parents might feel compelled to defer to professional judgment. One of these is lack of information about options, or information that is biased by the informant having a vested interest in preserving a particular form of education or having a limited perspective on disability. Cullen and Brown (1992) recognised this problem and proposed that procedures be set up to ensure that parents receive information about options that is unbiased towards either regular or special school. Options also need to be presented in terms that are familiar to the parent, rather than in legal terms. Parents' lack of familiarity with procedures and options in special education could also influence the perceptions that professionals hold of them and indirectly limit their roles in decision making (Strickland, 1982). Parents often perceive professionals as having greater expertise, or lack assertiveness in the face of professional advice. Conversely, professionals may perceive parents as being uninterested or unwilling to be involved in decisions about placement.

Resources and funding

A further trend is a general recognition that integration of students with disabilities into regular schools cannot proceed without adequate resources. Tempting though it may be to governments seeking economies in their education budgets to close special schools and relocate special education students into regular classes, the level of resources needed and the associated costs to support a student with a disability do not seem to vary much on average between settings. However, there seems to be no ideal way for funding special education. Indeed, where special education had been funded largely through resources provided outside the regular classroom, early integration programmes often proceeded without much consideration of resource needs, or how additional funding could be provided to support students who receive much of their education within the regular class. Inadequate accountability procedures have subsequently been revealed to result in considerable inequities in the allocation of funding. For example, in Victoria, where resource funding became closely identified with the provision of integration aides, some regions attempted to spread available funding thinly to all who needed additional support, resulting in inadequate support for many students (Auditor-General, Victoria, 1992). Others funded only those with the most intense needs for support, or on a 'first come first served' basis, leaving some students without any support.

In the United Kingdom, the Audit Commission (1992) found that individual statements often described resource needs in vague terms. Local education authorities tended to retain control over funds, providing their own support staff, so that accountability procedures from schools to local authorities were not always in place. Thus there was no way of ensuring effective use of resources in relation to student progress.

There have been several attempts to redress problems of inequity and inefficient use of funds. The Alberta Education Response Centre (1990) set out some useful principles against which funding methods should be evaluated. These included effective use of public resources, ease of administration, sensitivity to variations in the number of students with disabilities and the need for flexibility of programmes at a local level. Procedures should avoid unnecessary labelling of students, instead reflecting their functional needs and abilities. Finally, funding methods should be comparable to other systems of educational funding allocation.

In line with these principles, in 1984 individual category-based grants were replaced with block grants based on the number of students overall residing in each school jurisdiction (Alberta Education Response Centre, 1990). The aim was to allow school boards flexibility in providing for special needs, rather than to encourage segregation as the only way to obtain a grant. The block grant assumed a similar proportion of students with disabilities in each area. Subsequently an equity grant was introduced to provide additional support to areas in which the proportion of students with severe disabilities exceeded the average, but without designating funds for specific students or programmes.

In the United Kingdom, the Audit Commission (1992) recommended introduction of formula funding with the aim of reducing the flow of students into special schools. Special school budgets would be based on the predicted number of places needed, rather than on the actual number of places. The local education authority would remain responsible for ensuring that all students with statements received the resources specified in their statement.

In Victoria, new funding procedures recommended by Pickering (1993) have helped to address the inequitable distribution of resources, while at the same time ensuring that parents can choose either a special school or a regular school programme without losing entitlement to resources. Funding is a two-stage process. In the first stage, students are assessed by conventional methods for eligibility to receive support. In the second stage, specific resource needs are identified, and the student is placed in one of four bands of funding on the basis of those needs. The funding is then allocated to the school in which the student enrols. This may be a regular school or a special school. Each student with a disability has a Programme Support Group which consists of teaching and administrative staff involved in the student's programme, as well as the parents and, if appropriate, students themselves. This group decides on an appropriate educational programme for the student and the allocation of funding to purchase needed resources. These resources may include an integration aide, special equipment or a therapy programme, for example, and funding may also contribute to the salary of an integration teacher. These procedures are school-based, but a centralised check on eligibility and needs assessment procedures is designed to ensure accountability.

The future of funding for special education is perhaps its greatest concern. While commending increased school autonomy in financial management, Wedell (1993) expressed a concern that schools experiencing difficulties in achieving a balanced budget may choose not to enrol students with disabilities whose needs place an additional strain on budgeting. The other side of the coin is a concern that has been expressed in the Victorian context that the allocation of funding directly to schools to support students with disabilities may lead some schools to enrol students with disabilities in order to gain extra funds, rather than out of commitment to inclusive education. Accountability procedures need to ensure that money allocated to support an individual student is used for the benefit of that student. However, it is clear that some economies can be achieved through the sharing of resources when a school enrols a number of students with disabilities.

Further, the funding of students at different levels according to the intensity of their needs may mean a higher proportion of students identified as having more severe needs (Lovitt, 1993). On the other hand, if funding based on either category or individual service is replaced by a blanket allocation to a school or district to meet special educational needs, those with the most intense needs may suffer. We need to work through these problems to devise safeguards against misuse of limited funds, while ensuring that needs are met as economically and effectively as possible.

THE FUTURE

Of equal concern may be the operational climate into which education generally is moving. Hampson (1991) referred to such concepts as accountability, cost effectiveness, relevance and the full utilisation of resources as reflecting an industrial model in which education is viewed as a business rather than as a service. According to Hampson, these concepts are tangible concerns that have little to do with either educational theory or the ways in which students learn. In an industrial model, governments will invest funding only where returns are most likely. The kinds of returns most highly valued by governments are likely to be measurable achievements such as entry to tertiary education or employability. The returns on special education are less readily apparent, and are more likely to be in terms of avoiding long-term problems rather than the achievement of society's most valued outcomes. Hampson's concerns have been echoed by Wedell (1993), who suggested that the provision of services to students with special needs could not be operated on market economy principles. In particular, the purchase of services by schools could be subject to budgetary constraints, and there would be no guarantee that the most effective services would be the most economic.

These comments perhaps reflect a broader malaise in special education. In the words of Hallenbeck and Kauffman (1994: 408):

> The present context of educational reform is one in which special education is struggling with its identity and viability in a public education system obsessed with international economic competition, yet apparently dedicated to the education of all children.

Kauffman (1993) proposed that there are three critical tasks for special education. Firstly, he suggested that it is necessary to keep the issue of location of education in perspective. Kauffman pointed out that different settings vary in their expectations and in what occurs in those settings. We know little about how a student's placement might affect possibilities for instruction and its outcomes, although, as Kauffman pointed out, there is no evidence that setting is the key to improvement of educational outcomes. Kauffman also pointed to an absence of evidence that low social status and isolation of students with disabilities are the direct result of being taught outside the regular classroom.

As Lovitt (1993) suggested, we have given too much energy to trying to compare one form of delivery with another. We need more flexible models of delivery which allow education to take place outside the school setting, and others besides teachers to take part in some elements of instruction. In particular, there will need to be some resolution to the problems associated with the education of students with severe and multiple disabilities, for whom medical and health needs may override educational needs, and for whom access to a core curriculum in the mainstream may have little benefit. In terms of numbers, this is a relatively small proportion of the population of students with disabilities, but their support needs are disproportionate to their overall numbers.

Norwich (1990) has predicted that the future is likely to see fewer special schools providing for students with disabilities. The majority of students with special needs – those with moderate learning difficulties or sensory and motor problems – can eventually be provided for in a regular school either in resource rooms or in the regular class with specialist support. Those with severe and multiple disabilities and behavioural and emotional difficulties are more likely to remain in special schools or units, but according to Norwich there is no reason why these cannot be based in regular schools to encourage closer links between students with disabilities and their non-disabled peers. Attitudinal issues will continue to need attention, and more effort needs to be given to initiating extra-curricular programmes that ensure positive and productive interactions.

Other problems remain to be addressed. These include issues of identification for special needs support. More recently, inclusive schooling has implied a continuum of need, with no cut-off point – that is, support is provided to any student who needs it. This is an important issue. In the past we have tended to focus on students with more clearly identified disabilities and the means of providing them with support, to the neglect of those students struggling in the mainstream without any obvious reason, or for reasons that are social and cultural. Inclusive schooling is supposed to remedy this problem, but in times of economic constraint and requirements for account-ability criteria for receiving additional support may need to be more stringently applied. We have not yet devised a satisfactory alternative to psychometric assessment. Undoubtedly tests have their faults, and inaccuracies in assessment may result as much in under-identification as they do in over-identification. For example, according to Lovitt (1993) 15 per cent of students who are assessed in New York City are not subsequently identified as having a disability. Unfortunately, this does not address the issue of why they were referred for assessment in the first place. Winzer (1994: 380) expressed this problem succinctly in the Canadian context:

There is not yet a quantitative measure of how great a handicap must be for special services to be offered, nor is there yet established an absolute number or combination of characteristics that must be identified before a pupil is diagnosed as exceptional.

Another persistent issue is the need to address outcomes of special education generally, not just for integration. Many special school programmes have hitherto not been subject to critical appraisal. The industrial model may have some benefits if only to focus on critical evaluation and ensure that limited funds are not spent on programmes that have little value. Special education has been particularly vulnerable to fads and fashions in education. Much effort has been wasted in programmes that subsequently have been shown to have no scientifically demonstrable value. Special education needs to be justified in terms of its benefits not only to individuals but to education generally. We also need to decide on outcome criteria for students with disabilities, which cannot always be the same as for the majority of students. The current emphasis is on standardised achievement measures, and ultimate entry to tertiary or technical and further education. These outcomes are not appropriate expectations for all students. Lovitt (1993) suggested alternative approaches to assessing outcomes for students with disabilities. These include curriculum-based measures directly related to activities that have actually been taught, evaluation in terms of individual programme objectives, a portfolio approach which includes student work samples and dynamic assessment which examines the student's learning in the assessment context. We also need to maintain a flexible approach to curriculum.

We have yet to see the full impact of changes in special education on the mainstream. The inclusive schools movement has been inextricably tied to better provision for individual differences at all levels in the regular classroom. To equate these two aspects is to overlook the very real needs of many students which may be better catered for outside the classroom – for example in the community. It is a further injustice to make provision for the many students with specific learning needs, who do not at present receive any formal support, contingent on integration of students with the most intense needs. At present, provision for students with disabilities does not seem to be a major concern in education generally. We also need to avoid confusing fanaticism for new movements, programmes or techniques with genuine enthusiasm for progress in the education of students with disabilities, and seek methods of research that will provide useful answers to questions about the outcomes of special education.

The future of special education needs to be considered in a rational context free of emotive pressures or hidden agenda, and in the context of the purpose of education generally. Yet although many problems have still to be overcome, the achievements of special education over the past twenty years are enormous and should not be underestimated. The debate has moved away from arguments about setting to a rapprochement between special and regular education. A more balanced approach is emerging that recognises the need for flexibility and choices. Attention is turning to effective use of resources to support students with special needs in either regular or special settings. Debate about appropriate curriculum and instructional methods is a healthy sign that more thought is being given to the content of special education. New models of provision are being developed to ensure that students with disabilities can participate in regular education activities and interact with their age peers while also learning many of the functional skills that they will need as adults in the community. In the long term, this more balanced view can only be for the benefit of all students.

References

AGAR, L., BELL, G.H., CARR, N., CORDINER, E., HALL, C. and HUFFORD, D. (1989). 'Studying the curriculum', in BELL, G.H. and COLBECK, B. (eds), *Experiencing Integration: The Sunnyside Action Inquiry Project*, London: Falmer, pp. 21–52.

AINSCOW, M. (1991). 'Effective schools for all: An alternative approach to special needs in education', *Cambridge Journal of Education*, 21, 293–303.

ALBERTA EDUCATION RESPONSE CENTRE (1990). *Special Education Review: A Discussion Paper*, Edmonton, AB: Author.

ALBERTA EDUCATION RESPONSE CENTRE (1992). *Integrated Services Review: Yellowhead School Division No. 12*, Edmonton, AB: Author.

ALBRIGHT, K.Z., BROWN, L., VANDEVENTER, P. and JORGENSEN, J. (1989). 'Characteristics of educational programs for students with severe intellectual disabilities', in BIKLEN, D., FERGUSON, D. and FORD, A. (eds), *Schooling and Disability: Eighty-eighth Yearbook of the National Society for the Study of Education*, Chicago, IL: National Society for the Study of Education, pp. 59–76.

ANDERSON, E. (1973). *The Disabled Schoolchild*, London: Methuen.

ARTILES, A.J. and TRENT, S.C. (1994). 'Overrepresentation of minority students in special education: A continuing debate', *Journal of Special Education*, 27, 410–437.

AUDIT COMMISSION (UK) (1992). *Getting in on the Act. Provision for Pupils with Special Educational Needs: The National Picture*, London: HMSO.

AUDITOR-GENERAL, VICTORIA (1992). *Special Report No. 17: Integrated Education for Children with Disabilities*, Melbourne: Government Printer.

BALSHAW, M. (1991). *Help in the Classroom*, London: Fulton.

BARTON, L. and TOMLINSON, S. (1984). *Special Education and Social Interests*, London: Croom Helm.

BELL, G.H. and COLBECK, B. (eds) (1989). *Experiencing Integration: The Sunnyside Action Inquiry Project*, London: Falmer.

BIKLEN, D.P. (1989). 'Redefining schools', in BIKLEN, D., FERGUSON, D. and FORD, A. (eds), *Schooling and Disability: Eighty-eighth Yearbook of the National Society for the Study of Education*, Chicago, IL: National Society for the Study of Education, pp. 1–24.

BILLINGSLEY, F.F. and KELLEY, B. (1994). 'An examination of the acceptability of instructional practices for students with severe disabilities', *Journal of the Association for Persons with Severe Handicaps*, 19, 75–83.

BLACK-BRANCH, J.L. (1993). 'The nexus between policy and practice regarding special needs students: The experiences and opinions of Canadian school administrators', *British Columbia Journal of Special Education*, 17, 148–156.

BLACKHURST, A.E., BOTT, D.A. and CROSS, D.P. (1987). 'Noncategorical special education personnel preparation', in WANG, M.C., REYNOLDS, M.C. and WALBERG, H.J. (eds), *Handbook of Special Education: Research and Practice*, Vol. 1, New York: Pergamon, pp. 313–329.

BLESS, G. and AMREIN, C. (1992). 'The integration of pupils with learning difficulties: The results of research into the effects of integration', *European Journal of Special Needs Education*, 7, 11–19.

BOVAIR, K. (1993). 'A role for the special school', in VISSER, J. and UPTON, G. (eds), *Special Education in Britain after Warnock*, London: Fulton, pp. 110–125.

BRADY, M.P., McDOUGALL, D. and DENNIS, H.F. (1989). 'The schools, the courts, and the integration of students with severe handicaps', *Journal of Special Education*, 23, 43–58.

BUNCH, G. (1994). 'An interpretation of full inclusion', *American Annals of the Deaf*, 139, 150–152.

CARLBERG, C. and KAVALE, K. (1980). 'The efficacy of special versus regular class placement for exceptional children: A meta-analysis', *Journal of Special Education*, 14, 295–309.

CARPENTER, B., FATHERS, J., LEWIS, A. and PRIVETT, R. (1988). 'Integration: The Coleshill experience', *British Journal of Special Education*, 15, 119–121.

CASEY, W., JONES, D., KUGLER, B. and WATKINS, B. (1988). 'Integration of Down's syndrome children in the primary school: A longitudinal study of cognitive development and academic attainments', *British Journal of Educational Psychology*, 58, 279–296.

CENTER, Y. and CURRY, C. (1993). 'A feasibility study of a full integration model developed for a group of students classified as mildly intellectually disabled', *International Journal of Disability, Development, and Education*, 40, 217–235.

CENTER, Y. and WARD, J. (1989). 'Attitudes of school psychologists towards the integration (mainstreaming) of children with disabilities', *International Journal of Disability, Development, and Education*, 36, 117–131.

CENTER, Y., WARD, J., PARMENTER, T. and NASH, R. (1985). 'Principals' attitudes towards the integration of disabled children into regular schools', *The Exceptional Child*, 32, 149–161.

CHINN, P.C. and SELMA, H. (1987). 'Representation of minority students in special education classes', *Remedial and Special Education*, 8, 41–46.

CLAYTON, T. (1989). 'The role of welfare assistants in supporting children with special educational needs in ordinary primary schools', in EVANS, R. (ed.), *Special Educational Needs: Policy and Practice*, Oxford: Blackwell Education, pp. 103–108.

COLE, P. and CHAN, L. (1990). *Methods and Strategies for Special Education*, Sydney: Prentice-Hall.

COLE, T. (1989). *Apart or a Part? Integration and the Growth of British Special Education*, Milton Keynes: Open University Press.

COLLINS, M.K. (Chairman) (1984). *Integration in Victoria. Report of the Ministerial Review of Educational Services for the Disabled*, Melbourne: Department of Education.

COPE, C. and ANDERSON, E. (1977). *Special Units in Ordinary Schools*, London: University of London Institute of Education.

CROLL, P. and MOSES, D. (1994). 'Policy-making and special educational needs: A framework for analysis', *European Journal of Special Needs Education*, 9, 275–286.

CULLEN, R.B. and BROWN, N.F. (1992). *Integration and Special Education in Victorian Schools: A Program Effectiveness Review*, Melbourne: Department of School Education.

DALE, D.M.C. (1984). *Individualised Integration: Studies of Deaf and Partially-Hearing Students in Ordinary Schools and Colleges*, London: Hodder and Stoughton.

DANBY, J. and CULLEN, C. (1988). 'Integration and mainstreaming: A review of the efficacy of mainstreaming and integration for mentally handicapped pupils', *Educational Psychology*, 8, 177–195.

DE LEMOS, M.M. (1994). *Schooling for Students with Disabilities*, Canberra: AGPS.

DENO, E. (1970). 'Special education as developmental capital', *Exceptional Children*, 37, 229–237.

DEPARTMENT FOR FURTHER EDUCATION (UK) (1994). *Code of Practice on the Identification and Assessment of Special Educational Needs*, London: Central Office of Information.

DEPARTMENT OF SCHOOL EDUCATION, NEW SOUTH WALES (1993). *Special Education Policy*, Sydney: Author.

DESAI, I. (in press). 'Primary school principals' attitudes toward mainstreaming in Victoria, Australia', *International Journal of Disability, Development, and Education*.

DESSENT, T. (1987). *Making the Ordinary School Special*, London: Falmer.

DIAMOND, S.C. (1995). 'Special education and the great god, inclusion', in KAUFFMAN, J.M. and HALLAHAN, D.P. (eds), *The Illusion of Full Inclusion*, Austin, TX: Pro-Ed, pp. 247–254.

DIRECTORATE OF SCHOOL EDUCATION, VICTORIA (1991). *Integration: Teacher Policy and Guidelines*, Melbourne: Author.

DIRECTORATE OF SCHOOL EDUCATION, VICTORIA (1995). *Guidelines for Implementing the Curriculum and Standards Framework for Students with Disabilities and Impairments*, Melbourne: Author.

DUNN, L.M. (1968). 'Special education for the mildly retarded – is much of it justifiable?', *Exceptional Children*, 35, 5–22.

EDGAR, E. and POLLOWAY, E.A. (1994). 'Education for adolescents with disabilities: Curriculum and placement issues', *Journal of Special Education*, 27, 438–452.

EDUCATION DEPARTMENT, TASMANIA (1983). *Integration of Special Children into Ordinary Schools*, Hobart, Tas: Author.

ELKINS, J. (1994). 'The school context', in ASHMAN, A.F. and ELKINS, J. (eds), *Educating Children with Special Needs*, 2nd ed., Sydney: Prentice-Hall, pp. 71–103.

EURIDICE UNIT (1993). *Information Dossiers on the Structures of the Education Systems in the European Community 1993: The Netherlands*, Netherlands: Ministry of Education and Science.

EVANS, I.M. and WELD, E.M. (1989). 'Evaluating special education programs: Process and outcome', in BIKLEN, D., FERGUSON, D. and FORD, A. (eds), *Schooling and Disability: Eighty-eighth Yearbook of the National Society for the Study of Education*, Part II, Chicago, IL: University of Chicago Press, pp. 232–255.

FALVEY, M.A. (1989). *Community-based Curriculum: Instructional Strategies for Students with Severe Handicaps*, Baltimore, MD: Brookes.

FENRICK, N.J. and PETERSEN, T.K. (1984). 'Developing positive changes in attitudes towards moderately/severely handicapped students through a peer tutoring program', *Education and Training of the Mentally Retarded*, 19, 83–90.

FISH, J. (1984). 'The future of the special school', in BOWERS, T. (ed.), *Management and the Special School*, London: Croom Helm, pp. 6–20.

FISH, J. (1989). *What is Special Education?*, Milton Keynes: Open University Press.

FLETCHER-CAMPBELL, F. (1992). 'How can we use an extra pair of hands?', *British Journal of Special Education*, 19, 141–143.

FLETCHER-CAMPBELL, F. with HALL, C. (1993). *LEA Support for Special Educational Needs*, Slough: National Foundation for Educational Research.

FORD, B.A. (1992). 'Representation of minority students in special education classes for students with mild mental retardation', *Exceptional Children*, 59, 107–114.

FOSTER, S. (1989). 'Reflections of a group of deaf adults on their experiences in mainstream and residential school programs in the United States', *Disability, Handicap and Society*, 4, 37–56.

FREDERICKSON, N. and WOOLFSON, H. (1987). 'Integration: The social dimension', *Educational Psychology in Practice*, 3, 42–48.

FREEZE, D.R. and RAMPAUL, W. (1991). 'Consultative-collaborative resource teaching as a means of improving special education service delivery', in UPTON, G. (ed.), *Staff Training and Special Educational Needs*, London: Fulton.

FUCHS, D. and FUCHS, L.S. (1994). 'Inclusive schools movement and the radicalisation of special education reform', *Exceptional Children*, 60, 294–309.

GALLAGHER, J.J. (1995). 'The pull of societal forces on special education', in KAUFFMAN, J.M. and HALLAHAN, D.P. (eds), *The Illusion of Full Inclusion*, Austin, TX: Pro-Ed, pp. 91–103.

GAMBLE, B. and PALMER, J. (1989). 'The adjustment class as an integrating part of the main school', in BELL, G.H. and COLBECK, B. (eds), *Experiencing Integration: The Sunnyside Action Inquiry Project*, London: Falmer, pp. 127–149.

GASH, H. (1993). 'A constructivist attempt to change attitudes towards children with special needs', *European Journal of Special Needs Education*, 8, 106–125.

GENT, P.J. and MULHAUSER, M.B. (1988). 'Public education of students with handicaps: Where it's been, where it's going, and how it's getting there', *Journal of the Association for Persons with Severe Handicaps*, 13, 188–196.

GIANGRECO, M.F., DENNIS, R., CLONINGER, C., EDELMAN, S. and SCHATTMAN, R. (1993). ' "I've counted Jon": Transformational experiences of teachers educating students with disabilities', *Exceptional Children*, 59, 359–372.

GIANGRECO, M.F. and MEYER, L.H. (1988). 'Expanding service delivery options in regular schools and classrooms for students with severe disabilities', in GRADEN, J.L., ZINS, J.E. and CURTIS, M.J. (eds), *Alternative Educational Delivery Systems: Enhancing Instructional Options for all Students*, Washington, DC: National Association of School Psychologists, pp. 241–267.

GOACHER, B., EVANS, J., WELTON, J. and WEDELL, K. (1988). *Policy and Provision for Special Educational Needs: Implementing the 1981 Education Act*, London: Cassell.

GOTTLIEB, J. (1981). 'Mainstreaming: Fulfilling the promise?', *American Journal of Mental Deficiency*, 86, 115–126.

GRBICH, S. and SYKES, S. (1992). 'Access to curricula in three school settings for students with severe intellectual disability', *Australian Journal of Education*, 36, 318–328.

GRESHAM, F.M. (1982). 'Misguided mainstreaming: The case for social skills training with handicapped children', *Exceptional Children*, 48, 422–433.

HALLAHAN, D.P. and KAUFFMAN, J.M. (1994). 'Toward a culture of disability in the aftermath of Deno and Dunn', *Journal of Special Education*, 27, 496–508.

HALLAHAN, D.P. and KAUFFMAN, J.M. (1995). 'From mainstreaming to collaborative consultation', in KAUFFMAN, J.M. and HALLAHAN, D.P. (eds), *The Illusion of Full Inclusion*, Austin, TX: Pro-Ed, pp. 5–17.

HALLAHAN, D., KELLER, C., McKINNEY, J., LLOYD, J. and BRYAN, T. (1988). 'Examining the research base of the regular education initiative: Efficacy studies and the adaptive learning environments model', *Journal of Learning Disabilities*, 21, 29–35.

HALLENBECK, B.A. and KAUFFMAN, J.M. (1994). 'United States', in MAZUREK, K. and WINZER, M. (eds), *Comparative Studies in Special Education*, Washington, DC: Gallaudet University Press.

HAMPSON, E. (1991). 'A not-so-modest proposal: The fate of special education', *British Columbia Journal of Special Education*, 15, 127–136.

HARKER, B. and HILL, L. (1988). 'Self-esteem building: Integration of Townsville special school students at Townsville High School', in ASHMAN, A.F. (ed.), *Integration 25 Years On* (Exceptional Child Monograph No. 1), St Lucia, Qld: Schonell Special Education Research Centre, pp. 103–107.

HART, S. (1992). 'Evaluating support teaching', in BOOTH, T., SWANN, W., MASTERTON, M. and POTTS, P. (eds), *Learning for All: Curricula for Diversity in Education*, London: Routledge, pp. 105–113.

HARVEY, D.H.P. (1989). 'Integration in Victoria: Teachers' attitudes after six years of a no-choice policy', *International Journal of Disability, Development, and Education*, 39, 33–45.

HASAZI, S.B., JOHNSTON, A.P., LIGGETT, A.M. and SCHATTMAN, R.A. (1994). 'A qualitative policy study of the least restrictive environment provision of the Individuals with Disabilities Education Act', *Exceptional Children*, 60, 491–507.

HASS, J. (1994). 'Role determinants of teachers of the visually impaired', *British Columbia Journal of Special Education*, 18, 140–148.

HAYES, A. and GUNN, P. (1988). 'Success in mainstreaming: How judged?', in ASHMAN, A.F. (ed.), *Integration 25 Years On* (Exceptional Child Monograph No. 1), St Lucia, Qld: Schonell Special Education Research Centre, pp. 63–67.

HEGARTY, S. (1988). 'Supporting the ordinary school', *British Journal of Special Education*, 15, 50–53.

HEGARTY, S. (1991). 'Toward an agenda for research in special education', *European Journal of Special Needs Education*, 6, 87–99.

HEGARTY, S. (1993). *Meeting Special Needs in Ordinary Schools: An Overview*, 2nd ed., London: Cassell.

HEGARTY, S. and POCKLINGTON, K. (1981). *Educating Pupils with Special Needs in the Ordinary School*, Windsor: NFER-Nelson.

HENDERSON, R.A. (1988). 'Integration: Similarities and differences – Australia and the United States', in ASHMAN, A.F. (ed.), *Integration 25 Years On* (Exceptional Child Monograph No. 1), St Lucia, Qld: Schonell Special Education Research Centre, pp. 29–40.

HERR, S.S. (1993). 'Special education as a human and legal right', in MITTLER, P.,

BROUILLETTE, R. and HARRIS, D. (eds), *Special Needs Education: World Yearbook of Education*, London: Kogan Page, pp. 38–50.

HODGSON, A., CLUNIES-ROSS, L. and HEGARTY, S. (1984). *Learning Together: Teaching Pupils with Special Educational Needs in the Ordinary School*, Windsor: NFER-Nelson.

HOLBORN, P. and McPHIE, J. (1994). *Perspectives on Inclusion: An Exploration of the Focus Group Process*, Richmond, BC: Richmond School District and Richmond Teachers' Association.

HOLMEISTER, R.A.M. and FRIEDMAN, S.G. (1986). 'The application of technology to the education of persons with severe handicaps', in HORNER, R.H., MEYER, L.H. and FREDERICKS, H.D.B. (eds), *Education of Learners with Severe Handicaps: Exemplary Service Strategies*, Baltimore, MD: Brookes.

HOWARTH, S.B. (1987). *Effective Integration: Physically Handicapped Children in Primary Schools*, Windsor: NFER-Nelson.

INNES, J.J. (1994). 'Full inclusion and the deaf student: A deaf consumer's view of the issue', *American Annals of the Deaf*, *139*, 152–156.

IRESON, J. (1992). 'Collaboration in support systems', *British Journal of Special Education*, *19*, 56–58.

JENKINS, J.R., PIOUS, C.G. and JEWELL, M. (1990). 'Special education and the regular education initiative: Basic assumptions', *Exceptional Children*, *56*, 479–491.

JENKINSON, J.C. (1982). *The Integration of Trainable Mentally Retarded Children into the Normal Classroom*, Burwood, Vic: Victoria College Press.

JENKINSON, J.C. (1983). 'Correlates of sociometric status among TMR children in regular classrooms', *American Journal of Mental Deficiency*, 88, 332–335.

JENKINSON, J.C. (1987). *School and Disability: Research and Practice in Integration*, Hawthorn, Vic: Australian Council for Educational Research.

JENKINSON, J.C. (1993). 'Integration of students with severe and multiple learning difficulties', *European Journal of Special Needs Education*, 8, 320–335.

JENKINSON, J. C. (1995). *Parent Choice in the Education of Students with Disabilities*, Paper presented at 19th National Conference of Australian Association of Special Education, Darwin, NT.

JOHNSON, D.W. and JOHNSON, R.T. (1986). 'Impact of classroom organisation and instructional methods on the effectiveness of mainstreaming', in MEISEL, C.J. (ed.), *Mainstreaming Handicapped Children: Outcomes, Controversies, and New Directions*, Hillsdale, NJ: Erlbaum, pp. 219–250.

JOHNSON, G.O. (1975). 'The education of mentally retarded children', in CRUICKSHANK, W.M. and JOHNSON, G.O. (eds), *Education of Exceptional Children and Youth*, 3rd ed., Englewood Cliffs, NJ: Prentice-Hall.

KAUFFMAN, J.M. (1993). 'How we might achieve the radical reform of special education', *Exceptional Children*, 60, 6–16.

KAUFFMAN, J.M. (1995). 'The Regular Education Initiative as Reagan–Bush education policy: A trickle-down theory of education of the hard-to-teach', in KAUFFMAN, J.M. and HALLAHAN, D.P. (eds), *The Illusion of Full Inclusion*, Austin, TX: Pro-Ed, pp. 125–155.

KAUFFMAN, J.M. and HALLAHAN, D.P. (eds) (1995). *The Illusion of Full Inclusion*, Austin, TX: Pro-Ed.

KAUFMAN, M., AGARD, J. and SEMMEL, M. (1978). *Mainstreaming: Learners and their Environment*, Baltimore, MD: University Park Press.

KNOX, M. and PARMENTER, T.R. (1990). 'Transition from school to adult life:

Views of school leavers with disabilities', *International Journal of Disability, Development, and Education*, 37, 45–55.

KUBICEK, F.C. (1994). 'Special education reform in light of select state and federal court decisions', *Journal of Special Education*, 28, 27–42.

KYLE, C. and DAVIES, D. (1991). 'Attitudes of mainstreamed pupils towards mental retardation: Pilot study at a Leeds secondary school', *British Journal of Special Education*, 18, 103–106.

KYLE, J.G. (1993). 'Integration for deaf children', *European Journal of Special Needs Education*, 8, 201–220.

LACEY, P. (1991). 'Managing the classroom environment', in TILSTONE, C. (ed.), *Teaching Pupils with Severe Disabilities*, London: Fulton.

LALKHEN, Y. and NORWICH, B. (1990). 'The self-concept and self-esteem of adolescents with physical impairments in integrated and special school settings', *European Journal of Special Needs Education*, 5, 1–12.

LEE, B. (1991). *Extending Opportunities: Modern Foreign Languages for Pupils with Special Educational Needs*, Slough: National Foundation for Educational Research.

LEINHARDT, G. and PALLAY, A. (1982). 'Restrictive educational settings: Exile or haven?', *Review of Educational Research*, 52, 557–578.

LEWIS, A. (1995). *Children Understanding Disability*, London: Routledge.

LEYSER, Y., KAPPERMAN, G. and KELLER, R. (1994). 'Teacher attitudes towards mainstreaming: A cross-cultural study in six nations', *European Journal of Special Needs Education*, 9, 1–15.

LIEBERMAN, L.M. (1992). 'Preserving special education . . . for those who need it', in STAINBACK, W. and STAINBACK, S. (eds), *Controversial Issues Confronting Special Education*, Boston, MA: Allyn and Bacon, pp. 13–25.

LIEBERT, D., LUTSKY, L. and GOTTLIEB, A. (1990). 'Post-secondary experiences of young adults with severe physical disabilities', *Exceptional Children*, 57, 56–63.

LIPSKY, D.K. and GARTNER, A. (eds) (1989). *Beyond Separate Education: Quality Education For All*, Baltimore, MD: Brookes.

LIPSKY, D.K. and GARTNER, A. (1992). 'Achieving full inclusion: Placing the student at the centre of educational reform', in STAINBACK, W. and STAIN-BACK, S. (eds), *Controversial Issues Confronting Special Education*, Boston, MA: Allyn and Bacon, pp. 3–12.

LOVITT, T.C. (1993). 'Recurring issues in special education', in GOODLAD, J.I. and LOVITT, T.C. (eds), *Integrating General and Special Education*, New York: Merrill.

LYNAS, W. (1986). *Integrating the Handicapped into Ordinary Schools: A Study of Hearing-Impaired Pupils*, London: Croom Helm.

McDONNELL, J. (1987). 'The integration of students with severe handicaps into regular public schools: An analysis of parents' perceptions of potential outcomes', *Education and Training in Mental Retardation*, 22, 98–111.

McGAW, B., PIPER, K., BANKS, D. and EVANS, B. (1992). *Making Schools More Effective: Report of the Australian Effective Schools Project*, Hawthorn, Vic: Australian Council for Educational Research.

McLESKEY, J. and PACCHIANO, D. (1994). 'Mainstreaming students with learning disabilities: Are we making progress?', *Exceptional Children*, 60, 508–517.

MACMILLAN, D.I. and HENDRICK, I.G. (1993). 'Evolution and legacies', in GOODLAD, J.I. and LOVITT, T.C. (eds), *Integrating General and Special Education*, New York: Merrill, pp. 23–48.

MALE, M. (1994). *Technology for Inclusion: Meeting the Special Needs of all Students*, Boston, MA: Allyn and Bacon.

MALOUF, D.B. and SCHILLER, E.P. (1995). 'Practice and research in special education', *Exceptional Children*, 61, 414–424.

MANN, L. and KENOWITZ, L.A. (1985). 'Towards an actuarial data base for special education interventions', *Studies in Educational Evaluation*, 11, 5–11.

MAROZAS, D.S. and MAY, D.C. (1988). *Issues and Practices in Special Education*, New York: Longman.

MARSTON, D. (1988). 'The effectiveness of special education: A time series analysis of reading performance in regular and special education settings', *Journal of Special Education*, 21, 13–26.

MINISTRY OF EDUCATION, VICTORIA (1986). *Curriculum Guidelines*, Melbourne: Author.

MINISTRY OF EDUCATION, WESTERN AUSTRALIA (1993). *Report of the Ministerial Task Force on the Education of Students with Disabilities and Specific Learning Difficulties*, Perth, WA: Author.

MITHAUG, D.E., HORIUCHI, C.N. and FANNING, P.N. (1985). 'A report on the Colorado statewide follow-up survey of special education students', *Exceptional Children*, 51, 397–404.

MITTLER, P. (1992). 'International visions of excellence for children with disabilities', *International Journal of Disability, Development, and Education*, 39, 115–126.

MITTLER, P. (1993). *Teacher Education for Special Educational Needs*, Stafford: National Association for Special Educational Needs.

MITTLER, P. (1995). *Education for All or for Some: An International Perspective*, Keynote Address, 19th National Conference of Australian Association of Special Education, Darwin, NT.

MITTLER, P. (n.d.). *Towards a Society for All for Persons with an Intellectual Impairment*, University of Manchester unpublished manuscript.

MITTLER, P. and FARRELL, P. (1987). 'Can children with severe learning difficulty be educated in ordinary schools?', *European Journal of Special Needs Education*, 2, 221–236.

MONTGOMERY, J.K. (1987). 'Mainstreaming orthopedically handicapped students in a regular public school', in BERRES, M.S. and KNOBLOCK, P. (eds), *Program Models for Mainstreaming*, Rockville, MD: Aspen, pp. 169–189.

MOSTERT, M.P. (1991). 'The regular education initiative: Strategy for denial of handicap and the perpetuation of difference', *Disability, Handicap and Society*, 6, 91–101.

NORWICH, B. (1990). *Reappraising Special Needs Education*, London: Cassell.

NORWICH, B. (1994a). 'The relationship between attitudes to the integration of children with special needs and wider socio-political views: A US–English comparison', *European Journal of Special Needs Education*, 9, 91–106.

NORWICH, B. (1994b). *Segregation and Inclusion: English LEA Statistics 1988–92*, Bristol: Centre for Studies on Inclusive Education.

O'HANLON, C. (1993). *Special Education Integration in Europe*, London: Fulton.

OLSEN, K. (1994). 'Have we made progress in fifteen years of evaluating the effectiveness of special education programs?', *Special Services in the Schools*, 9, 21–37.

ORGANISATION FOR ECONOMIC CO-OPERATION AND DEVELOPMENT

(1994). *The Integration of Disabled Children into Mainstream Education: Ambitions, Theories and Practices*, Paris: Author.

O'SHEA, L.J., O'SHEA, D.J. and ALGOZZINE, B. (1989). 'The regular education initiative in the U.S.: What is its relevance to the integration movement in Australia?', *International Journal of Disability, Development, and Education*, 36, 5–14.

PICKERING, D. (Chair) (1993). *Cullen Brown Implementation Advisory Committee Report*, Melbourne: Directorate of School Education.

PICKERING, D. and DICKENS, E. (1991). *Special Schools: Students, Parents, Teachers*, Burwood, Vic: Victoria College Press.

POLLOWAY, E.A. and SMITH, J.D. (1988). 'Current status of the mild mental retardation construct: Identification, placement and programs', in WANG, M.C., REYNOLDS, M.C. and WALBERG, H.J. (eds), *Handbook of Special Education: Research and Practice*, Vol. II, New York: Pergamon, pp. 7–22.

PUGACH, M.C. and WARGER, C.L. (1993). 'Curriculum considerations', in GOODLAD, J.I. and LOVITT, T.C. (eds), *Integrating General and Special Education*, New York: Merrill, pp. 125–148.

PUTNAM, J.W. (1993). *Cooperative Learning and Strategies for Inclusion: Celebrating Diversity in the Classroom*, Baltimore, MD: Brookes.

RAPPORT, M.J.K. and THOMAS, S.B. (1993). 'Extended school year: Legal issues and implications', *Journal of the Association for Persons with Severe Handicaps*, 18, 16–27.

REID, D.L., ROBINSON, S.J. and BUNSEN, T.D. (1995). 'Empiricism and beyond: Expanding the boundaries of special education', *Remedial and Special Education*, 16, 131–141.

REYNOLDS, M.C., WANG, M.C. and WALBERG, H.J. (1987). 'The necessary restructuring of special and regular education', *Exceptional Children*, 53, 391–398.

RICHMOND, R.C. and SMITH, C.J. (1990). 'Support for special needs: The class teacher's perspective', *Oxford Review of Education*, 16, 295–310.

ROBERTS, C. and ZUBRICK, S. (1992). 'Factors influencing the social status of children with mild academic disabilities in regular classrooms', *Exceptional Children*, 59, 192–202.

RUEBAIN, D. (1987). 'The development of an integration scheme: A governor's view', in BOOTH, T. and SWANN, W. (eds), *Including Pupils with Disabilities: Curricula for All*, Milton Keynes: Open University Press, pp. 195–200.

SAFRAN, S.P. (1989). 'Special education in Australia and the United States: A cross-cultural analysis', *Journal of Special Education*, 23, 330–341.

SAILOR, W. (1989). 'The educational, social, and vocational integration of students with the most severe disabilities', in LIPSKY, D.K. and GARTNER, A. (eds), *Beyond Separate Education: Quality Education For All*, Baltimore, MD: Brookes, pp. 53–74.

SCHECHTMAN., Z., REITER, S. and SCHANIN, M. (1993). 'Intrinsic motivation of teachers and the challenge of mainstreaming: An empirical investigation', *Special Services in the Schools*, 7, 107–124.

SCHINDELE, R.A. (1985). 'Research methodology in special education: A framework approach to special problems and solutions', in HEGARTY, S. and EVANS, P. (eds), *Research and Evaluation Methods in Special Education*, Windsor: NFER-Nelson, pp. 3–24.

SEMMEL, M.I., ABERNATHY, T., BUTERA, G. and LESAR, S. (1991). 'Teacher perceptions of special education reform: An empirical study of the Regular Education Initiative', *Exceptional Children*, 58, 9–24.

SEMMEL, M.I., GERBER, M.M. and MACMILLAN, D.L. (1995). 'A legacy of policy analysis research in special education', in KAUFFMAN, J.M. and HALLAHAN, D.P. (eds), *The Illusion of Full Inclusion*, Austin, TX: Pro-Ed, pp. 39–57.

SEMMEL, M.I., GOTTLIEB, J. and ROBINSON, N.M. (1979). 'Mainstreaming: Perspectives on educating handicapped children in the public school', in BERLINER, D.C. (ed.), *Review of Research in Education*, Vol. 7, Washington, DC: American Educational Research Association, pp. 223–279.

SHELDON, D. (1991). ' "How was it for you?" Pupils', parents' and teachers' perspectives', *British Journal of Special Education*, 87, 107–110.

SIMPSON, R.G. (1992). 'Quantitative research as the method of choice within a continuum model', in STAINBACK, W. and STAINBACK, S. (eds), *Controversial Issues Confronting Special Education*, Boston, MA: Allyn and Bacon, pp. 235–242.

SITLINGTON, P.L., FRANK, A.R. and CARSON, R. (1992). 'Adult adjustment among high school graduates with mild disabilities', *Exceptional Children*, 59, 221–233.

SLOPER, P., CUNNINGHAM, C., TURNER, S. and KNUSSEN, C. (1990). 'Factors relating to the academic attainment of children with Down's syndrome', *British Journal of Educational Psychology*, 60, 284–298.

SMITH, M.L. and NOBLE, A.J. (1993). 'Toward a comprehensive program of evaluation', in GOODLAD, J.I. and LOVITT, T.C. (eds), *Integrating General and Special Education*, New York: Merrill, pp. 149–170.

SNELL, M.E. and DRAKE, G.P. Jr (1994). 'Replacing cascades with supported education', *Journal of Special Education*, 27, 393–409.

STAINBACK, W. and STAINBACK, S. (1989). 'Practical organisational strategies', in STAINBACK, S., STAINBACK, W. and FOREST, M. (eds), *Educating all Students in the Mainstream of Education*, Baltimore, MD: Brookes.

STAINBACK, W. and STAINBACK, S. (1990). *Support Networks for Inclusive Schooling: Interdependent Integrated Education*, Baltimore, MD: Brookes, pp. 71–87.

STAUB, D. and HUNT, P. (1993). 'The effects of social interaction training on high school peer tutors of schoolmates with severe disabilities', *Exceptional Children*, 60, 41–57.

STIELER, S. (1994). 'Children with physical disabilities', in ASHMAN, A.F. and ELKINS, J. (eds), *Educating Children with Special Needs*, 2nd ed., Sydney: Prentice-Hall.

STOBART, G. (1986). 'Is integrating the handicapped psychologically defensible?', *Bulletin of the British Psychological Society*, 39, 1–3.

STOREY, K. (1993). 'A proposal for assessing integration', *Education and Training in Mental Retardation*, 28, 279–287.

STRAIN, P.S. and KERR, M.M. (1981). *Mainstreaming of Children in Schools: Research and Programmatic Issues*, New York: Academic Press.

STRICKLAND, B. (1982). 'Parental participation, school accountability, and due process', *Exceptional Education Quarterly*, 3, 41–49.

SWANN, W. (1987). ' "Firm links should be established." A case study in conflict and policy-making for integration', in BOOTH, T. and SWANN, W. (eds), *Including Pupils with Disabilities: Curricula for All*, Milton Keynes: Open University Press, pp. 201–217.

SYKES, S. (1989). 'Integration in Victorian schools: A review of policy and progress

(1984–1989)', *International Journal of Disability, Development and Education*, 36, 85–106.

THE ASSOCIATION FOR PERSONS WITH SEVERE HANDICAPS (TASH) (1993). *Resolution on Inclusive Education*. (Reprinted in KAUFFMAN, J.M. and HALLAHAN D.P. (eds) (1995), *The Illusion of Full Inclusion*, Austin, TX: Pro-Ed, pp. 314–316.)

THOMAS, D. (1985). 'The determinants of teachers' attitudes to integrating the intellectually handicapped', *British Journal of Educational Psychology*, 55, 251–263.

THOMASON, J. (1987). 'Educating students with severe handicapping conditions "side-by-side"', in BERRES, M.S. and KNOBLOCK, P. (eds), *Program Models for Mainstreaming*, Rockville, MD: Aspen, pp. 105–123.

TILSTONE, C. (1991). 'The class teacher and stress', in TILSTONE, C. (ed.), *Teaching Pupils with Severe Learning Difficulties*, London: Fulton, pp. 130–142.

TINDAL. G. (1985). 'Investigating the effectiveness of special education: An analysis of methodology', *Journal of Learning Disabilities*, 18, 101–112.

TRICKEY, G. and STOBART, G. (1987). 'Integration: A needlessly cosmetic revolution?', *Educational Psychology in Practice*, 3, 33–37.

VISSER, J. (1993). 'A broad, balanced, relevant and differentiated curriculum', in VISSER, J. and UPTON, G. (eds), *Special Education in Britain after Warnock.*, London: Fulton, pp. 10–12.

WADE, B. and MOORE, M. (1992). *Patterns of Educational Integration*, Wallingford, OX: Triangle Books.

WANG, M.C. and BAKER, E.T. (1985–86). 'Mainstreaming programs: Design features and effects', *Journal of Special Education*, 19, 503–521.

WARD, J. and CENTER, Y. (1990). 'The integration of children with intellectual disability into regular schools: Results from a naturalistic study', in FRASER, W.I. (ed.), *Key Issues in Mental Retardation Research*, London: Routledge, pp. 354–365.

WARE, J. (1989). 'The Fish Report and pupils with learning difficulties', in JONES, N. (ed.), *Special Educational Needs Review*, Vol. 2, London: Falmer, pp. 115–126.

WARE, J. (1990). 'The National Curriculum for pupils with learning difficulties', in DANIELS, H. and WARE, J. (eds), *Special Educational Needs and the National Curriculum: The Impact of the Educational Reform Act*, London: Kogan Page–University of London, pp. 11–18.

WARE, J., SHARMAN, M., O'CONNOR, S. and ANDERSON, M. (1992). 'Interactions between pupils with severe learning difficulties and their mainstream peers', *British Journal of Special Education*, 19, 153–158.

WARNOCK, H.M. (1978). *Report of the Committee of Enquiry into the Education of Handicapped Children and Young People*, London: HMSO.

WATTS, B.H., ELKINS, J., HENRY, M.B., APELT, W.C., ATKINSON, J.K. and COCHRANE, K.J. (1978). *The Education of Mildly Intellectually Handicapped Children in the Eastern States of Australia*, Canberra: AGPS.

WATTS, T. (1987). *The Wisdom of Solomon: A Review of Integration between Belvoir Special Developmental School and Wodonga West High School*, Melbourne: Department of Education.

WEDELL, K. (1990). 'Overview: The 1988 Act and current principles of special educational needs', in DANIELS, H. and WARE, J. (eds), *Special Educational Needs and the National Curriculum: The Impact of the Educational Reform Act*, London: Kogan Page–University of London, pp. 1–10.

WEDELL, K. (1993). 'Special needs education: The next 25 years', *National Commission on Education: Briefing No. 14*, May.

WEISEL, A. (1988). 'Contact with mainstreamed disabled children and attitudes towards disability: A multi-dimensional analysis', *Educational Psychology, 8,* 161–168.

WHITE, R. (1984). 'Paraprofessionals in special education', *Social Policy, 44–47.*

WILTON, K. (1994). 'Special education policy for learners with mild intellectual disability in New Zealand: Problems and issues', *International Journal of Disability, Development, and Education, 41,* 143–158.

WINZER, M. (1994). 'Canada', in MAZUREK, K. and WINZER, M. (eds), *Comparative Studies in Special Education,* Washington, DC: Gallaudet University Press, pp. 370–378.

WOLFENSBERGER, W. (1972). *Normalisation,* Toronto: National Institute on Mental Retardation.

WOLRAICH, M.L. (1986). 'The consequences for health professionals in mainstreaming handicapped children', in MEISEL, C.J. (ed.), *Mainstreaming Handicapped Children: Outcomes, Controversies, and New Directions,* Hillsdale, NJ: Erlbaum, pp. 149–164.

YORK, J., VANDERCOOK, T., MACDONALD, C., HEISE-NEFF, C. and CAUGHEY, E. (1992). 'Feedback about integrating middle school students with severe disabilities in general education classes', *Exceptional Children, 58,* 244–258.

YSSELDYKE, J.E. and THURLOW, M.L. (1994). 'What results should be measured to decide whether instruction is working for students with disabilities?', *Special Services in the Schools, 9,* 39–94.

ZABEL, R.H. (1987). 'Preparation of teachers for behaviourally disordered students: A review of the literature', in WANG, M.C., REYNOLDS, M.C. and WALBERG, H.J. (eds), *Handbook of Special Education: Research and Practice,* Vol. 2, New York: Pergamon, pp. 171–193.

ZIGLER, E. and HALL, N. (1995). 'Mainstreaming and the philosophy of normalisation', in KAUFFMAN, J.M. and HALLAHAN, D.P. (eds), *The Illusion of Full Inclusion,* Austin, TX: Pro-Ed, pp. 293–303.

Index